NEW BRUNSWICK AT THE CROSSROADS

NEW BRUNSWICK AT THE CROSSROADS

LITERARY FERMENT AND SOCIAL CHANGE IN THE EAST

TONY TREMBLAY,
EDITOR

WILFRID LAURIER
UNIVERSITY PRESS

This book has been published with the help of a grant from the Federation for the Humanities and Social Sciences, through the Awards to Scholarly Publications Program, using funds provided by the Social Sciences and Humanities Research Council of Canada. Wilfrid Laurier University Press acknowledges the support of the Canada Council for the Arts for our publishing program. We acknowledge the financial support of the Government of Canada through the Canada Book Fund for our publishing activities. This work was supported by the Research Support Fund.

LIBRARY AND ARCHIVES CANADA CATALOGUING IN PUBLICATION

New Brunswick at the crossroads : literary ferment and social change in the east / Tony Tremblay, editor.

Includes bibliographical references and index.
Issued in print and electronic formats.
ISBN 978-1-77112-207-8 (softcover).—ISBN 978-1-77112-208-5 (PDF).—
ISBN 978-1-77112-209-2 (EPUB)

1. Canadian literature—New Brunswick—History and criticism. 2. Literature and society—New Brunswick—History. 3. New Brunswick—Social conditions. I. Tremblay, M. Anthony (Michael Anthony), [date], author, editor

PS8131.N3N49 2017   C810.9'97151   C2017-900216-3
                                        C2017-900217-1

Cover and text design by Sandra Friesen.

© 2017 Wilfrid Laurier University Press
Waterloo, Ontario, Canada
www.wlupress.wlu.ca

Every reasonable effort has been made to acquire permission for copyright material used in this text, and to acknowledge all such indebtedness accurately. Any errors and omissions called to the publisher's attention will be corrected in future printings.

No part of this publication may be reproduced, stored in a retrieval system, or transmitted, in any form or by any means, without the prior written consent of the publisher or a licence from the Canadian Copyright Licensing Agency (Access Copyright). For an Access Copyright licence, visit http://www.accesscopyright.ca or call toll free to 1-800-893-5777 .

CONTENTS

FOREWORD   vii
Christl Verduyn

PREFACE AND ACKNOWLEDGEMENTS   xix

INTRODUCTION   1
The Cultural Geography of New Brunswick
Tony Tremblay

CHAPTER 1   19
Loyalist Literature in New Brunswick, 1783–1843
Gwendolyn Davies

CHAPTER 2   45
Emergent Acadian Nationalism, 1864–1955
Chantal Richard

CHAPTER 3   73
The Fredericton Confederation Awakening, 1843–1900
Thomas Hodd

CHAPTER 4   101
Mid-Century Emergent Modernism, 1935–1955
Tony Tremblay

CONTENTS

CHAPTER 5   129
Modernity and the Challenge of Urbanity in Acadian Literature, 1958–1999
Marie-Linda Lord

AFTERWORD   155
Congruence and Recurrence in the Literatures of New Brunswick
David Creelman

WORKS CITED   167

CONTRIBUTORS   193

INDEX   195

FOREWORD

Christl Verduyn

New Brunswick at the Crossroads: Literary Ferment and Social Change in the East can be placed firmly at the forefront of the evolving landscape of twenty-first-century literary criticism in Canada. This study of literary New Brunswick confirms some of the most compelling analytical approaches to Canadian literature today and asserts a more central place for New Brunswick in the country's cultural history.

Recent critical work suggests that contemporary Canadian literary studies comprise a shifting, changing, unsettled, and even a troubled landscape. Troubled, Smaro Kamboureli states, "because 'Canadian' minus any qualifiers evokes the entirety of the geopolitical space it refers to, but it also siphons off large segments of this space and its peoples into oblivion at worst, and circumscribed conditions at best" (*Trans.Can.Lit.* ix). Kamboureli's concern here is for the adequate inclusion and assessment of Indigenous and diasporic contributions to Canadian cultural history.[1] The present collection shows that her concern for oversight is equally applicable to New Brunswick. This province's rich and varied literary contributions continue to be among the least studied of the country, editor Tony Tremblay observes. *New Brunswick at the Crossroads* sets out to address this neglect in two ways. First, it demonstrates that New Brunswick has been a dynamic cultural place of multiple spatial and temporal frames and distinct periods of literary ferment that have been more significant and influential in Canadian literary history than may be recognized.[2] Secondly, *New Brunswick at the Crossroads* illustrates a contemporary shift in Canadian literary studies

FOREWORD

toward broader, multidisciplinary—in this context, non-literary—critical approaches.

The development of a more multidisciplinary framework for Canadian literary criticism is charted in recent work by critics such as Smaro Kamboureli in her TransCanada project and its three collections of essays, *Trans.Can.Lit: Resituating the Study of Canadian Literature* (Kamboureli and Miki 2007), *Shifting the Ground of Canadian Literary Studies* (Kamboureli and Zacharias 2012), and *Critical Collaborations: Indigeneity Diaspora, and Ecology in Canadian Literary Studies* (Kamboureli and Verduyn 2014). Other critics, as well, have opened the literary field to the multidisciplinary, including Diana Brydon and Marta Dvořák in *Crosstalk: Canadian and Global Imaginaries in Dialogue* (2012); Aloys N.M. Fleischmann, Nancy Van Styvendale, and Cody McCarroll in *Narratives of Citizenship: Indigenous and Diasporic Peoples Unsettle the Nation-State* (2011); Cynthia Sugars and Gerry Turcotte in *Unsettled Remains: Canadian Literature and the Postcolonial Gothic* (2009); Kit Dobson in *Transnational Canadas: Anglo-Canadian Literature and Globalization* (2009); Barbara Godard in *Canadian Literature at the Crossroads of Language and Culture* (2008); Chelva Kanaganayakam in *Moveable Margins: The Shifting Spaces of Canadian Literature* (2005); and Laura Moss in *Is Canada Postcolonial?: Unsettling Canadian Literature* (2003).

Likewise, work by Sneja Gunew (*Haunted Nations*), Stephen Slemon ("Climbing Mount Everest"), and scholars working from feminist, anti-racist, and multicultural perspectives during the last decades of the twentieth century contributed to a changing, more multidisciplinary cultural criticism in Canada. New publications by Indigenous scholars, such as Neal McLeod's *Indigenous Poetics in Canada* (2014) or *Introduction to Indigenous Literary Criticism in Canada* (2016) by Heather Macfarlane and Armand Garnet Ruffo, trace the changing landscape of Canadian literary criticism to anti-colonial work going back to the 1970s[3] by Indigenous writers such as Thomas King, Lee Maracle, Jo-Ann Episkenew, Daniel David Moses, and Daniel Heath Justice. "In hindsight," Macfarlane and Ruffo reflect, "we can see a convergence of the social and political that created the conditions necessary for these voices to emerge and claim their rightful place within Canada's literary culture" (xi).

The contributors to *New Brunswick at the Crossroads* take their place squarely among the ranks of these important scholars. Though coming from a different direction—New Brunswick and its cultural history—they work within the same critical framework of rethinking Canadian literary studies. They pay particular attention to the conditions—the socio-cultural circumstances—that have led to periods of literary ferment over the years, and in the process they draw important and overdue attention to the contribution of New Brunswick literature and literary criticism to Canadian cultural history.

In his introduction to this volume, Tony Tremblay explains that the idea of literary ferment serves as a conceptual and organizational portal or prism through which to look into the socio-cultural-intellectual environment and characteristics of five periods of intensive creative activity in New Brunswick: the period of Loyalist awakening, 1783–1843; emergent Acadian nationalism, 1864–1955; the broadly parallel period of post-Confederation ferment and the Fredericton School of Confederation poets, 1843–1900; the 1935–1955 period of the Ted Campbell Studio and the Fiddlehead School of emergent modernism; and the concomitant period of the second Acadian Renaissance, 1958–1999. For Tremblay, literary ferment is both a localizing and unifying phenomenon. He suggests that a kind of dialectic is at play, that "though seeds of ferment are often imported from the outside, the special features of ferment are modified by (and in turn modify) local circumstances." This framework or concept has a precedent in the work of New Brunswick historian Alfred G. Bailey, who suggested that intellectual ferment was essential to the province's turn toward to a more positive and productive future. The notion of literary ferment aligns as well with more recent concepts and methods for the analysis of the material conditions of cultural production, such as "emergent events" in Kamboureli's Trans-Canada project or "crosstalk" in Brydon and Dvořák's collection of that title.

Emergent events, Kamboureli and Zacharias explain in *Shifting the Ground* (2012), are not sudden, radical paradigm shifts. Rather, as the notion of "ferment" implies, they tend to materialize as part of an incremental process that eventually introduces and encourages new perspectives. As Maliseet scholar Andrea Bear-Nicholas observes of the growing non-Indigenous awareness of settler colonialism in Canada, "whether it is called settler colonialism or settler imperialism, scholars do agree that it is not a single event, but a structure or process that generally occurs over time" ("The Role of Colonial Artists" 27). Emergent events, then, may take different forms. They can emanate from individual works— Kamboureli cites the example of Joy Kogawa's 1981 *Obasan* or Lee Maracle's 1990 *Oratory: Coming to Theory*—or they can emerge from collective projects, such as the TransCanada conferences and publications (Verduyn, "Critical Allegiances"). Today's Idle No More movement or the 1990 "Oka

Crisis" offer further examples of emergent events: "1990, the year of the resistance at Kanehsatake ('the Oka Crisis') signifies a watershed for Indigenous literature and literary criticism in Canada," Macfarlane and Ruffo write (xv), noting the proliferation of publications by Indigenous writers following "the socio-political action associated with 'the Oka Crisis'" (xv). Idle No More has emerged as a similar watershed event, generating publications such as *The Winter We Danced: Voices from the Past, the Future, and the Idle No More Movement* (2014) by the Kino-nda-niimi Collective.

"Events" such as these have impact and significance beyond the strictly literary field. They cross disciplinary boundaries and take on meaning in other fields, such as Canadian history and politics, or Canadian multiculturalism and social justice. Like the notion of literary ferment, the concept of emergent events shifts the disciplinary ground by bringing material contingencies to bear from outside. In the case of literary analysis, this moves the focus from the more familiar critical terrain of imagery, genre, or theme to the conditions and contexts of literary production, which is front and centre in *New Brunswick at the Crossroads*. Attention focuses on the intellectual and artistic climate and socio-cultural circumstances of literary creativity rather than on the texts or writers. The contributors to the TransCanada project, for example, are as concerned with broader socio-economic matters—from the market sector and neoliberalism, to government departments and civil society, to social justice, the law, and the environment—as with literary analysis (Verduyn, "Critical Allegiances" 230).

In a similar gesture, Brydon and Dvořák propose "crosstalk" as a framing device and a point of entry for literary studies today. They use this framework in their collection's exploration of the dialogue between aesthetics and politics and of the ways in which "shifting relations between national and global imaginaries interact with cultural, theatrical, and literary imaginaries" (2). As with Kamboureli's TransCanada project, *Crosstalk* engages in a re-conceptualization of Canadian literature, perceiving it as "an institutionalized structure of exchange between texts and readers, which is both unravelling and rearticulating itself within the contexts of a changing world system" (1). Among other questions, contributors to the collection ask how the literary and cultural spheres interact in an era of new media technologies (7). In their responses they are concerned with a wide range of topics, from the nation-state and citizenship to visual culture and public sphere theory, to the Hérouxville affair[4] and the Bouchard-Taylor Commission report on it, and to jazz as a model for political, cultural, and ethical dialogue.

FOREWORD

Such broader analytical approaches to Canadian literature, including that of *New Brunswick at the Crossroads*, were encouraged by a number of earlier Canadian critics who called for more attention to the "circumstances" of the work of literature. In the late 1980s, Francesco Loriggio, for example, advocated for the role of social, historical, and political contexts, conditions, or circumstances of literary production in literary analysis (54). Arun Mukherjee's 1994 *Oppositional Aesthetics* likewise enjoined Canadian literary critics to pay attention to the aspects of literary production that for her were the most important considerations, including "poverty, exploitation, social inequality, social and political conflicts, imperialism, racism" (iii). Indigenous scholars have also brought awareness of the impact and legacy of settler colonialism to the study of Canadian literature. Considerations and concerns such as these helped move Canadian literary studies away from what Diana Brydon summarized as "the great themes of the nation-building narrative" of Canadian literary studies: "transportation and communication; a movement from east to west, from sea to sea, from civilization to wilderness; a march of progress; a resistance to north–south pulls and to the ethos of the United States" ("Metamorphoses" 13).

Under Tony Tremblay's editorial leadership, the contributors to *New Brunswick at the Crossroads* have participated in this reorientation of Canadian literary studies. In their essays for the volume, they investigate the material or social and cultural contexts of five periods of creative activity in New Brunswick, thereby joining forces with others who are reshaping contemporary literary analysis in Canada. The spatial and temporal contexts identified and explored in *New Brunswick at the Crossroads* confirm New Brunswick's contribution to the country's cultural history. Late-twentieth and early-twenty-first-century changes and contexts were enormously consequential and significant for both literary and cultural production and analysis. The result was the gradual evolution and acceleration of a new generation of conceptual frameworks, literary theories, and innovative approaches to cultural criticism.

THE CHANGING FIELD OF CANADIAN LITERARY STUDIES

What were some key or seminal changes in contexts or circumstances that led to the reshaping of literary analysis in which *New Brunswick at the Crossroads* takes part? To begin, Canada's demographic composition underwent enormous transformation with postwar waves of immigration and the country's development into one of the world's most multicultural nations. This led to changes in Canadian law and policy, including its immigration and multicultural policies, and generated extensive political discussion, debate, and ideas. These developments were a subset of a broader phenomenon that came to be characterized as globalization and that reflected widespread liberalization and movement of goods and services, capital and investment, people and labour, cultural ideas and tastes, supported by new technologies and new forms of communication.

Accompanying these social, political, and economic transformations were a swirl and melange of critical and cultural movements that reacted to, were informed by, and in turn shaped global developments. From feminism and anti-racism to post-colonialism, transculturalism, transnationalism, and the ongoing resistance to settler colonialism by Indigenous scholars, these movements unfolded at both national and international levels and encouraged critical thinking across disciplines, a thinking that contested inherited assumptions about knowledge and traditions. Scholars from political science, economics, sociology, legal studies, literary studies, and Indigenous studies embraced increasingly multidisciplinary concepts and approaches in their work. The resulting multidisciplinary perspectives offered intriguing and innovative frameworks for new analyses of what had also become an increasingly complex and varied Canadian cultural and literary landscape.

Among these frameworks, the combination of feminist, multicultural, and anti-racist perspectives offered a particularly powerful analytical matrix during the last decades of the twentieth century. The transformation of social, political, cultural, and economic circumstances in the globalized environment foregrounded themes of difference and diversity, from gender and sexual orientation to ethnic and racialized identification. Feminist theory played a critical role in this context, notably in the work of women authors who were also writing as critics. Theorizing the intersection of gender, ethnicity, and race in collections such as *Language in Her Eye: Views on Writing and Gender in Canadian Women Writing in English* (Sheier et al. 1990), *La Théorie, un dimanche* (Bersianik et al. 1988), or *Telling It: Women and Language across Cultures* (Telling It Book Collective 1990) had significant impact on Canadian literary criticism. Along with the powerful expansion of writing by women, the postwar period saw a literal explosion of immigrant and ethnic minority writing reflecting the demographic changes noted above as well as the subsequent policy changes that brought in official multiculturalism. In an ongoing dialectic, this resulted in and was subsequently shaped by the acceleration of critical work in the developing interdisciplinary fields of women's studies, ethnic studies, and Canadian studies. The resulting methodologies and areas of investigation reinvigorated literary and critical exploration of social and political issues such as immigration, multiculturalism, and language, as well as gender and class. The increasingly complex cultural and social realities of Canadian experience, critics like Enoch Padolsky asserted in "Canadian Diversity and Canadian Literature" (1991), called for a pluralistic, cross-cultural, and interdisciplinary approach to Canadian literary studies, the kind of approach that parallels that of *New Brunswick at the Crossroads*.

It was imperative and inevitable that Canadian literary studies address the issue of race, which came to the fore in the context of globalized demographics and modern migration. A new Canadian discourse on race developed during the final decades of the twentieth century, expanding the literary and critical corpus in important ways. This development was influenced by a number of critical socio-political and cultural events during the 1990s,[5] including the "appropriation debates,"[6] the 1994 "Writing Thru Race" conference in English Canada, and the 1997 *pure laine* controversy in Quebec.[7] These events heightened social and political awareness of racism within Canadian society, including the arts communities (Tator, Henry, and Mattis, *Challenging Racism in the Arts*), underscoring the part played by socio-political conditions and tensions in cultural production, as seen in the periods (earlier and contemporary) and place (New Brunswick) examined in *New Brunswick at the Crossroads*.

From the contexts of feminist and anti-racist theoretical frameworks, Canadian literary studies evolved toward a contemporary global terrain and discourse, mirroring political, economic, and social developments nationally and internationally. This shift was informed by theories of postcolonialism, transnationalism, transculturalism, and globalism. Canadian literary criticism was animated anew by postcolonial theory and its concepts of the subaltern, the uncanny, the unhomely, the haunted, the liminal, the spectral, ambivalence, and hybridity.[8] Over the next decade, important studies appeared both in the form of edited collections—such as Laura Moss's *Is Canada Postcolonial?: Unsettling Canadian Literature* and Cynthia Sugars's *Home-Work: Postcolonialism, Pedagogy, and Canadian Literature* (2004) and *Unhomely States: Theorizing English-Canadian Postcolonialism* (2004)—and as individual contributions by critics like Stephen Slemon ("Climbing Mount Everest"), Diana Brydon, and Sneja Gunew (*Haunted Nations*). As the new millennium advanced, the impact of globalization, transnationalism, or transculturalism on Canadian literary studies emerged as another critical focus—and another instance of opening the field of literature to different critical approaches.

FOREWORD

Smaro Kamboureli's co-edited collections from 2007, 2012, and 2014; Diana Brydon and Marta Dvořák's 2012 *Crosstalk;* and work by Winfried Siemerling, Kit Dobson, Daniel Coleman, Norman Cheadle and Lucien Pelletier, among others, measured and assessed this impact. Kamboureli's TransCanada project placed Canadian literary studies within the broader contexts of "globalizing processes and critical methodologies ... [and] institutional structures such as the Humanities, the cultural industries, curricula and anthologies" (Kamboureli, *Trans.Can.Lit.,* xii–xiii). In *Crosstalk,* Brydon and Dvořák addressed Canadian literature and culture from a global perspective, exploring "what it means for Canadian literature (and to a lesser extent, culture) to re-envision its participation within a field of transnational production, circulation, and reception: a field where the Canadian may not disappear but may well become destabilized and rearticulated" (10). In similar ways, contributors to *Canadian Cultural Exchange/Échanges Culturels au Canada: Translation and Transculturation/ Traduction et Transculturation* adopted a transcultural approach to literary analysis. Following Fernando Ortiz's notion of transculturalism, the editors of that collection noted the "turbulent and unpredictable process resulting from the interaction among cultures in contact ... which potentiates, in spite of unequal power relations, the emergence of new cultural forms" (Cheadle and Pelletier xi).

Writing and critical work by mixed-raced writers comprised yet another powerful field of creative change in Canadian literary studies. This is particularly the case of work exploring mixed immigrant and Indigenous experience. In their work, authors such as Fred Wah, Lawrence Hill, SKY Lee, and Larissa Lai investigate relations with and within white society, as well as the complex relationship between immigrant and ethnic minority Canadians and Canada's Indigenous populations. SKY Lee's novel *Disappearing Moon Café* (1990), for example, explores the relatively unmapped terrain of the interrelations of Asian and Indigenous Canadians. Donna Bennett, in "Getting Beyond Boundaries" (2005), proposed the term polybridity to describe "inheritance from more sources than two," provided that inheritance is understood in all its complexities, "not just in terms of the gene pool but also as describing influences and cultural mixing" (12). Binary systems, even those of hybridity, Bennett argued, are "inadequate to the complex narratives that describe the history of colonization and immigration and the personal stories of its citizens that form Canada" (12).

The history of settler colonialism in Canada and stories of its impact on Indigenous peoples comprise a key narrative of cultural criticism in the country today. As the twenty-first century unfolds, Canadian literature and literary criticism continue to reflect the growing sociological and ethnic complexity and the increasing cultural sophistication of modern Canada. In turn, theoretical and conceptual approaches to the study of the country's literary and cultural history trace the contours of growing critical consciousness and diverse, multifaceted changes to Canadian society. Recently, approaches such as legal studies—in particular Indigenous legal studies (Henderson "First Nations Legal Inheritances" and "Postcolonial Indigenous Legal Consciousness")—have joined the wide array of interdisciplinary work that literary scholars are adopting in their study of Canadian literature. Critic Len Findlay, for example, has found useful models for literary criticism in the methods and principles developed in the legal system to protect Indigenous rights and treaties. Quite simply, Findlay states, "literary scholars and cultural workers need to know as much about this legal-jurisprudential *turn* as they do about linguistic and cultural and ethical turns" (247).

If today, as Smaro Kamboureli reflects, Canadian literature and literary criticism includes work by Indigenous, Métis, South Asian Canadian, Japanese Canadian, Trinidadian Canadian, and Italian Canadian authors, the field nevertheless remains "a tradition that bears the signs of its troubled trajectory" (*Trans.Can.Lit.* ix). Kamboureli points to an ongoing project and challenge for Canadian literary criticism: a constant rethinking of its history and ongoing identification and assessment of what has been circumscribed or marginalized in that history. As noted, her concern is for Indigenous and diasporic contributions to the country's cultural history. The parallel concern in *New Brunswick at the Crossroads*, arrived at differently, but displaying the same desire for reassessment and renewal, is for the contribution and importance of New Brunswick's cultural story, particularly in the five periods of literary ferment identified therein.

Taking its place in the shifting landscape of Canadian literary studies, *New Brunswick at the Crossroads* will prove to be enormously important and influential for the evolution of literary analysis both in Canada in general and in New Brunswick in particular. This volume successfully establishes the importance of New Brunswick's cultural story, in itself and as part of the Canadian landscape. In addition, it illustrates and contributes to the innovative and multidisciplinary approaches that have informed the most powerful and consequential literary analyses nationally and internationally in recent decades. The identification and sophisticated analysis of five crucial periods of literary ferment provides a narrative and interdisciplinary prism for an estimation of the substance and consequences of

FOREWORD

New Brunswick's cultural story. *New Brunswick at the Crossroads* expands the terrain and substance of Canadian literary criticism and in its focus on material, social, political, economic, and cultural circumstances, contributes significantly to the welcome shift to a broader, multidisciplinary approach to contemporary Canadian literary studies.

NOTES

1   "[T]he term conveys a semblance of plenitude ... [one that] has been forged by means of occlusion and repression, marginalizing particular idioms of English, as the language has been othered by indigeneity and diaspora" (Kamboureli, *Trans.Can.Lit.* ix).

2   In his editorial outline, Tremblay identifies other instances of ferment in Canadian literature, such as the Ottawa School (Lampman and Scott); the McGill Fortnightly group (Smith, Scott, Klein); the Montreal 40s group (Layton, Dudek, Sutherland); Frye's Mythopoets (Atwood, Reaney); and the TISH group (Davey, Bowering, etc.). Each has influenced the literature of the country in unique ways, Tremblay states, and most have been well studied. The New Brunswick ferments, however, with the exception of the Fredericton School of the Confederation Poets, have not, and most certainly have not been acknowledged as providing the stimulus that they did to other movements in the country. That is one purpose of the essays in this collection.

3   The collection includes E. Pauline Johnson's important 1892 essay "A Strong Race Opinion: On the Indian Girl in Modern Fiction," but focuses on the period 1970–2000.

4   Diana Brydon ("Negotiating Belonging in Global Times: The Hérouxville Debates" 253–71) offers the following account of the Hérouxville affair: "In January 2007, a small town in Quebec posted a declaration of 'norms' for immigrants on the town website as its contribution to an ongoing controversy in the province regarding the accommodation of religious and cultural minorities. This act became a media event" (253). It led to the creation of the Commission de consultation sur les pratiques de l'accommodement reliées aux différences culturelles/the Consultation Commission on Accommodation Practices Related to Culture Difference, chaired by Gerard Bouchard and Charles Taylor. They issued their report, *Building the Future: A Time for Reconciliation*, in 2008.

5   For example, the 1989 *Vision 21* protest at the 1989 PEN conference in Toronto, which involved a public dispute between M. NourbeSe Philip and June Callwood about the representation of minority writers; the 1989 "Into the Heart of Africa" exhibition at the Royal Ontario Museum, which in Toronto's black community's view glorified the imperial conquest of Africa; two American

FOREWORD

musicals—*Miss Saigon* and *Show Boat*—staged in Toronto in 1993. For analysis, see NourbeSe Philip (*Frontiers*) or Tator, Henry, and Mattis (*Challenging Racism*).

6 In 1988, at both The Women's Press in Toronto and the Third International Women's Book Fair in Montreal, protest arose against the way some women appeared to be "speaking for" others—most notably white middle-class feminists speaking for women from Canada's Indigenous and black communities. The controversy related both to cultural outsiders writing about the experience of racialized groups (thus contributing to the exclusion of writers *from* those groups) and to feminist groups that claimed to represent women, but did so largely from a white, middle-class perspective that marginalized other experiences. The events sparked national debate on the issue of cultural appropriation. The discussions were carried forward by minority writers, spreading from feminist communities to organizations such as the Writers' Union of Canada. In 1989, Indigenous writers Lenore Keeshig-Tobias and Daniel David Moses called for the creation of a Writers' Union task force to look into issues of artistic appropriation and accessibility. An ad hoc committee was established, and in 1992 it organized a three-day retreat on the topic of "The Appropriate Voice." Among its recommendations was that the ad hoc committee be renamed the Racial Minority Writers' Committee and that the Writers' Union address voice appropriation, which the committee identified as the misrepresentation of cultures and the silencing of their peoples.

7 This was a fiery exchange about being a *Québécois de souche* versus being an immigrant Quebec writer. The Sroka-LaRue debate, Patricia Smart explains, arose out of a short essay on Quebec literature and pluralism, *L'Arpenteur et le navigateur*, by novelist Monique LaRue, which was harshly criticized by then-editor of *La Tribune juive*, Ghila Sroka, in an editorial entitled "De LaRue à la poubelle." LaRue's essay, which Smart describes as "a call for greater openness to 'the other,' i.e. the non-Québécois" (15), was characterized by Sroka as a "racist discourse [suggesting] that Quebec had produced only sublime *Québécois pure laine* writers and that all the others can be dismissed" (qtd. in Smart 16). Support for and criticism of both writers ensued (see also Maïr Verthuy in Verduyn *Literary Pluralities*). The term *Québécois de souche* refers to the descendants of the first French colonists, or old-stock Quebeckers.

8 English departments were slow in taking up the study of minority writing. Arun Mukherjee, for instance, remarked that, "If one looks at the 1984 ACCUTE [Association of Canadian College and University Teachers of English] conference program, one gets the impression that the only officially sanctioned valid response to literary works is structuralist-formalist" (*Oppositional Aesthetics*

451). Chelva Kanaganayakam points out that "postcolonial studies is a fallout from Empire and that English departments tend to be custodians of postcolonial literature" ("Pedagogy and Postcolonial Literature" 730); he wonders if practitioners of postcolonial studies "may be guilty of recolonizing the field" (728).

PREFACE AND ACKNOWLEDGEMENTS

This book had its genesis in a Standard Research Grant from the Social Sciences and Humanities Research Council of Canada. In the earliest phase of this project, our team of English- and French-language literary scholars in New Brunswick took its cue from health researchers in asking a basic, but complex, question about literature: namely, what are the determinants of *the literary*? Is literature mostly the creation of hypersensitive antennae of the race, as Marshall McLuhan suggested (*Gutenberg Galaxy* 269), or is the artist enmeshed in social matrices of language, narrative, and history that speak through, and thus index, artistic creation? In the pages that follow, we not only historicize that question and the tensions that follow from it, but also locate its address in distinct periods of New Brunswick literary history.

We are concerned primarily with social determinants, the *latent* complex of forces that contributed to periods of literary ferment or flowering in New Brunswick. To extend the flowering metaphor, we focus less on the smell of the rose, or its sheen, or its symbolic resonance, than we do on the soil it grows in, the water it consumes, the air quality around it, and the attentions of its quirky gardeners. Thus, we are not setting out to describe the *manifest* components of distinct periods of literary ferment in New Brunswick (key figures and achievements), but to examine the conditions that were in place to enable, stifle, or augment production.

In adopting that approach to understanding a provincial culture, we do not imply that social conditions are *solely* responsible for an artist like Herménégilde Chiasson, or that a straight line can be drawn from social factors to literary achievement, but contend that a focus on social conditions provides a starting point for literary interpretation. Establishing the contextual frame, in other words, is the logical place to start for understanding a literature as understudied as New Brunswick literature is. How, for example, can we comprehend the many dimensions of a figure like Chiasson if we do not know the tensions, negotiations, material apparatus, and complex of conditions that underlie and prefigure contemporary Acadie?

In the chapters that follow, then, we examine the multivalent social factors that were congruent with periods of intense literary activity in New Brunswick, and we ask what the sum of those factors tells us about New Brunswick as a distinct, albeit plural, cultural space.

The *primary* goal of our research is to create new knowledge about New Brunswick literature and culture by examining the province's most active periods of literary output. To do that, we examine five key periods of ferment in the province, the first beginning in the 1780s and the most recent extending into the 1990s.

A *secondary* goal of our work is to provide a forum for English- and French-language scholars in the province to collaborate. Though New Brunswick is small, it is still a place of two solitudes where intercultural work is rare. English and French scholars do not know each other well, nor do they know the literature and scholarship produced in the other language. This project bridges that divide, an especially important goal given that New Brunswick is Canada's only officially bilingual province, and therefore possesses a culture of rich, if largely misunderstood, plurality.

The seven scholars making up our research team, and present in this collection, were chosen for the project because they have been the most active researchers in New Brunswick literature in the last decade. Our opening point of consensus was to publish our work first in English and then in French, thereby communicating research results to both dominant language groups in the province and beyond. This book is the first part of that commitment.

Our work, we hope, will bring attention to the neglected field of New Brunswick literature at a time when the province has embarked on a sweeping program of renewal that invites studies of culture and identity (Hodd 196–209; Tremblay "Harnessing" 369–77). And while the cultivation of a collaborative program of research with scholars of New Brunswick literature meets part of that expectation, we also hope our work will have a positive impact on raising the profile of New Brunswick studies among students, our future researchers. In recent years, many of our most promising

ACKNOWLEDGEMENTS

students have gone elsewhere to pursue graduate work, citing the lack of defined nodes of humanities research focused on the province. Our work in this book endeavours to address that problem, and thus supports the goals expressed in the *Action Plan to Transform Post-Secondary Education in New Brunswick*. Simply put, we all have a stake in aligning research with goals of sustainability, whether of communities or cultural systems.

ACKNOWLEDGEMENTS

We gratefully acknowledge the financial support of the Social Sciences and Humanities Research Council of Canada, whose funding enabled us to begin this work, to support the undergraduate and graduate students who assisted with it, and to publish the results. Beyond that simple acknowledgement, we feel it is also important to state how invaluable SSHRC support is to small universities in distant regions of the country, for without that support projects such as this one would never be completed.

Parts of most of these chapters have been delivered as papers at scholarly conferences around the region. We wish to thank conference organizers for enabling us to bring our early work before peer audiences. Additionally, we wish to thank the many research and administrative assistants, as well as librarians, archivists, and colleagues who helped with this project. Those who played direct and significant roles were Tammy Armstrong, Jean Babineau, Patricia Belier, David Lloyd Bent, Denis Bourque, Cynthia Bouzanne, Margaret Conrad, Stephen Davidson, Michael Dawson, André Duguay, Billy Johnson, Patti Auld Johnson, Koral LaVorgna, Gayle MacDonald, Margie Reed, and Ellen Rose. Especially significant was the work that Sara Dunton did to get the manuscript into shape. Also helpful and accommodating were staff at Archives and Special Collections (Harriet Irving Library, UNB), the Provincial Archives of New Brunswick, and the Centre d'Études Acadiennes Anselme Chiasson. For hosting our annual research symposia, we are grateful to facilities and conference management staff at St. Thomas University, Université de Moncton, and Mount Allison University.

Just before this work was completed, scholars in the region lost a valued colleague and a champion of Atlantic Canadian literature. Herb Wyile of Acadia University was not only a colleague, however, but also a cherished friend of the contributors to this collection, and so it is to his memory that we dedicate this work.

Tony Tremblay
Fall 2016

INTRODUCTION

THE CULTURAL GEOGRAPHY OF NEW BRUNSWICK

Tony Tremblay

> Before it takes the air in greener shoots
> A seed is nurtured by surrounding soil
> And patterned by whatever streams can coil
> Where worms and borers worked their slow pursuits;
> And though it wills to grow a crown that fruits
> In skies where lightnings break and thunders clap,
> It can't escape the source that feeds its sap:
> No tree belies its soil, outgrows its roots.
> (Fred Cogswell, "New Brunswick" 12)

The signature of every region or locale is, in the broadest sense, cultural. And culture, likewise, is an equally vast and, for Raymond Williams, "complicated" (87) admix of language, history, ethnicity, and social and economic factors that coalesce to form signifying and symbolic patterns that change over time. Dynamism is normative in cultural systems, observed Walter Ong, because "species themselves ... are not fixed but develop through natural selection brought about by open interaction between individuals and environment" (324). Where there is high culture, there is also low; where one language dominates, there are always others on the periphery. Consensus about history and culture, as a result, always has a short half-life.

Such has been the case with New Brunswick, a territory originally inhabited by Mi'kmaq, Maliseet (Wolastoqiyik), and Passamaquoddy peoples, settled by Acadian, Planter, German, and Scottish farmers and fishermen, and resettled, forcibly, by a patchwork of pro-British Loyalists fleeing the new Republic of America. For Sally Armstrong's fictional Charlotte Taylor, this mélange of peoples and traditions forms the unique bricolage of New Brunswick, a place where "[t]here's a piece of everyplace else ... language, customs, traits, even recipes. My own hearth could be described as Acadian, British and Micmac!" (374).

To approach New Brunswick as a cultural space, then, is to enter multivalent and uneven geographies. Historically, the province's Indigenous matrix was characterized by the seasonal migrations of sea-based northern Mi'kmaq and St. John River-based Wolastoqiyik and Passamaquoddy, their differences presaging the differences between northern and southern settler populations. After the Expulsion of the Acadians (1755–1762), this broad division of north and south re-established itself along French and English lines, with the more bureaucratically dominant English Loyalists settling in the southern part of the province and the returning French population occupying less-habitable lands north and east of the fertile St. John River valley. Configurations of labour and settlement followed those divisions, as did the "occupational pluralism" that rendered small communities fixed and inviolate (McCann 94). Resource economies developed in the north and central parts of the province—the result of river transport systems and abundant forests—while commercial and institutional enterprises flourished in the south, the effect, originally, of Saint John's global port. Disparities in personal wealth emerged, as did sociological differences between the mostly rural/small-town north and the urban south. It was those differences that led to Premier Louis J. Robichaud's program of Equal Opportunity in 1964, a program meant to close the service gaps between urban and rural, south and north, and rich and poor populations of New Brunswickers. Prior to Equal Opportunity, dirt roads, inadequate health systems, inequitable tax structures, and sub-par schooling was the norm in northern and rural New Brunswick. That the early literature of the province is mostly associated with the urban south, namely Fredericton and Saint John, the locales that were first to move from subsistence demands to leisure, reflects this larger human geography.

Today, despite the equalizing intent of Robichaud's reforms, much the same cultural geography exists in New Brunswick. The province is made diverse, and its people, by extension, diffused, by differences in latitude (north and south), language (French and English), sociology (rural and urban), ethnicity (Aboriginal, Acadian, Scots, Irish), religion (Catholic and Protestant), and wealth distribution (rich and poor). No one representation adequately reflects this diversity, nor has one writer or filmmaker managed to express the dissonance of the province's tenors, which have remained stubbornly separate and insular into the twenty-first century. In the fullest history of New Brunswick to date, W.S. MacNutt observed this separation as a feature of the province's settlement: "There was nothing to compel a man to live in proximity to and in emulation of his neighbours. The element that explained the remarkable local initiative of New England, the orderly development of townships that thrust responsibility as well as privileges upon individuals, was completely absent in New Brunswick" (*New Brunswick* 55).

Absent, too, was any sense of or desire for unanimity among the province's peoples, who shared neither language nor nationality, only the fact that each was vanquished: the First Nations by systemic erasure, the Lowland and Highland Scots by land restrictions and clearances, the Acadians by the Expulsion, the Loyalists by republican victory, and the Irish by famine. Alistair MacLeod had this historical fact in mind when writing of the tribal attachment to place that vanquished peoples from distant lands or times re-created in the region. "That they were alone with their landscape for a long, long time," he observed, and that those landscapes "went into them somehow," explains their sense of intransigent attachment (269). Suspicion and xenophobia followed, those emotions manipulated by a political class that used sectarian differences for partisan advantage. And so division became both institutional and structural.

The result was balkanization. New Brunswick was cast into distinct imaginative territories, not only of dominant Acadian and anglophone sensibility, but also microsensibilities of larger ethnic and linguistic groups (H. Chiasson, "Une Acadie triangulaire"). The imagined worlds of Bliss Carman (Fredericton), Raymond Fraser (Miramichi), and Rose Després (Moncton) reflect this balkanization and the uniquely syncretic worldviews in evidence across the province.

While these separate regions of the province have produced a rich array of distinct literary and artistic voices, they have also, in their diversity, resisted containment under unifying critical labels. The consequence has been a dearth of critical efforts to understand the province. To put the matter bluntly, New Brunswick has been characterized by a paucity of venues for, and scholarly personnel committed to, critical explorations of provincial culture and heritage. And though there are degrees of difference between English and Acadian New Brunswick in this regard (Acadians are much more advanced than their English neighbours in cultural and critical enterprise), the fact remains that no contemporary history of the province has yet been written, no general provincial encyclopedia exists, no free press interrogates vital issues of the day, and no publishing house has emerged that focuses exclusively on provincial matters. In terms of its identity enterprise, New Brunswick is therefore still very much in its infancy, a fact surprising for a province that attained its charter in 1784.

If cultural geography teaches us anything about this situation, however, it is that diversity, while unsuited to reductive schema, *can* be represented by methodologies open to diversity, which is both the rationale and organizational strategy of this book.

The scholars assembled in this volume share the view that the province can only be understood as a constellation of microcultures that have changed over time. New Brunswick is certainly not the Victorian Elysium represented in Charles G.D. Roberts's *In Divers Tones* (1886), nor is it, on the other hand, the squalor of Flea Island in Antonine Maillet's *La Sagouine* (1971). Rather, it is both and neither of those fictions, just as Fredericton, as capital and symbolic centre of the province, is and is not a reflection of the province's heterogeneity.

Given that condition, the following principles govern the critical approach of the contributors to this volume:

First, that multiple spatial and temporal frames are the best means by which New Brunswick can be understood as a cultural matrix;

Second, that a literary sociology rather than an overarching theory is the functional methodology best suited to critical inquiry of such an uneven landscape;

And, *third*, that a study that examines the intersections of ideas and art—including the vital creative reactions that occur when a multiplicity of forces coalesce in place and time—is useful not only for understanding New Brunswick literature, but also for understanding New Brunswick history and society as well. Because of the paucity of scholarly work on the province, such an approach offers the widest possible application to the province as a whole.

WHAT IS LITERARY FERMENT?

In scientific parlance, ferment implies discharge: an agent is brought into a stable system, causes a reaction, and energy is released. In more general terms, ferment usually connotes a multiplicity of causes that give rise to an intense array of effects. The inference is that ferment is not benign, that whatever the cause, the result is agitation, a rumpus, or upheaval of some significant sort. Ferment, then, normally implies excitation. As the end result of a chemical process, it can be explosive. When sugar is added to yeast, gasses are released that cause bread to rise or bubbling to form. As every brewer knows, keeping the lid loose on a primary fermenter is the only way to avoid an explosion.

Social scientists use the same language and metaphors for social upheaval, though the effects they track are measured not by degrees of excitation but by magnitude of transformational change. Media ecologist Neil Postman's work is useful for understanding the difference. Identifying technology as an agent of social change, Postman posits that "technological change is neither additive nor subtractive. It is ecological," by which he means transformative: "one significant change generates total change" (*Technopoly* 18). To illustrate, Postman argues that the introduction of rabbits into a biome that had never had rabbits is not merely the old system plus rabbits (additive) but a totally new biome. Likewise with the computer and the portable phone: their introduction to society did not result in the old society plus the computer and phone but a radically different society. History records the effects of similar agents of transformational change (tools, media, ideas) over time, each resulting in changed social systems.

In this study we treat ferment, specifically "literary" ferment, as social scientists like Postman and Charles Weingartner do: namely as "the study of transactions among people, their messages, and their message systems" (*Soft Revolution* 139). We isolate historical periods in New Brunswick when literary activity is intensified and we study the agents that give rise to large-scale releases of creative energy within those periods. By "agents" we mean the material and symbolic forms that effect transformational change: influential teachers and schools; institutional apparatuses (publishing houses, journals, and professional associations); pioneering writers and critics; a social climate that cultivates intellectual or artistic habits of mind; material wealth in abundance to turn select individuals and whole classes from subsistence to leisure pursuits; access to other ports of culture and cosmopolitanism; a political awareness of the importance of arts in social health; stimulation (or agitation) by others, either like-minded or opposed; and the nebulous but insistent notion that culture, as an expression of identity and self-determination, is a fundamental human right, whether recognized as such or not.

LITERARY FERMENT AND CULTURAL SOCIOLOGY AS METHODOLOGY

The adoption of the concept of *literary ferment* as the point of entry into this study was not without scholarly precedent. The broad research question that guided us was first posed by New Brunswick historian Alfred G. Bailey, author of the influential "Creative Moments in the Culture of the Maritime Provinces." While pursuing graduate studies in history and anthropology at the University of Toronto, Bailey came under the influence of Harold Innis, whose theory of alignment between staples production and social organization focused Bailey's attention on cultural sociology. In an interview many years later, Bailey synthesized Innis's influence in the form of a question. He asked what would also become our own foundational question: "Is the socio-cultural environment responsible for innovation, or is the individual?" (qtd. in Lane, "Interview" 227). The question resided at the heart of Bailey's scholarship and it became manifest in a series of important essays, the most influential of which are the aforementioned "Creative Moments," as well as "Evidences of Culture Considered Colonial" and "Literature and Nationalism in the Aftermath of Confederation," all of which appear in *Culture and Nationality* (1972).

The essays in that book pursue lines of inquiry that are grounded in the essential premise that each citizen's larger environment is a dynamic field that shapes the conditions for both assent and revolt. Hence the recurring historical dramas of stability and rupture that Bailey observes: specifically, that in every region and nation there are distinct periods of intellectual unease when small groups of artists and cultural workers coalesce around the view that inherited traditions are restrictive or outmoded. The resulting desire for reform sometimes swells into a literary ferment, sometimes not. Each period, however, is characterized by an upswing of creative energy that redefines the relationship of artists to their communities and their craft. Literary ferment is therefore both a localizing and a historicizing phenomenon, and though the seeds of ferment are often imported from the outside, the special features of ferment are modified by (and in turn modify) local circumstances.

Considered in the wider realm of critical theory, Bailey's question and the thinking it engendered enter the arena of *cultural sociology*, a field generally associated with the dialectical materialism of Lukàcsian Marxism. In *The Historical Novel* (1937) and *Studies in European Realism* (1950), Georg Lukàcs theorized that human science is mediated by social totality and that literature, as an aspect of that totality, is constitutive, not causative, in the historical evolution of consciousness. In other words, social systems prefigure individuals, no matter how powerful or unique those individuals are. Lukàcs's thinking was most vigorously pursued by two figures whose work bears summarizing here.

The first is Lucien Goldmann, who was deeply influenced by Lukàcs's dialectical methodology in *History and Class Consciousness* (1923). That work in particular enabled Goldmann to move beyond the static structuralism of traditional Marxism—with its emphasis on rationalism and bourgeois politics—and develop a theory of "genetic structuralism" (494), which he defined as the coherent mental framework of a social group that is discernable in great works of literature. With the seeming contradiction between each individual's narrow empiricism yet expansive subjectivity foremost in mind, Goldmann advances the idea that "mental structures ... are not individual phenomena, but social phenomena," thus structurally homologous in ways that individual subjectivity, dominated by the ego, refuses to acknowledge (495). From that point he is able to argue that "the very peaks of literary creation" are "complex[es] of significant [social] reactions" (495–96), a perspective that directs his own inquiries into the major literary figures and events of Europe. His work on Jean Racine is instructive in that regard. Though Racine's plays, Goldmann begins, bear the mark of the writer's youth in Port-Royal, his association with people of the theatre and court, and his familiarity with the Jansenists, the more direct key to understanding Racine's work is through the sociology that contains and prefigures it. In other words, "the existence of the tragic vision was already a constituent element of the situations forming the starting-point from which Racine was led on to write his plays" (497). Goldmann's point is that authorship is a function of a collective that is historically constituted, and his implication is that research must therefore attend to a "genetic" structure— similar to Foucault's notion of genealogy—that is the ultimate producer of both author and the objects of that author's creation.

The utility of Goldmann's work for later scholars of culture is, admittedly, limited. That utility is *not* in his positivist insistence that research must seek to locate and quantify those structures (or *vision du monde*) that govern all imaginative production, but rather in the more general view that structural surroundings are determinative in aesthetic practice. Goldmann's advance beyond the "great man" theories of Thomas Carlyle and Matthew Arnold, which harnessed creative achievement and critical assessment to the individual psychology of artists, is significant and, as Walter Ong has suggested, more accurately representative of humans as an interactive species. Moreover, in the emerging field of cultural studies in mid-century, Goldmann's work was important in contesting the still-influential New Critical insistence on textual autonomy. Thus, though the cultural sociology of the 1960s would move away from Goldmann's positivism—the idea that the critic should unlock great works to discern laws of structural coherence—contemporary scholars of literature are indebted to his notion that the literary and artistic are constituted by the non-literary and the non-aesthetic: that, in effect, the work of art does not stand at the apex of a society but sits, instead, at its busiest crossroads.

It is this notion of relational totality that the post-Goldmann group of cultural sociologists adopts, thanks, in large part, to Malcolm Bradbury's interpretations of M.H. Abrams, Leo Lowenthal, and Raymond Williams—and thanks, also, to the popularity of sociology as critical practice that Émile Durkheim effected. Just as Goldmann extended Lukàcs's thought, so did Bradbury extend Abrams, Lowenthal, and Williams, finding in *The Mirror and the Lamp* (Abrams 1953), *Literature and the Image of Man* (Lowenthal 1957), and *Culture and Society* (Williams 1958) the protracted analysis of social bias that made Goldmann's ideas normative. By the early 1970s, Bradbury could jettison Goldmann's positivist structuralism while maintaining his focus on social totality, the evidence of which appears in Bradbury's introduction to *The Social Context of Modern English Literature*. The definition of literature Bradbury advances in that introduction is thus indebted to Goldmann's work, but is free from the *science* of sociology that Goldmann used to authenticate his ideas: "Literature can be regarded as primarily an activity of mind, a creative and self-conscious enterprise—though one that is socially formed in the sense that the writer is part of the current of human thought, shares the language, attitudes and tones of voice of his fellows, and expresses values that come from a discernable context in a society, a nation, a period" (xx).

For Bradbury, there is no latent social reality that manifests itself coherently in art, nor is it possible to "transliterate the insights of literature into sociological terms" (xxii). Rather, there is only a writer and that writer's mediation of "a tradition, a stock of language, [and] a social frame" (xxiv), all of which coalesce in different combinations with unpredictable results. In light of this, Bradbury suggests an alteration in interpretative practice: namely, that what should replace the preoccupation with systemic coherence is a focus on epochal change, historical moments "when 'style' shifts and the structure of perception among artists significantly alters, and when the environment and the prevailing assumptions of art are so radically recreated that it seems no longer to be witnessing to the same kind of world, or employing structure, material or language in the same way as before" (xxvii). It is the critic's job, then, to be attentive to what Canadian historian Ian McKay would later call "matrix events": "moment[s] that reshape hegemony at both its profoundest structural levels and its conscious level" (95). Those moments of "creativity and innovation," adds Allen Scott, must be "understood as social phenomena rooted in ... [a] geographic milieu" (814). Spatial differences matter, writes Scott, because communities "are not just foci of cultural labour in the narrow sense, but are also vortexes of social reproduction in which critical cultural competencies are generated and circulated" (809). For McKay, Scott, and the generation of socio-cultural critics that followed Bradbury, history's moments of renovation and intellectual unease provide the clearest views to creative practice and spatial poetics, and should therefore be the portals for understanding culture. "One way to look at [innovation]," concludes Bradbury, "[is] to consider in detail the work of the most important writers of [a] period ... and to see their evaluation of their society and their literary context. But it seems useful to begin with a broader base—to consider what sort of change this was that is being brought to intellectual and artistic focus over this period" (xxxiv).

Our own work and methodology now comes into clearer focus. Wanting, first, to find a way to examine New Brunswick literature and society across different temporal frames, and seeking, as well, a method that freed us from the totalizing pressures of Goldmann and Durkheim, we chose a flexible cultural sociology that was neither Marxist nor Hegelian—that, in other words, did not reify literature as "the illusion of truth" (Hegel 55) nor bind literature to the production-based apparatus of consciousness (Goldmann). Instead, endeavouring to understand literature as mediation, we looked for key moments in the literary history of New Brunswick and focused our critical attentions on the social complexities of each. While followers of Hegel and Goldmann, to provide a cognate example, might have studied the Italian Renaissance via its key figures—who they were, what they believed in, and how their art cohered as social form—the alternate method of cultural sociology considers the social factors that enabled that renaissance to incubate: the dominance of the Church, the rise of the middle class within a humanist Catholic tradition, the political climate in fourteenth-century Italy, the cosmopolitanism of Florence, the unique twinning of science and self-awareness that came from the contagion of the plague, the towering influence of Dante, the republican ethos among wealthy patrons of art, the Copernican revolution, and the broadening of perspective that followed Columbus's 1492 voyage (Hay 10–26, 58–75). In pursuing this second avenue of inquiry, research would foreground that complex of factors that shaped the conditions for Michelangelo and da Vinci to emerge, while also reserving "a favoured place" for the work of art, that favoured place related to art's primacy as the "datum to be explained ... and the principal evidence to be used to explain what appears to be happening in the field" (H. White 99). Literature is not sidelined or forgotten, then, but repositioned in a wider social drama.

The contributors to this volume have taken the second avenue of inquiry as the means best suited to understanding New Brunswick literatures that are as performative of social dramas as they are discursively constructed: that is, as M.H. Abrams would say, as literatures that hold *both* a mirror and a lamp to society—and in so doing, reflect and shape the historical periods they inhabit. "For those who want an account of the evolution of literary forms more sophisticated than mere chronicle," observes Hayden White, "there can be no ignoring of the problem of the relationship between the literary works that make up the chronicle and the various artists, contexts, and audiences that comprise the other irreducible elements of the literary field" (110). Cultural sociology is thus *flexible* enough to carry the polyvalence of New Brunswick culture, *rigid* enough to enable us to display the changing historical contexts of the New Brunswick literary field, and *accommodating* enough to contain the wider extra-literary inquiries that a province as understudied as New Brunswick needs.

METHODOLOGY AS PRACTICE AND ORGANIZATIONAL STRUCTURE

Working within that broad methodological frame, the contributors to this volume adopted and revised Bailey's question about the socio-cultural environment. If, as Bailey and the Marxists asserted, innovation exists at the nexus of local circumstance, we asked further: "What are the socio-cultural characteristics of the distinct periods of literary ferment in English and French New Brunswick, and what do the sum of those characteristics tell us about New Brunswick as a dynamic cultural space?"

The chapters in this book address those questions. To start, we identified the most active periods of literary ferment in New Brunswick. Those were broadly delineated in the scholarship of Bailey ("Literature and Nationalism"), Cogswell ("Literary Traditions"), Boudreau and Maillet ("Acadian Literature"), and Zénon Chiasson ("Acadian Theatre"). We then applied Hayden White's schema of revolutionary change to each period to determine if it met the criteria for epochal transformation: that it was a period when "new systems of encodation and transmission of messages are being constituted" and when "*language itself* has fallen under question" (108; italics in original). We disregarded periods of literary change and coalescence of styles or address—for example, the Miramichi and Tantramar ferments of the mid-twentieth century in New Brunswick—if no lasting extra-literary or ideological movement resulted, or if language was not brought under crisis, a necessary condition of renovation that White finds in neo-classicism, realism, postmodernism, and other periods of historical rupture. On that basis, we chose *only* the historical periods that met White's definition of cultural moments that first fermented and then solidified as fully dimensioned literary movements. (We ultimately rejected the Miramichi and Tantramar ferments because they did not fit White's definition of what was *innovative, lasting, influential, paradigm-shifting, localized,* and *autonomous.*) Had we extended our treatment of ferment forward, however, or had we undertaken this work twenty-five years into the future, we would have included the cultural moments fermenting today, foremost among those the excitation in First Nations communities. New Brunswick's First Nations artists, musicians, writers, and filmmakers are mobilizing currently, as are First Nations artists in other parts of Canada; however, that mobilization is current and thus out of our (admittedly historical) purview. That said, the utility of our approach to considering moments of ferment and their impacts on cultures makes our book extremely relevant to populations undergoing cultural and social change, as the First Nations currently are.

The five periods that met both White's criteria for epochal transformation and the sanction of New Brunswick literary historians are the following, each of which is treated in a separate chapter in this book:

1   The period of Loyalist Awakening (1783–1843)
2   The period of Emergent Acadian Nationalism (1864–1955)
3   The period of Confederation Awakening (1843–1900)
4   The period of Mid-Century Emergent Modernism (1935–1955)
5   The period of Modernity and Urbanity in Arcadian Literature (1958–1999).

The book begins with a foreword by Christl Verduyn that situates our project in contemporary Canadian critical and literary contexts. Verduyn observes that recent work by an array of Canadian scholars and critics traces a shift toward a broader, multidisciplinary framework for literary studies in Canada, one that foregrounds the role and importance of the material conditions of cultural production. In their examination of the socio-cultural characteristics of five periods in New Brunswick's cultural history, the chapters in *New Brunswick at the Crossroads*, Verduyn concludes, are part of this notable shift in contemporary Canadian literary criticism.

In the first chapter, Gwendolyn Davies contextualizes the post-1783 influx of Loyalist refugees into what became the province of New Brunswick at the conclusion of the American Revolution, focusing on newspapers, handbills, and theatrical prologues as populist literary vehicles for exposing the follies and foibles of the new society. The chapter also identifies the increasing importance of Saint John as a catalyst for literary production and distribution in early-nineteenth-century New Brunswick. Examining Walter Bates's *The Mysterious Stranger* (1817) and Oliver Goldsmith Jr.'s *The Rising Village* (1825) as examples of regionally based British cultural values, Davies identifies how the vernacular newspaper satire of the 1830s and 40s eroded a lingering Loyalist mythology in the province. The chapter further suggests that the emergence of the ambitious literary periodical *The Amaranth* in the 1840s not only valorized the genres of historical fiction and the sporting sketch, but also opened a venue for New Brunswick writers Douglas Huyghue and Moses Perley to deal sympathetically with the province's Indigenous peoples.

In chapter two, Chantal Richard then maps the quite-different social terrain of French New Brunswick a generation later, examining the conditions for the emergent Acadian nationalism of the nineteenth century. Following a century of silence after the Expulsion, Acadian identity up to the middle of the nineteenth century, she contends, had been largely defined by outsiders such as Edmé Rameau de Saint-Père and Henry Wadsworth Longfellow, but in the second half of the century, and for the first time in its history, Acadians started developing the means to express and disseminate their identity within their own territory. Collège Saint-Joseph, founded in 1864, became a nexus of social and literary activity, and the appearance of the first French-language Acadian newspaper in 1867 provided a venue for the publication of identity-promoting texts. The Conventions Nationales Acadiennes, from 1881 to 1937, further cemented collective identity through the choice of national symbols, and place-specific literature flourished in the works of Antoine Léger, Pascal Poirier, James Branch, and others who, Richard suggests, would define the collective vision of Acadians for over half a century. During the ensuing Acadian Renaissance, a body of literature emerged that was not only nationalist, but also accelerated the forces of social and cultural reawakening.

Considering roughly the same period of the mid- and late nineteenth century, Thomas Hodd turns his attention in chapter three to the Confederation climate in English New Brunswick, exploring the socio-cultural conditions in which the pioneers of a distinctly *Canadian* literature navigated the politics of imperialism and national autonomy. He begins by charting Fredericton's cultural awakening from 1840 to 1860 before focusing on the significance during the 1870s and 1880s of the four-block microcommunity in downtown Fredericton where future Confederation poets such as Charles G.D. Roberts, Bliss Carman, Barry Straton, and Francis Sherman spent their formative years. Within that close-knit community, Hodd suggests, were key sites of influence that had an enormous impact on the young coterie's individual and collective creative psyche, such as the Rectory, the University of New Brunswick (UNB), the St. John River, and the surrounding wild forests. Equally important were the group's literary mentors, such as the Carman sisters, Sir George Parkin, and UNB professors like Thomas Harrison who cultivated within these young writers a love of literature and the wider literary world. The result of the mix of such social and cultural factors was the flowering of an original kind of local literature by a new generation of New Brunswick writers rooted in common childhood experiences and social standing, a shared love of the outdoors, and a collective sense of pride in their own landscape.

In chapter four, Tony Tremblay surveys the New Brunswick social landscape at the dawn of modernism. He investigates both the social temper of anti-modernist sentiment in the province and the development of an institutional apparatus for cultural production that accompanied the formation of the postwar New Brunswick state. Beginning in Saint John among a group of intellectuals and artists associated with Ted Campbell's studio (among whose number were A.G. Bailey, P.K. Page, Kay Smith, and John Sutherland), social energies moved north to Fredericton, where Bailey recruited figures such as Desmond Pacey, Fred Cogswell, and Elizabeth Brewster to radically localize cultural expression. *The Fiddlehead*, Brunswick Press, and a diversity of other developments, from new academic departments to significant library expansions, resulted, as did the realization that New Brunswick, though culturally isolated, could also participate in larger aesthetic movements while meeting its own needs for self-expression.

In chapter five, Marie-Linda Lord focuses on the city of Moncton as both cultural incubator and literary subject. Her treatment of underlying social, economic, and political forces covers the period from the late 1950s to the end of the 1990s, and establishes the growing centrality of Moncton as the urban and imaginative hub of Acadian consciousness. Beginning with Quebec's Quiet Revolution, she charts the maturing of this consciousness from Premier Louis Robichaud's Equal Opportunity reforms through the building of intellectual infrastructure (the Université de Moncton, key media outlets and publishing houses, and arts organizations) to the flowering of cultural Acadie in the works of Antonine Maillet, Raymond Guy LeBlanc, Guy Arsenault, and Herménégilde Chiasson. In the process, Lord shows how Acadian identity shifted from the agrarian sensibility of the Church fathers to the much more modern sensibility of urban secularism. The contemporary Acadie she identifies is one that comfortably accepts the contradictions and negotiations of current artists and citizens alike, and functions as a model of pluralism for not only New Brunswick but also a multicultural Canada.

Taken together, these chapters seek to understand the *historical* relationship between literary ferment and the socio-cultural conditions within which that ferment occurred. In doing so, each contributor considers the conditions underlying cultural production, distribution, and reception: specifically, the political, social, and economic factors that predominated during each period of ferment, and how those factors inflected literary activity. Contributors also consider whether the literature of each period was reactionary, and, if so, why literary artists in the province felt the need to renovate inherited traditions, the most salient features of which are language and its metaphoric and technical applications. Toward similar ends, each contributor examines the social apparatus that supported literary production in particular periods, seeking to understand the relationship, if any, between ferment and building the capacity for production and attention, whether in media and schools or through the efforts of select groups, small magazines, or professional associations. Lastly, contributors consider the public expectations of literary artists in New Brunswick during each period of creative excitation, asking if artists had to contravene those expectations to achieve their aims. What function did different reading publics ascribe to New Brunswick's writers, we ask, and what role did those functions play in the matrices of production and reception?

In the afterword, David Creelman extracts the features common to each period of literary ferment with the intention of understanding New Brunswick as a cultural space. He asks: Are there consistencies across periods and languages in terms of the apparatus and attitudes that underlie ferment, and, as importantly, how were those forms and attitudes modified to fit local circumstances? He asks, similarly, if there is congruency in the public response to literary expression across eras, both in the ways that expression was understood to avow or contest institutional power (that is, in how the role of the literary artist was interpreted by the public), and in what that expression addressed in English and French New Brunswick. Finally, as a summative question, he considers what is unique about New Brunswick literature and society that is discernable from its moments of creative ferment. Based on the evidence of the five chapters before him, Creelman concludes that "epochal transformation" occurs when four socio-cultural conditions are present: compression and concentration of ideological interests, adversarial tensions, propitious aesthetic conditions, and individuals of daring and genius who work together as a collective. His pursuit of recurring features and social conditions is not aimed at resuscitating a methodology we rejected—namely, Goldmann's desire to codify the coherent structure of a social genetic—but at determining whether New Brunswick's unique cultural geography can be understood as the sum of social conditions that gave rise to its most florid moments of literary output. His afterword illustrates, then, that while our specific research objective is to learn much more about New Brunswick literature and culture than is currently known, our more general aim is to think about the province as a constellation of meanings that have shifted over time, thereby understanding New Brunswick as a dynamic cultural landscape.

ALIGNING METHODOLOGY WITH THE CULTURAL ECONOMY OF HAVE-LESS PROVINCES

Work proximate to our study has been done piecemeal in the region, much of it under the banner of intellectual history. See, for example, scholarship by Bailey ("Creative Moments"), Boudreau (R. Boudreau, "Poetry as Action"), Gibbs ("Three Decades"), Gwyn ("Newfoundland Renaissance"), Harvey ("Intellectual Awakening"), Lord ("Identité et urbanite"), Mailhot ("La 'Renaissance acadienne'") Maillet (M. Maillet, *Histoire de la literature acadienne*), O'Flaherty (*The Rock Observed*), Ross ("A Strange Aesthetic"), and Runte (*Writing Acadia*). Little work has been done, however, on literary ferment in New Brunswick, and no cross-cultural/historical study of the province's literatures has been undertaken since *A Literary and Linguistic History of New Brunswick* (1985), a full thirty years ago. Both as signifier and site of production, then, New Brunswick continues to be the least studied province in the country. And this despite the rich literary heritage it has enjoyed; the international reach of many of its writers (Jonathan Odell, Julia Beckwith Hart, James De Mille, Placide Gaudet, Pascal Poirier, Napoléon

Landry, Charles G.D. Roberts, Bliss Carman, Francis Sherman, A.G. Bailey, Elizabeth Brewster, Fred Cogswell, Antonine Maillet, Herménégilde Chiasson, Gérald Leblanc, Alden Nowlan, David Adams Richards, Anne Compton, and Serge Patrice Thibodeau); and the fact that each of its major periods of literary ferment intersected with and altered cognate national movements that have been thoroughly studied. Well known, for instance, is the influence that Charles G.D. Roberts's work had on Archibald Lampman and the Ottawa School of Confederation poetry (Bailey, "Overture" 81; Pacey, "Archibald Lampman" 116; Bentley, *Lampman* 272, 276–77), as is the education in literary modernism that pioneering editor John Sutherland received from New Brunswick's A.G. Bailey (Gibbs, "English Poetry" 126). That education shifted the focus of second-generation modernism in Montreal and Toronto (Whiteman x; Tremblay and Rose 17–18), yet is seldom traced back to New Brunswick.

In light of those intersections, the advice of the late critic Barbara Godard concerning new directions in Canadian scholarship seems apposite: particularly, that new thinking should "pay systematic attention to the highly selective processes of appropriation and realignment that have taken place throughout the history of the Canadian literatures" (182). That advice invites the kind of study that has informed the recent rethinking of regional literatures in Canada, evident in the reassessment of "Prairie" in the work of Calder and Wardhaugh, and Thacker, and the reassessment of "Maritime" in the work of Creelman, Fuller, and Wyile.

Our study pays similar "attention" to those processes of "appropriation and realignment" in New Brunswick, offering an assessment of creative energies and cultural undercurrents that will destabilize many of the myths of New Brunswick's backwardness that have circulated freely in the absence of more fulsome research.

Especially relevant to our study in this regard is the recent work on cultural economies, including Richard Florida's theorizing about creative communities. Florida's work charts the economic shift to post-industrial growth centres, arguing that particular social conditions give rise to a creative class—in effect, to cultural and economic ferment. The widespread public interest in Florida's work—former Ontario Premier Dalton McGuinty commissioned him to write a socio-economic study of the province in 2009—provides a context for thinking more deeply about what constitutes *the creative* in Canadian society, especially in largely rural, "have-less" provinces like New Brunswick (Savoie, "Reviewing" 173). Despite the fact that Florida's proscriptive "3 T's" of "technology, talent and tolerance" (249) are cosmopolitan features of concentrations of high-skilled information workers—concentrations that have rarely existed in Atlantic Canada—distinct periods of creative energy *did* nevertheless coalesce in non-cosmopolitan "hinterlands" (Savoie, *Visiting* 48) such as New Brunswick. Our study, then, both challenges and also nuances Florida's work. In that sense, it takes up the suggestion of historian Steven High, who, in rebuking Florida's urban-centrism, called for research that particularizes moments of creative energy in variant spaces and times, thereby contesting "the work of futurist consultants like Richard Florida, who issue sweeping generalizations with little or no regard for people, place, or past" (33).

In the age of frenetic post-nationalism, an age that disguises neo-liberal economics in the glittery robes of globalization, the work of resuscitating place, especially rural places, grows vitally important. Prairie critic Alison Calder echoes Steven High almost exactly in summarizing what the stakes are, and how critics should respond: "At a time when we are being told that place and referentiality no longer matter, that there is no national literature, and that we are living in a world without boundaries, those of us who call the have-not political regions home are becoming aware that placing ourselves, and our literatures, is more important than ever" (60).

This study, then, is an act of *emplacement* that models ways that cultural vibrancy can be understood (and even enhanced) in rural, have-less areas like New Brunswick. As such, our work adds an important chapter to the many studies of cultural economy that focus almost exclusively on the creative capital of what urbanist Charles Landry termed "renaissance cities," cities such as Hong Kong, Singapore, Canberra, and Glasgow. Despite the histrionics of those who proclaim the end of geography (Arjun Appadurai, Joshua Meyrowitz, and Frances Cairncross, to name a few), as well as the general thrust of neo-liberalism to concentrate power in growth-pole centres of efficiency, thus artificially accelerating changes to normative spatial geographies, our research investigates strategies of creative invention and social resiliency that contest current assumptions about the locus of creative capital. What our work shows clearly is that the social conditions that index culture can coalesce in any time and place. Our hope is that policy-makers in New Brunswick and other have-less or rural regions will view this research as offering historical frames through which to view the admix of social ingredients and material interventions that characterize imaginatively vibrant communities. Though we do not aim to be instrumental in this hope—and, unlike many urban theorists of the creative economy, we do not view our work as offering a toolkit for cultural development—we do believe that when policy-makers, citizens, and artists know the conditions within which culture thrives there are clear markers for where investments in the cultural economy can be directed. Since cultural GDP in a province as small as New Brunswick is worth $641 million annually (Statistics Canada), a figure that supports over 9300 jobs, the stakes are high enough to warrant attention. This, again, is not to say that we have patented a prescription for cultural or rural health but a statement of the relevance of our work. Simply put, all economies and societies, large or small, have vested interests in culture—and our study aims to understand how creative cultures coalesce.

CHAPTER 1

LOYALIST LITERATURE IN NEW BRUNSWICK, 1783–1843

Gwendolyn Davies

"NOVA SCOTIA IS MY DWELEN PLAS / AND INGLAND IS MY NASHON"
In his 1976 autobiography, *In My Time*, Maritime novelist Thomas H. Raddall describes an eighteenth-century Nova Scotian privateer's book of sailing directions on which was written: *Francis Kempton is my nam / Seaman is my stashon / Nova Scotia is my dwelen plas / And Ingland is my nashon* (233). The doggerel could be dismissed as a seemingly evocative piece of folk culture, but taken in the context of post-Revolutionary British North America—and of the questions of place, identity, and nationhood facing the approximately 33,000 Loyalist refugees who came into the Maritime provinces circa 1783—the doggerel assumes more resonance.

The world of the Loyalists who flooded into Nova Scotia—including what in 1784 was to become the province of New Brunswick—was a "fluid" one, notes historian J.M. Bumsted, "emphasizing the ambivalences felt by many with regard to self-identification with things British and things American" (220). Indeed, most Loyalists, like Raddall's privateer, probably began the war self-identifying with *my stashon* and *my dwelen plas*, whether the latter were Dutchess County, New York; Germantown, Pennsylvania; or Stamford, Connecticut. "Direct exposure to wartime trauma" inevitably disrupted daily life, notes historian Liam Riordan, making "political allegiance a matter of public scrutiny as never before," and forcing "politics beyond traditional boundaries" (43). Moreover, as war progressed, a large body of male combatants became further defined by their regiments, the very names of which suggested origins rooted in American provinces (for example, the 1st Battalion New Jersey Volunteers, the Westchester Volunteers, or the Maryland Loyalists). By the time that they were evacuated to the east coast of British North America as refugees, most of the Maritime Loyalists had also spent years living in temporary accommodations behind British lines in places such as New York or Long Island, totally disconnected from the rhythms of American community life they had once known (Van Buskirk 26–43). As well, while being part of British civil society remained an ideal of social order for which many Loyalists had been prepared to sacrifice, most exiles nonetheless recognized that by both experience and community affiliation they were less British than North American. Thus, they brought to New Brunswick in 1783–1784 a certain discursiveness, because, as Bumsted argues, in the 1780s, there was no "common understanding of the meaning of nationalism." "In a very real sense," he adds, "nationalism both as a concept and a movement was in its infancy during the period 1760–1783, and one should be careful about reading back into those times later developments" (220).

It could be argued that this sense of shifting identity in the eighteenth-century Atlantic world might help to explain why, in spite of a common experience of war and exile, there was an edginess, a sense of insecurity and suspicion in a newly established Loyalist city such as Saint John in the early 1780s. And it may explain why the initial impulse in English-language literary writing in New Brunswick was to turn to the populist traditions of doggerel, invective, letters, dramatic dialogues, pamphlets, prologues, and public history—sources familiar to the Loyalists from their Revolutionary War experience—as an expression of resistance to perceived forces of politics or privilege threatening the potential for stability. Literary critic Ray Palmer Baker has theorized that no school of Loyalist literature evolved in the Maritime provinces because of the bitter backward-turning sense of loss of its formal public poets, Jacob Bailey, Joseph Stansbury, and Jonathan Odell. "Whatever they wrote was conditioned largely by the struggle in which they had played such an absorbing part," he has argued. "When that struggle receded in their memories, there were no aesthetic impulses, no dreams of the future, to take its place" (Baker 51).

Yet what Baker failed to recognize was that it was emphatically the "dreams of the future"—indeed, the *necessity* for a future—that inspired the writing of poetry, parody, history, doggerel, dialogues, diaries, letters, theatrical prologues, and even sermons that found their way into the newspapers and printers' shops of Saint John, and later Fredericton, from 1783 onward. And, it was the subversiveness of common citizens—their penchant for irony and "kicking against the pricks" (*Holy Bible*, Acts 26:14)—that Baker overlooked in the work of the Loyalists and their literary descendants in a province such as New Brunswick, largely because he, like critics after him, looked to public poets in the classical tradition as representative of the populace. In doing so, he failed to recognize that the newspaper, the prologue, and the periodical, *not the book*, often captured the prevalent literary voice of the post-1783 period. Nor, indeed, did he acknowledge that the majority of the 33,000 Loyalist exiles who came into the Maritimes at the cessation of war were by-and-large literate, with a populist background, notes Harvard historian Maya Jasanoff, that emerged in "what would become a recurring official commentary on loyalist refugees: American loyalists could shockingly resemble American patriots" (170).

Nowhere was this incipient ferment better illustrated than in the instant city of Saint John where, from May to November of 1783, thousands of refugees had been shipped to the shores of what Loyalist diarist Sarah Frost described as "the roughest land I ever saw" (122). Having sought safety behind the lines in New York City and Long Island from 1777 onward as the British gradually lost the war, many of the incoming Loyalists had endured inadequate accommodation, icy winters (the Hudson froze in 1779-1780), food shortages, financial loss, and uncertainty in a New York that had become "a thoroughly uneasy place" (Van Buskirk 21, 179). Landing in waves from May 1783 onward at the site of what was to become Saint John, the disembarking Loyalists faced boundary lines, building lots, and cross streets for the new city only cursorily identified by roughly-cut fir posts or by blazes upon trees (Rees 74; Jack 63-70). Yet by 1784, when the province of New Brunswick (numbering about 17,000 Loyalists) had been partitioned from Nova Scotia, and by 1785, when the first provincial election was being called, a new city of Saint John, divided into the Lower Cove (primarily working class and disbanded soldiers) and the Upper Cove (lawyers, merchants, officers), had already been created and incorporated (MacNutt, *New Brunswick* 58-59).

Even before the Loyalist evacuees had left New York, notes historian David Bell, 600 heads of refugee households had signed a memorial against the proposal that fifty-five upper-middle-class Loyalists receive individual fiefdoms of 5,000 acres of the best land in Nova Scotia (and what was to be New Brunswick)—at the expense of the disbanded military and refugee families awaiting passage (*Early Loyalist* 64-65). Although assured by General Sir Guy Carleton in New York that he would forward "their remonstrance to Governor Parr," the incoming Loyalists brought their sense of grievance and ferment with them to Saint John. Within two years, anger over the effrontery of the "Fifty-Five," discontent over the perceived foot-dragging of land agents, and suspicion of elitist initiatives to rig the 1785 election of representatives to the province's first Assembly, had erupted in violence. Stones ricocheted in the streets of Saint John, windows were broken, and soldiers were summoned to break up a politically inspired riot at Mallard's tavern (Bell, *Loyalist Rebellion* 110–23; MacNutt, *New Brunswick* 61). "The political climate of early Saint John assumed an aspect so grave," notes David Bell, "that many likened it to the mood of the old colonies on the eve of the Revolution" (*Early Loyalist* 62). Or as Jasanoff has noted in her 2011 study of the Loyalist diaspora: "the tumults in New Brunswick also plainly revealed that political schisms among British subjects did not simply end with the war. They highlighted an important continuity, forged by loyalist refugees, from the pre-revolutionary into the post-revolutionary British Empire" (188).

Such discord might inevitably inspire caricature, satire, even parody, but it was not the Revolution's most trenchant Tory satirist, Jonathan Odell, now comfortably ensconced in Fredericton as the Provincial Secretary of the newly created province of New Brunswick, who took up the pen during this period of fraught tensions. Rather, it was the common people, anonymous citizens, who resorted to doggerel, to a proposed proletarian history of the Loyalists, and to mock dialogues to give literary expression to their sense of social and political frustration. Turning for their outlet to the *Royal St. John's Gazette*, the province's first newspaper, begun on 18 December 1783 only seven months after the arrival of the Spring Fleet, the anonymous agitators found in printers and former New York newspaper partners William Lewis and John Ryan sympathetic support. On 29 January 1784, Lewis and Ryan published an extraordinary sixty-line poem by "A Spectator." Cursed by "frozen ink and fretful fire," the versifier began by defining the Loyalists' plight ("By various scenes of fortune toss'd, / Lock'd up by one eternal frost; / An iron shore, ordain'd by fate, / For Loyalists their last escape"). Then—after documenting a range of suffering ("a scanty meal of meat," "a shameful peace," the loss of "prime and youth," "Friends and relations far from here," "A piece of barren ground that's burnt")—the embittered versifier turned to a denunciation of agents, directors, and politicians. In particular, "A Spectator" attacked the Reverend John Sayre, agent of the "Fifty-Five," who, in spite of being on his deathbed with dropsy, was treated with venom: "May he, the author of our woes, / Far fiercer than our rebel foes, / Have his due portion near a lake, / Which is ordain'd to such by fate; / May living worms his corps devour, / Him and his comrades fifty-four: / A scandal to both church and state, / The rebel's friend, the public's hate" (*Royal St. John's Gazette* 29 January 1784).

On 26 February 1784, only a month after the "Spectator" poem had so scathingly attacked the authorities, the *Gazette* published a dramatic dialogue by "A Plain Dealer." This also focused on the land distribution question, including the perceived lethargy with which authorities were surveying new properties or escheating old ones for Loyalist distribution. By 4 March 1784, when an anonymous letter by "A Soldier" was published in the *Saint John Gazette* threatening the authorities with feeling "the force of a justly enraged soldier" if things did not change, Lewis and Ryan were compelled to reveal the source of their published material and, on 10 March 1784, were arraigned before the Sunbury County Grand Jury for printing seditious and scandalous libel (Tremaine 598; Bell, *Early Loyalist* 74–78). Thus a blow against literary free speech was struck early in the Loyalist newspaper history of New Brunswick, a move that Lewis and Ryan challenged on 9 September 1784 by publishing the prospectus of what promised to be a polemical three-hundred-page history of the Loyalists written by New Brunswick refugee David Melville. Allegedly exposing the "Fifty-Five" and, among other targets, the perceived tardiness of agents in escheating land, Melville's text has not survived (Bell, *Early Loyalist* 100; Bell, *Loyalist Rebellion* 106). However, references suggest the importance of the proposed work as a transfer of the Revolution's polemical pamphlet traditions into the literary discourse of New Brunswick. Ryan and Lewis's inclusion of a hard-hitting letter by "Americanus" on 22 February 1786 again brought them before the courts. Found guilty of sedition and heavily fined on 2 May 1786 (Tremaine 598; Bell, *Loyalist Rebellion* 130–31), Lewis and Ryan dissolved their partnership, leaving Ryan alone to carry on with a renamed and reconfigured newspaper, *The St. John Gazette & Daily Advertiser*.

One can only speculate on the impact of this heavy-handed judicial intrusion into authorial and editorial freedom on the development of irony, parody, and satire in New Brunswick literature over the next fifty years. Clearly, although "the adversities of war had produced a powerful cohesion" among the Loyalists during the 1775–1783 Revolutionary period, notes W.S. MacNutt, the "circumstances of the first settlement" in New Brunswick had revealed cracks of both "diversity and difference" (*New Brunswick* 63). Thus the initial meeting of the New Brunswick legislature in January 1786 after the debacle in Saint John (where the proletarian Lower Covers had won the election but had been denied victory by the middle-class Upper

Covers' invocation of a technicality) marked the "commencement" of what was to be a "robust political life" in the province throughout the late eighteenth and early nineteenth centuries (63). Indeed, "instead of the unified, vigorously led community of their dreams," adds historian Ann Condon, Loyalist leaders found a New Brunswick society "racked by dissension and virtual paralysis during its first two decades," including a split between inland and coastal interests that pitted the Fredericton government and judiciary against the trading and timber economy of centres such as Saint John, St. Andrews, and the Miramichi (Condon, *Loyalist Dream* 158–59; MacNutt, *New Brunswick* 100–12; Bell, *Loyalist Rebellion* 148–54). Adding to these challenges, notes historical geographer Graeme Wynn, the province in its early decades was "a backwater of empire, peripheral to, and poorly connected with, the North Atlantic World" (*Timber Colony* 25). The population was scattered, the climate was harsh, overland communication was difficult, and the "forest, scarcely altered by the hand of man, spread over almost the entire province in 1800" (12).

Yet despite the grim challenges outlined by Wynn, a spirit of wry humour emerges in the ephemeral literature of the day. The clever Aesopian fable of "Weazels/Elephant/and Ape" that appeared in the *Royal Gazette* in January 1786 (Bell, *Loyalist Rebellion* 146*)*, and the handbill doggerel of the local News-Carriers' New Year's "Addresses" (Fleming 12–13), were typical in integrating prickly politics into often clever vernacular literature for popular consumption. As well, locally written prologues to amateur productions of British plays, often laced with propagandistic subtexts, enhanced the taste for theatricals that Loyalists had brought with them into New Brunswick as part of their process of cultural transfer (Van Buskirk 31–32). Thus, in the midst of the intensifying 1790s political confrontations between the interior capital, Fredericton, and the growing Bay of Fundy port, Saint John, the anonymous prologue written for a production of *All the World's A Stage* performed at Mallard's Long Room in Saint John typified a coastal perspective in prognosticating a provincial future based on the naval and commercial hegemony of the port city: "What rais'd this City on a dreary coast, / Alternately presenting rocks and frost, / Where torpid shell-fish hardly found a bed, / Where scarce a pine durst shew a stunted head? / 'Twas commerce—commerce smooth'd the rugged strand, / Her streets and buildings overspread the land; / Her piers the mighty Fundy's tides control, / And navies ride secure within her mole" ("Prologue," *Royal Gazette* 20 January 1795; M.E. Smith, *Too Soon* 7; Davies, *Studies* 37). Not to be outdone, inland proponents of an agriculturally based provincial economy did not miss an opportunity to present an equally polarizing prologue before the lieutenant-governor and "a numerous and crowded audience" in Fredericton in May 1803 at a production of *Speed the Plough*:

> The air we breathe is wholesome, pure and good,
> And our strong minds require *substantial* food:
> Here active *industry* (as yet) prevails,
> Ourselves, our children, live by Plough and Flails.
> We need not pamper'd minions—half a score
> To drive the wretched from the great man's door,
> Nor systematic soups to feed *our* poor.
> The man who labours *here* has nought to dread,
> He's sure to earn his honest daily bread—
> In *such* a land—you'll certainly allow
> Our play's well chosen—It is *Speed the Plough*.
> ("Theatrical: Prologue," *Saint John Gazette*, 21 May 1803)

While both prologues propagandize a geographical agenda (coastal versus inland), they must also be contextualized within the broader divisive issues facing New Brunswick in the 1790s and at the turn of the century. A financial depression, war with France beginning in 1793, and political resistance to "the Carleton government's determination to impose its centralized elitist goals upon the province" (Condon, "Young Robin Hood" 123) all intensified a growing atmosphere of tension between Governor Carleton's appointed Council in Fredericton and the provincially elected House of Assembly. Typical of the way in which economic and class confrontations in New Brunswick became catalysts for literary ferment in this period was reformer James Glenie's 1795 *Substance of* MR. GLENIE's *Address to the* FREEEHOLDERS *of the County of Sunbury*, which, on the cusp of a provincial election, attacked the perceived privilege-oriented performance of Governor Carleton's regime in vitriolic terms (Condon, "Young Robin Hood" 123; MacNutt, *New Brunswick* 102, 104). Glenie's agriculturally based constituency of Sunbury, settled in 1761 by Bunyan and Bible-reading New England Planters (some of whom had fought for the Patriot cause during the Revolution in the 1776 siege of Fort Cumberland), reflected only part of the complexity of a province that saw the Mi'kmaq, Maliseet, Acadians, New England Planters, Yorkshire Settlers, Scots, Irish, and 17,000 Loyalists all jostling to find their place within the fluid boundaries of a nascent eighteenth-century provincial economy. Even among themselves, the Loyalists represented a diverse lot, with 36% coming from New York, 20% from New Jersey, 12% from Connecticut, and fewer than 7% from each of the other states (E.C. Wright, *The Loyalists* 155).

Faced with such diversity on the eve of the 1795 election—and with issues ranging from the need for a reformed marriage act to a "vigilant defence of the assembly's, and thus the people's rights"—Glenie proposed in his pamphlet to extend the range of the Supreme Court beyond Fredericton by carrying "the administration of Justice by that Court into every County and to every Man's door as much as possible" (Godfrey "Glenie, James"; Godfrey, "James Glenie" 19–29; Condon, "Young Robin Hood" 120–43). However, the imagery of "every man's door" was to reverberate on Glenie, when, in 1795, Loyalist satirist Edward Winslow, member of Council and an associate of Governor Carleton, responded to the ferment of the hustings with the poison of the pen. His satirical pamphlet play, *Substance of The Debates, In The Young Robin Hood Society*, reduced Glenie to parody as the character Issachar, in particular exploding his metaphor of justice's being carried "to every Man's door" by farcically portraying the fully robed Supreme Court and "Gentlemen of the Bar" literally trundling their wheelbarrows of legal records around the province "bringing justice" to each humble doorstep (Condon, "Young Robin Hood" 126). Predating by almost thirty years Joseph Howe and Thomas Chandler Haliburton's creation of a mock Nova Scotian "club" as a literary conduit for contemporary political satire (Davies, *Studies* 88–106), Winslow's apocryphal *Young Robin Hood Society* was cleverly designed to entertain as well as persuade. The targets of his caricatures (the Reverend Jonathan Odell and James Glenie) were reduced to indignity, including the Hogarthian bawdiness of foil-figure Zedikiah's (Glenie's) exhortations that the Congregationalist and New Light constituents of Sunbury County's electorate "lay the whore of Babylon flat upon her back. Your shoulders are to her—therefore tug away—in the Lord's name tug away" (Condon, "Young Robin Hood" 133). The play's apocryphal library, to be established in Glenie's fundamentalist religious constituency, allegedly included titles such as *The Religious Courtship* and *Hooks and Eyes for Believers Breeches* (Condon, "Young Robin Hood" 126). And Glenie's mathematical prowess, which had earned him membership in the Royal Society in London in 1779, received Swiftian dismissal as he (Issacher) was described as having "an amazing proficiency in ciphering—He would undertake Sir, in five minutes to calculate how many grains of Flour there were in a barrel of Ginger-bread ... [H]e understood the principles of motion, and he had such a mechanical genius that he invented a Dumb-Betty upon a new construction to wash without water, and made great improvements upon wooden Clocks" (Condon, "Young Robin Hood" 141).

If Winslow's 1790s New Brunswick emerges as a world of topsy-turvy turmoil in the *Young Robin Hood Society*, Britain itself, in the words of historian Roy Porter in *English Society in the 18th Century*, was going through a decade of seething social unrest, with "the prospect of civil strife and even bloody revolution" being "sudden and traumatic" (348). Discord emanated from "a long-term build-up of stress-points," notes Porter (348), a parallel that 1790s observers of New Brunswick politics might find equally apposite, particularly in the mounting abrasiveness between elected Glenie reformers and the lieutenant-governor's British-approved Council. Glenie "would accept as an ally any man who carried a grievance," notes W.S. MacNutt, and there was nothing "half-hearted in his abuse of the lieutenant-governor and his officials. Allen was 'an illiterate moon-struck judge', Ludlow an 'illiterate, strutting chief-justice', Billop, 'an ignorant, uncouth Dutch boor'" (*New Brunswick* 102). In February 1797, verbal warfare culminated in a duel, with Glenie wounded in a confrontation with political enemy John Coffin in the woods across the river from Fredericton (Godfrey, "Glenie, James").

That politics in New Brunswick should somehow echo international edginess, particularly framed against the uncertainties generated by war with revolutionary France, finds resonance in the Robin Hood Club of London's being a hotbed of what Porter calls "para-political invective" (349). Thus the subtlety of Winslow's title, the "Young Robin Hood Society," for his own "para-political invective" would not be lost on the cognoscenti in New Brunswick, particularly as political dissent continued to be a catalyst for literary production as the province entered the 1802 election. Throughout this period Glenie's abrasiveness informed a pamphlet war that ranged from Samuel Denny Street's *A Statement of the Facts Relative to the Proceedings of the House of Assembly on Wednesday the Third, and Thursday the Fourth of March, 1802, at the Close of the Last Session* by "Creon," to Edward Winslow's "rather vicious" (Vincent, *Narrative Verse* 120) *A Statement of facts relative to the Standfasts and Runaways, Or Sammy Creon's Pamphlet Turn'd Right Side Outwards*. Pithy citizen letters and verse in *The Royal Gazette* and *The Saint John Gazette* (Vincent, *Narrative Verse* 120) intensified political passion leading up to the election, culminating in the publication of Samuel Denny Street's satirical long poem, *Creon*, in *The Saint John Gazette* on 23 October and 6, 13, and 20 November 1802. While the poem can be read in the tradition "of eighteenth-century Augustan satire," notes Thomas Vincent (*Narrative Verse* 121), it must also be seen as resorting to the same literary conventions employed by Loyalist poets Jonathan Odell, Jacob Bailey, and Joseph Stansbury during the American Revolution. "In their satires," argues Vincent, the loyal Tories had been presented as "upholders of Reason, Justice, Law and Order," while the rebels had been perceived as having "played fast and loose with these precious gifts, compromising social stability in order to achieve selfish ends" (122). By inverting that model—by portraying the Assembly's reformers as the agents of Reason, Justice, Law and Order—Street "implicitly set the political problems of New Brunswick in 1802 against the background of the American Rebellion and Whig-Tory politics of eighteenth-century England" (122).

Despite the inverted analogy between Street's contemporary literary strategies and those of the Loyalist poets of the Revolution, Jonathan Odell, that "most powerful and most unrelenting of the Tory satirists" of the 1775-1783 conflict (Tyler 98), remained aloof from the Glenie-Winslow-Street exchange of the 1790s and early 1800s, even when Glenie caustically employed the liturgical conventions of Odell's Anglican clerical background to pillory his privileged Council position in verse satire ("Beloved of all Britons, Men of men, head of heads ...").[1] But the outbreak of the War of 1812—a reopening of old wounds for many Loyalist survivors of 1775-1783—drew Odell back into writing public declarative verse. As New Brunswick's still largely Loyalist citizenry rallied around the 104th Regiment of Foot as it marched 1,100 kilometres overland from Fredericton to Kingston in the winter of 1813 to fight at Sackets Harbour, Fort Erie, and Niagara, Odell generated patriotic fervour in provincial newspapers by publishing poems such as *Song for the 104th* (1811) and *The Battle of Queens Town, Upper Canada* (1812). By far the most ambitious of these works was *The Agonizing Dilemma*, inspired by American General Stephan Van Rensselaer's battle report published in the New York *National Intelligencer* on 31 October 1812 and recirculated in the Saint John *Royal Gazette* on 16 November (Vincent, *Narrative Verse* 175). Odell composed his satirical long poem on the defeated American general with speed and alacrity, publishing it in the *Gazette* on 28 December 1812 and 4 January 1813 (Vincent, *Jonathan Odell* 17). "Employing the actual first person narration of Van Rensselaer's report as a baseline to expose the ineptitude of the Americans, Odell nonetheless tempered the venom of his political satire," notes Vincent, because he wanted to detract from neither the war nor the gallant victory of the British forces (*Narrative Verse* 176–77). His death five years later, adds poet Robert Gibbs, marked the passing of a literary voice that had remained committed to "deeply held convictions, a way of seeing and responding to the world and to life" throughout his exile in New Brunswick (Gibbs, Introduction ix).

Like Odell, other members of the founding generation of Loyalist leaders and writers were also beginning to age and retire just at a time when "the last seven years of the great war against Napoleon" were bringing "a degree of unprecedented prosperity" to New Brunswick and were effectively establishing "the character of the colony for fifty years following" (MacNutt, *New Brunswick* 144). The British government's wartime intervention in protecting shipping commerce by convoys (thereby lowering insurance rates), and its inclusion of both Saint John and St. Andrews under the "Free Port Act" to facilitate the flow of wartime goods, had been complemented by its growing dependence on New Brunswick pine after the blockade of Baltic timber (MacNutt, *New Brunswick* 150; Wynn, *Timber* 33). By the end of the Napoleonic Wars in 1815, the growth of the timber trade, the increase in international commerce and immigration, and the ongoing demand for masts and shipbuilding supplies (MacNutt, *New Brunswick* 144–56) all promised to feed New Brunswick's aspirations to become a buoyant player in Atlantic world trade (Wright, *Saint John Ships* 8). "Diversification of the New Brunswick economy" also became a theme, notes Wynn, with "exhortations almost always" endeavouring "to draw men away from lumbering and into farming" ("Deplorably Dark" 171). To this end, an Agricultural and Emigrant Society was founded in 1825, working with other organizations to disseminate information, improve stockbreeding, and distribute seeds (172). Ultimately, as Wynn argues, by mid-century there would be "a widespread pattern of occupational pluralism" in New Brunswick, where, for example, "on the coasts, fishermen farmed and farmers fished" (176). And as late as 1850, an external report on the province's agricultural state was to report that many farmers were "lumberers before they were farmers, and it was by lumbering they got their farms stocked, etc." (178).

SAINT JOHN, LITERARY POPULISM, AND SOCIAL ORDER

By 1824, the year of New Brunswick's first census, the province's population had grown to 74,116 (compared to 25,000 circa 1800), with some of that increase reflecting postwar immigration from Scotland, Ireland, and the United States (MacNutt, *New Brunswick* 162–63). When Lady Sir Martin Hunter had arrived in Fredericton in 1804 as the wife of the lieutenant-governor, she had described it as a "bucolic village" of "about one hundred and twenty houses" "scattered on a delightful common of the richest sheep pasture I ever saw, and flocks grazing close up to our door" (Rees 80). By

1832, notes geographer Ronald Rees, Fredericton had lost its "village-like look," but was "still no more than two principal streets running parallel with the river, and containing about twelve hundred inhabitants" (81). By contrast, coastal Saint John had grown to approximately 12,000 by 1824 (MacNutt, *New Brunswick* 164; Thomas and Tracy 114) and projected a bustling mercantile image, including a handsome courthouse, market, post office, city hall, chamber of commerce, and Bank of New Brunswick (Wynn, *Timber* 45), all centrally located close to the Market Slip. In the Subscription Room at Cody's Exchange Coffee House local entrepreneurs consulted the latest *Lloyd's List* as well as London, New York, Boston, and Halifax newspapers (available to paying members), while the Freemason, Saint George's, and St. Andrews' Societies met there regularly (Thomas and Tracy 137). Although it would be devastated numerous times during the nineteenth century by major fires (1826, 1837, 1839, 1841, 1849, and 1877), Saint John nonetheless always rebounded. "A less resilient city might have wasted away, but in cities, as in real estate," notes Rees, "location is everything. The valley and the New Brunswick shore of the Bay of Fundy needed a fulcrum—an organizing, marketing, and supply centre—and there was no better place for it than the two rocky headlands at the mouth of the Saint John River" (104).

Saint John's pivotal position not only made it a driver of the province's commerce and international trade but also a catalyst for literary production and distribution—including newspapers, almanacs, pamphlets, and sermons—throughout the post–Napoleonic War years. From the earliest days of Loyalist settlement, the city's merchants had advertised fresh shipments of books arriving from Britain, and bookseller and stationer William Reynolds was typical, advertising on 10 July 1816 in the *Saint John City Gazette* such popular Sir Walter Scott editions as *Marmion, The Lady of the Lake*, and *Lord of the Isles* (the latter just published in 1815). Equally current was the Saint John Society's "Library" list for 1816 revealing that, among other recent imports from Great Britain, Jane Austen's *Pride and Prejudice* was being circulated to readers only three years after publication in London, a revelation of Saint John's integration into the cultural Atlantic at a time when Austen references are extremely rare in the Maritimes (List of Books Imported, 1816).[2] The city's history of fires in the nineteenth century has resulted in a significant loss of publishing records, but a surviving contract between Sheriff Walter Bates of Kingston and printer William Durant of Saint John dated 17 January 1826 illustrates the interactive responsibilities of writer and printer in this era of literary production in the province, making it clear that, for Durant's printing of 1,000 copies of Bates's proposed collection of essays, the author was bound to cover printing costs of £50 ("Special Agreement"). While distribution details for Bates's Saint John reprints of his 1817 *The Mysterious Stranger* (initially published in the United States and Britain) remain unclear, it was an indication of the city's role as cultural catalyst in the province that Peter Fisher's *Sketches of New Brunswick* (the first history of the province, 1825), Anthony Lockwood's "superb" 1825 *Map of New Brunswick* (Wynn, *Timber Colony* 46), Peter Fisher's *The Lay of the Wilderness* (1833), Oliver Goldsmith's revision of *The Rising Village* (1834), and Peter Fisher's *Notitia of New Brunswick* (1838) all emerged from Saint John publishers at a time when, elsewhere in Canada, "local literary works were rare, most readers preferring imported and inexpensive publications" (Fleming, Gallichan, Lamonde 71).

Despite Saint John's initiative in literary production in the post-Napoleonic era, the fortunes of the city and the province were always to be responsive to "the fluctuations" of "nineteenth century business cycles in Britain" (Wynn, *Timber Colony* 53). It is within the uncertainties of this ongoing framework of a "boom and bust" provincial economy that literary initiatives such as Walter Bates's *The Mysterious Stranger* (1817) and Oliver Goldsmith's *The Rising Village* (1825) were to be published and republished, each illustrating a taste for regional culture in what had hitherto been a largely politically driven literary environment. Of the two, it was rural-based Sherriff Walter Bates who seemed least likely to be authoring a book that would appear almost simultaneously in three countries and become the first bestseller in what is now Canada. But his trustworthiness as a representative "everyman" narrator in a period of social change in rural New Brunswick can be contextualized against his background in the American Revolution where his commitment to the concept of British civil rights had informed his Loyalism in the face of arrest, threats of execution, and demands that he betray his brothers in Connecticut (Cogswell, "Bates, Walter"). And, in the same way that Loyalists had imported into New Brunswick an appreciation for British law and order, so too had they brought with them a taste for the genre of crime and confessional literature that had been universally popular in England and America since the seventeenth century. Including execution broadsides, crime pamphlets, confessional texts, and newspaper trial descriptions that confirmed the triumph of authority in the face of social disruption, these tales of criminal aberration had, by the nineteenth century, often moved out of the "hellfire domain" of the clergy into the realm of entertaining, if moral, reading for a cross-section of society ranging from apprentices to housewives (Cohen 24–25, 34).

It was within this tradition of confessional crime literature that *The Mysterious Stranger* by Bates was published in rapid succession in 1817 in New Haven, Connecticut; London, England; and Halifax, Nova Scotia.[3] Rarely out of print in book or serialized newspaper form in New Brunswick throughout the nineteenth and twentieth centuries, Bates's retrospective memoir begins after he has reluctantly incarcerated a gentlemanly young man (Henry More Smith, alias Henry Moon, "the lunar rogue") in the Kingston, New Brunswick, jail on 24 July 1814 on a charge of suspected horse theft. Smith's subsequent bravado, trickery, escapes, and occasional madness titillate the reader with the conventions of popular melodrama, at the same time exposing the rogue's exploitation of the homespun populace of Windsor, Pictou, Saint John, Kingston, Gagetown, Maugerville, Woodstock, and Fredericton as he charmingly barters stolen goods and fine horse flesh in the years 1812 to 1814. Along the way, like the protagonist of an eighteenth-century picaresque novel, he is unmasked by a farmer in Norton; by an innkeeper in Upper Kingsclear; by an Anglican clergyman en route to Woodstock; and by a freed slave outside of Fredericton. What holds these disparate citizens—the fabric of New Brunswick society—together is a commitment to the rule of British law and a sense of regional community. While they might experience vicarious thrills by visiting Henry More Smith's clever marionette performances in the Kingston jail or by reading accounts of his nefarious behaviour in local newspapers, the tension between law and "outlaw" (that taxonomy of otherness that More Smith, alias Moon, represents) becomes an organic unifying factor in Bates's narrative—and, indeed, by implication, in New Brunswick society. To the end of their days, as a number of newspaper obituaries of the 1880–1899 period in New Brunswick indicate, provincial citizens remembered where they were from 1812 to 1815 in relation to More Smith's thefts, escapes, and antisocial activities ("Obituaries"). The War of 1812 may have been unfolding in the background, but it is the amorality of the con artist—not the amorality of war—that dramatized their immediate lives and gave them a cameo role in preserving the rule of common law in their society.

Just eight years after Bates's *The Mysterious Stranger* (described by Fred Cogswell as "comparable to the best work of Daniel Defoe in combining suspense with credibility" ["Bates, Walter"]), Oliver Goldsmith Jr.'s popular long poem, *The Rising Village,* was also to offer New Brunswick readers a vision of community social cohesion as a counterpoint to chaos. The grand-nephew and namesake of the famous Anglo-Irish writer Oliver Goldsmith Sr. (author of *The Deserted Village*), the New Brunswick Goldsmith, a son of Loyalists, embraced the theme of his uncle's 1770 long poem of Irish-enforced outmigration and exile by evoking in his own long poem, *The Rising Village*, an image of "the hardy bands" (55) of the dispossessed carving out fields from the wilderness as "by slow degrees a neighbourhood they form" (126). As David Bentley has argued, on one level Goldsmith was very much the product of eighteenth-century Enlightenment social scientific thought, organizing his poem around a "'four stages theory' of the development of civilizations from their rude wilderness beginnings to their refined maturity," culminating in institutions such as churches, stores, schools, and commerce ("Oliver Goldsmith" 33, 40–41, 46–54). But, in spite of its contextualization within a tradition of Britannia's "laws ... liberty ... splendour, science, power, and skill," notes Bentley ("Oliver Goldsmith" 26–28, 40), the poem also "addresses itself to local issues and a local audience and, for this reason, grounds itself in the life of its place and time" (32–34, 54).

Thus, reading Goldsmith's *The Rising Village* with its pronounced stages of settler community evolution—including the marginalization of Indigenous peoples—is to infer an analogy with the archetypal exile, wilderness encounter, economic uncertainty, and gradual social integration into a new region of the Loyalist narrative experience. Many New Brunswickers reading the poem (London pub. 1825; Montreal pub. 1826; Saint John pub. 1834) undoubtedly recognized the parallels between the imagined "rising village" in a stylized "Acadia" and the existing new settler conditions in their own province where a social infrastructure of roads, schools, churches, and stores was slow in developing. Indeed, notes historian Esther Clark Wright, "for many decades, lumber was king along the upper Saint John. Villages and towns grew or dwindled at its dictation" (*The Saint John River* 215). Goldsmith's poem can therefore be read in real as well as archetypal time, an inference enhanced by historical knowledge of the poet's own Loyalist family whose home, grist mills, woodlands, and sawmills near Goldsmith's Stream and Goldsmith's Lake in Waweig, New Brunswick, were destroyed by fire and flood in the approximate year of his birth in St. Andrews in 1794 (Myatt 30–32; 150). Eventually serving, like his father, in the Commissariat Service in Saint John, Oliver Goldsmith Jr. was surrounded by a crowd of nearly 2,000 people on a Saint John wharf to wish him bon voyage when he was transferred from New Brunswick to China in 1844. He was a man admired for his acrobatic skating in the Saint John public rink, for his gentle professionalism, for his role in the founding of the Mechanics' Institute in 1839, and for his 1834 version of *The Rising Village* published in Saint John. "Do we not then, as New Brunswickers," noted the Saint John *Morning*

News of 15 May 1844 as Goldsmith set sail for China, "part with a native of our own land," the encomium suggesting that, by mid-nineteenth century, the New Brunswick offshoots of Goldsmith's "rising village" had begun to self-identify with both the province and its constituents (Myatt 108–14).

That the province of Goldsmith's generation was in a state of rapid change by the time that the poet sailed for China in 1844 is clear from the way that the "Loyalist" image of the province had begun to shift (Barkley 7). Manifestations of this appeared in the "increasing scrutiny and criticism" of the province's "elite," notes historian Murray Barkley, in "what was the initial phase of the struggle for responsible government in New Brunswick" (7) and, in particular, in the impact of massive immigration. For example, between 1815 and 1851, 71% of the immigrants to the province were Irish, comprising, in 1851, 21.1% of the population (Barkley 12 n.28). This major influx of "seemingly unassimilable Irish Catholics" exacerbated "the Loyalist élite's growing anxieties and fear of being numerically displaced," argues Barkley, and encouraged their backward-turning search for a sense of validation in works such as Peter Fisher's 1825 *Sketches of New Brunswick Containing an Account of the First Settlement of the Province* and Robert Cooney's 1832 *A Compendious History of the Northern Part of the Province of New Brunswick* (8–9; Richard et al., "Markers"). In both, the record of exile and struggle against a literal "wilderness" helped to inform a process of mythologization: "Of sorrow and suffering they had sufficient ... if they were driven from home to seek a refuge in the wilderness, they carried with them the virtue they inherited from their ancestors" (Cooney, *A Compendious History* 19). Contiguous with this process was the literary valorization of the Loyalists as manifestations of the "children of Israel" wandering in the wilderness.[4] Certainly, by the time that a grand public dinner for all surviving Loyalists was held in Saint John on 18 May 1833, fifty years after the arrival of the Spring Fleet, a distinctive Loyalist mythology had begun to be "publicly and explicitly articulated," enhanced by the prospect "that the last living links with the first generation" would soon pass away (Barkley 10, 17). That this mythology would henceforth resonate with conventions of British loyalty, distrust of the American connection, and a tradition of self-sacrifice was intrinsic to its character, points out Barkley. Throughout the 1840s, particularly in Thomas Hill's newspaper, *The Loyalist, And Conservative Advocate* (Saint John; Fredericton), various New Brunswick "literary endeavours" would sustain the flame of the Loyalist myth, "including the Loyalists' elitist origins, their self-sacrifice for principle, and their struggle against nature" (14).

However, even as a Loyalist mythology was evolving in the 1830s around the fiftieth anniversary of the refugees' landing, a long-simmering battle over the taxing of crown lands and the sale of undeveloped provincial wilderness to external mercenaries was highlighting the changing power dynamic within the province, pitting the ambitions of commissioner of crown lands, Irishman Thomas Baillie, against both the House of Assembly and established Loyalist New Brunswick families. In *The Atlantic Provinces: The Emergence of Colonial Society,* historian W.S. MacNutt has explored the intricacies of the financial and constitutional confrontations over crown lands that engaged New Brunswick legislators, the British Colonial Office, and Commissioner Baillie between 1830 and 1837, culminating, notes MacNutt, in the province's success in gaining everything it "had demanded" (198). But, during that process, political ferment inspired literary ferment, generating the irony of the daring 1832 pseudonymous "John Gape Letters" published by second-generation Loyalist editor Henry Chubb in *The New-Brunswick Courier*. Entertaining readers with their homespun audacity, the Gape letters exposed "the financial extortions" and "unspeakable arrogance" of Baillie and his rangers (MacNutt, *New Brunswick* 234), each missive to "Dear Mr. Editor" being enriched by targeted addresses and local example: "John Gape will visit him with the utmost terror of his vengeance, *the scorn and contempt of the People and the Press!*" (Gape, *The New-Brunswick Courier* 26 January 1833). The product of Scottish-born Robert Gowan, a former piper to the 74th Highlanders and a Crown Lands Office clerk, the investigative Gape letters were superseded by Gowan's incisively clever "The Triumph of Intrigue," a drama in three parts, first appearing in *The Courier* on 23 February 1833 under the pseudonym "O.P." In what was the fiftieth anniversary year of the Loyalists' arrival in New Brunswick, Gowan satirized Baillie ("Tammy Baillie") and his father-in-law, William Franklin Odell ("Wily Oh'Deil"), son of the Loyalist satirical poet Jonathan Odell, as "presiding over the crown lands after the fashion of Scottish lairds" (MacNutt, *New Brunswick* 236, 476; MacNutt "Gowan, Robert"; Smith, "English Drama" 170–71). The furor emerging from the Gape and O.P. satires generated strong public support for the principles that would eventually lead to responsible government, inspiring local vernacular poet William Leggatt to speak out on behalf of the common man on 28 September 1833 in his "Song of Thousands," printed in *The Courier*:

> Here's to John Gape—whilst the light of his fame
> Dispels the dark mist from our shore.

> I have listened with feeling profound
> To the voice that holds tyrants in thrall—
> I have listened with pride, whilst the multitude found
> There was one who dared speak for us all.
> (qtd. in MacNutt, *New Brunswick* 476 n.17)

Leggett's vernacular verse on plebeian literary power—published nearly fifty years after the newspaper doggerel writers of 1785 had defended their property rights against the imperious "Fifty Five"—attests yet again to the efficacy of New Brunswick's eighteenth- and nineteenth-century press in providing a conduit for irony and satire, as well as literary speech. And "paradoxically, and in more than a figurative sense," it reinforces the observation of New Brunswick literary critic Alfred Bailey that a "satirized society is the author of the satire" (Bailey, "Creative Moments" 51–52).

NEW ECOLOGIES AND SELF-REFLECTIONS

Indeed, it is from what David Bentley has generically identified as "the ideas" or events prominent "in the air," part of the "mood," or "merely givens in the environment at the time" ("Reflections" 22), that much of the formative literary writing of a changing New Brunswick was to emerge in the 1840s. Although a financial depression crippled Saint John in the early 1840s, by 1845 its economy had begun to recover, underscoring the port city's "prominent role in an Atlantic communications system extending to Liverpool and London in one direction, Boston and New York in another" (Careless, "Aspects" 119). A spurt in shipbuilding (eighty-one new boats in the 1820s; one hundred and sixty-two in the 1840s), mass immigration, industrialization, telegraphy, gas illumination, steam navigation, American boundary resolutions, and the implications of railway interconnectivity all broadened the social horizons of New Brunswick residents and writers throughout the decade of the 1840s (Wright, *Saint John Ships* 11–16; "Growing Prosperity of St. John," *The Morning News* 28 April 1845). In Saint John, a new Market House had opened in Market Square in 1840 and the theatre at the Golden Ball corner could accommodate 600 patrons (Jack 127). Although geography challenged Saint John's interaction in the far north of the province—and it resentfully lost the new Anglican Cathedral to the seat of government, Fredericton, in 1845—the port city nonetheless dominated the province in mid-century in terms of "size, commercial importance, and nascent industrial character" (Wynn, *Timber Colony* 153; Careless, "Aspects" 119; MacNutt, *New Brunswick* 307). Floating "booms across the mouths of coves or inlets" around the harbour formed "storage ponds for ton timber and logs" (Wynn, *Timber Colony* 153), reminding citizens and visitors alike of the forest industry as an economic driver. And to the city's steam- and water-powered sawmills, shipbuilding yards, merchant wholesaler establishments, and commercial buildings "clustered around Market Slip" could be added the fine homes of successful entrepreneurs and shipbuilding families, all dominated by the presence on King's Square of the old stone Court House described by an 1830s visitor as "One of the best if not the best building of the kind in North America" (154).

Moreover, it was a measure of Saint John's growing sophistication as a city that in 1839–1840 a Mechanics' Institute was built empowering the public, particularly an upwardly mobile working class, to attend free lectures, utilize a well-stocked library of 5,000 books, and visit educational exhibitions (for example, a *Grand Bazaar* display of Aboriginal history and culture organized by fiction writers Douglas Huyghue and Moses Perley in 1842 [Huyghue, *Argimou* v]). The Victorian public, as John Gross has pointed out in *The Rise and Fall of the Man of Letters*, was one that craved intellectual guidance (89). And while the publication of inexpensive literary periodicals had lagged behind imports in New Brunswick, the January 1841 launch of the ambitious Saint John journal, *The Amaranth*, edited by Scottish-born Robert Shives, encouraged New Brunswick writers to submit poetry, fiction, essays, and travel literature to what was to be an inexpensive compendium of both international and regional material. Shives's inclusion of stories such as Gaeneye's "Life in Saint John. A Speculator," a Dickensian-style narrative of working-class life set "in that dark and unexplored recess, known as 'Drury Lane,' York Point" (August 1841, 230), or Junius's "A Journey to Fredericton," a confrontation between immigrant Yorkshire and elitist "King's College Fredericton" values ("he actually astonished my rusticity" [October 1842, 319]), reflects the way in which provincial class issues had begun to inform literary production. Even at its low price of 7s.6d per annum (1s.3d added for mailing), *The Amaranth* probably never reached Saint John's disempowered unemployed immigrants at York Point or "the poorest parts of Portland" where people were "living at the margins" (Wynn, *Timber Colony* 155–56). Rather, its anticipated audience in all likelihood included skilled mechanics, craftsmen, farmers, teachers, and merchants who had already made the New York *Albion* popular in New Brunswick (Beavan 40).[5] Symptomatic of this was Shives's inclusion in *The Amaranth* of a Mechanics' Institute lecture by George Blatch on correcting "Common Errors" in writing and speech, an initiative that foresaw "future merchants, magistrates, legislators, and public men" of New Brunswick emerging from "the homes of mechanics and humble people" (February 1843, 48). Or, as literary critic Queenie Leavis might have positioned the argument, the journal reinforced the dynamic of "Victorian uplift" (164).

If a mid-century Victorian emphasis on information and entertainment shaped the tone and tenor of *The Amaranth*, so too did a taste for public history. Thus, *The Amaranth's* March 1841 review of *An English Spelling Book, with Reading Lessons; for the Use of the Parish and Other Schools of New Brunswick* argued for the inclusion of local heritage material in provincial educational texts. "We think," the journal insisted, "that had the reading lessons been made subjects of simple and amusing, as well as instructive details of the settlement and advancement of the Province, including historical information, arranged in an easy and comprehensive style, it would have rendered the work a still greater means of imparting a correct and instructive familiarity with something more than plain words—and thus have served a double purpose" (Shives, "An English Spelling Book" 96). Provincially produced historical fiction in *The Amaranth*—written for a generation already addicted to reading Sir Walter Scott's novels of nation-building (Gerson 67)—also reflected Shives's interest in offering works that foregrounded local history and landscape, including a number of stories of Aboriginal-settler encounters. While *Amaranth* tales by Irish immigrant Emily Beavan of Long Creek stereotypically saw First Nations people through a literary lens of Gothic sensationalism—and stressed racial difference—those by Perley and Huyghue recognized the role played by Indigenous cultures in the history of the province, that recognition coming at a time, when, as Huyghue's narrator in *Argimou. A Legend of the Micmac* laments, "We rear the germ of a great city without casting a thought upon the generation crumbling beneath ..." (*Argimou* 3–4).

By the time that *The Amaranth* began publishing fiction such as Huyghue's (work based on the history of Aboriginal and European interaction in New Brunswick), the distressed state of Indigenous communities had already become a matter of public debate in the province's newspapers and Legislature. When the Loyalists had arrived in New Brunswick in the 1780s, notes historian John Reid, there had been approximately "1,000 Maliseet, Micmac, and Passamaquoddy" living in the province (*Six Crucial Decades* 70). Within a few years, the Maliseet had gradually been pushed back from the Fredericton area to "reserve lands at Kingsclear and elsewhere in the upper part of the valley" and "similar problems were experienced by the Micmac in areas further north in the province, especially on the Miramichi and Richibucto rivers" (J. Reid, *Six Crucial Decades* 78; Cuthbertson 1–18; Nicholas, "Shaping An Agenda" 21–57). By the late eighteenth and early nineteenth centuries, land not taken over "by Loyalists well armed with their land titles" (J. Reid, *Six Crucial Decades* 79) had often been lost to squatters (Conrad and Hiller 105). In 1783, for example, the Mi'kmaq had obtained a licence to occupy 20,000 acres on the Miramichi River, but by 1807, when the government set up the Eel Ground Reserve, half of that land was gone (105). When the British military officer Joseph Gubbins travelled in New Brunswick during the War of 1812 to assess and train the militia, he had noted in his journal that the decline of moose, "caribou," and "reindeer" in the province had forced Indigenous peoples to sell their lands, "hew fire wood," and till rented land to "grow potatoes and Indian corn on it after having cleared away the wood" (Gubbins 12–13). By the 1840s, local living conditions were often dire as violations of Maliseet and Mi'kmaq economic and property issues had escalated, particularly as immigrant squatters ignored aboriginal land titles. Debates raged, noted W.S. MacNutt, over whether Indigenous peoples should "remain in their native state" or be "assimilated to the ways of the white man" (*New Brunswick* 301).

The appointment of Planter descendant, author, and Saint John lawyer Moses Perley as an unpaid commissioner of Indian Affairs in New Brunswick in 1841 (Cuthbertson 30–31) was an attempt by government to gather further information and receive advice about the situation of Indigenous peoples. Perley toured the province extensively visiting Maliseet and Mi'kmaq communities before issuing his report to the House of Assembly in 1842. He protested against the encroachment of squatters on Indian property and recommended to the province that it hold Aboriginal lands, encourage the formation of village settlements, establish schools, and ensure medical attention for each community (Spray, "Perley, Moses Henry"; Cuthbertson 30–38, 100–103). His census identified 1,377 Indigenous people in the province (MacNutt, *New Brunswick* 301) and he found "Measles, Whooping Cough, Scarlet Fever, Croup, Tyfus, Small Pox, and a variety of other Diseases, to which Children are subject" running rampant throughout the population. "During my visit to the Miramichi," he added, "the Children were suffering dreadfully from Dysentery, and while at Burnt Church Point a death occurred almost daily" (J. Reid, *Six Crucial Decades* 42). Made a chief by both the Maliseet (1839) and the Mi'kmaq (1840) because of his efforts on their behalf, Perley was elected "Wunjeet Sagamore" (Chief Over All) in 1842, often spending months away from home visiting various reserves (Spray, "Perley, Moses Henry"). Perley's hopes that New Brunswick's Indian Act of 1844 would better protect First Nations lands from squatters and sales were to be disappointed (Nicholas, "The Role of Colonial Artists" 67; Cuthbertson 50). His subsequent investigations in 1845 (Northumberland County) and 1848 (Tobique) put him in conflict with the provincial government and led to his reform work for the Indigenous community being curtailed (Spray, "Perley, Moses Henry"; Cuthbertson 50–61).

Perley's intimacy with First Nations culture helped to shape his creative as well as his professional writing. Beginning in the 1830s and extending into the 1840s, he published a series of linked fictionalized sporting sketches in *The London Sporting Review* (1839–1841) and *The Amaranth* (1841–1843) that expanded the conventions of the genre by bringing his studies as an ichthyologist, his experience navigating the New Brunswick wilderness, and his appreciation of Maliseet language and storytelling to his first-person narratives. Enlivened by repartee with Aboriginal guides such as Tomah, Sabbatis, and Owkmawbish, Perley's integrated sketches—part campfire-tale, part forest epic, part First Nations oral history, and part personal *bildungsroman*—resonated with encounters with bears, portages, rapids, mosquitoes, and that peskiest of New Brunswick insects, the no-see-ums. Yet, while "weariness" of the world's "ways" drives the narrator to enjoy a "simple meal in peace and quietness by the river" in a sketch such as "La Belle Tolotah," he is nonetheless too much the urban Saint John Victorian not to cast his eye over the pristine unbroken "hill, river, lake, plain, valley and mountain pass" of wilderness New Brunswick in "The Forest Fairies of the Milicetes" and not envisage in its place "a thriving village," "the sound of the bell from the parish church," a brawling stream, a mill with "clacking" wheel, and carriages on the highways (Perley 193–94). Thus there is a tension underlying the highly entertaining and well-narrated stories of Perley's *Sporting Sketches*. On one hand, his admiration for the dignity, humour, and skill demonstrated by his First Nations companions in executing their traditional occupations—and his love of wilderness New Brunswick—prevails. But despite Perley's impassioned commitment to protecting the lifestyle values of Indigenous people (implied in the sporting sketches and articulated in his government recommendations), in his *Amaranth* sketches he is ultimately a worldly contemporary Victorian describing a wilderness lifestyle much cherished but already in flux.

As distressed by the contemporary challenges facing Indigenous communities as was his friend Moses Perley, fellow *Amaranth* writer Douglas Huyghue turned to Sir Walter Scott's historical-novel template of two cultures in tension, one ascendant and one descendant, to dramatize, in his 1842 *Argimou. A Legend of the Micmac*, the disenfranchisement of First Nations peoples in eighteenth-century New Brunswick.[6] A work influenced by the Romantic movement's interest in literary primitivism, the concept of the noble savage, and a sense of the past, *Argimou* also drew upon topographical conventions to develop a verbal mapping of the New Brunswick landscape ranging from the cold mists of the Tantramar Marshes to a dramatic dénouement on the reversing falls in Saint John. Thus, Huyghue, like Perley and a number of other regional *Amaranth* writers, marked a transitional shift from the politically reactive irony and satire of the literature of the Loyalist years of province-formation (1780s–1830s) to an active engagement, by the 1840s, with the landscape, history, changing population demographic, economics, and identity-formation of Victorian New Brunswick. Listening to the voices around them, Perley and Huyghue wrote as part of what British critic Marilyn Butler has called a "social process" (9). "Literature," she has noted, "like all art, like language, is a collective activity, powerfully conditioned by social forces, what needs to be and what may be said in a particular community at a given time" (9). Authors, she has added, "are not the solitaries of the Romantic myth, but citizens" (10). And it is as citizens that fiction writers Perley and Huyghue both responded to, and were shaped by, the spirit of their time.

While the Loyalist mythology of the 1783 exiles was to resurface periodically on anniversaries such as 1883 and 1933, the cultural self-confidence of social, historical, and wilderness writing represented by 1840s writers such as Huyghue and Perley was to be foundational. Charles G.D. Roberts's refinement of the wilderness tradition in internationally recognized stories of the campfire and the animal kingdom in the long Confederation period, as well as James De Mille's integration of vast stretches of Miramichi forest into a novel such as *Fire in the Woods* (1872) in his popular B.O.W.C. series published in the United States, spoke to the evolution of nature/sporting writing as a distinctive New Brunswick genre in nineteenth-century Maritime literature. Moreover, irony as a recurring literary trope (especially in the late-eighteenth- and early-nineteenth-century political sparring in New Brunswick) and the emergence of the press as the primary conduit of cultural delivery both reflect a distinctive interactive relationship between social ferment and literary expression in the first sixty years of the province. Ultimately, to borrow a concept from American critic/geographer Martin Brückner, New Brunswick's literary production had, by the 1840s, begun to reflect the "imaginings of a particularized commonality" (401). And in that spirit, one intuits that, sixty years on, Thomas Raddall's eighteenth-century privateer (who introduced this chapter) would have emerged with a very different sense of identity had he been sailing out of New Brunswick—instead writing into his log: *Francis Kempton is my name / Seaman is my stashon / Saint John is my dwelen plas / and New Brunswick is my nashon.*

NOTES

1. In "James Glenie and the Politics of Sunbury County," W.G. Godfrey notes that Glenie parodied the Anglican Creed in *The Book of Common Prayer* in 1800 to satirize the Reverend Jonathan Odell and various councillors serving Lieutenant-Governor Thomas Carleton. The Anglican Creed begins: "I believe in one God the Father Almighty, / Maker of heaven and earth, / And of all things visible and invisible: / And in one Lord Jesus Christ, the only-begotten Son of God, / Begotten of the Father before all worlds; / God, of God; / Light of Light; / very God, of very God; / Begotten, not made ..." (*Book of Common Prayer* 71). Glenie's "creed" included a condemnation of Odell, who was both secretary of the Council and an ordained Anglican clergyman: "I believe in J-N. O-L. S-Y of the Province of N.B. maker of Militia officers and Just Assess of the Peace, and plotter of all head quarter intrigues visible and invisible, the only beloved of Simple Tom, Beloved of all Britons, Men of men, head of heads, S-Y of S-Y's, beloved and not hated, being of one opinion with his Patron, by whom all Quonsillors are made ..." (Godfrey, "James Glenie" 27).

2. St. Andrews, on the Bay of Fundy, also had a Subscription Library. Opened in 1815 with fifty-seven subscribers (including women) and 271 titles of plays, novels, travel books, and classical works, its list, like that in Saint John, included contemporary writers such as Sir Walter Scott. The St. Andrews Subscription Library lasted until at least 1820. See Circulation Book for the St. Andrew's Library, 1815–1816, Lawrence F. Hachey Fonds, MC3185, Provincial Archives of New Brunswick, Fredericton, N.B.

3. Influenced by the portmanteau titles of the eighteenth-century novel, the full original title of Bates's 1817 book was *The Mysterious Stranger, or, Memoirs of Henry More Smith, alias Henry Frederick Moon, alias William Newman, who is now confined in Simsbury Mines, in Connecticut, for the crime of burglary: containing an account of his extraordinary conduct during his confinement in the gaol of King's County, province of New-Brunswick, where he was under sentence of death: with a statement of his succeeding conduct, before and since his confinement in Newgate/by Walter Bates, New Haven Conn.: Published by Maltby, Goldsmith & Co.: T.G. Woodward, Printer, 1817.* Two New Haven editions appeared in 1817. The book was also published as a co-piece with "some account of Caraboo, the

late female imposter at Bristol" in two editions in 1817 by Allman and Co. of London, with additional information in the title that Henry Frederic Moon was an alias of Henry Frederic More Smith, alias William Newman, a native of Brighthelmstone, Sussex, England. This edition also included "an introductory description of New Brunswick." The first Canadian publication appeared anonymously in the *Acadian Recorder*, Halifax, Nova Scotia, in 1817 on 10, 17, 24, and 31 May and 7, 14, and 21 June. The book was frequently reprinted in the Maritimes, especially New Brunswick, throughout the nineteenth and early twentieth centuries, including being serialized in local newspapers. No enumerative bibliography has ever been done on Bates's book.

4 An example of the analogy between the exiled Loyalists and the "Children of Israel wandering in the wilderness" can be found in the first stanza of an "original" poem entitled "1783" read by Charles Campbell at "Loyalist Day" in Saint John in 1904: "Like Israel to the wilderness / From bitter wrongs and shame, / Despoiled of homes and penniless, / But stern and steadfast in distress, / Our Loyal Fathers came." See "Loyalist Day," *Daily Sun* [Saint John], 19 May 1904, 5. I wish to thank Evelyn Costello, Library Assistant, Saint John Free Library, for identifying the source of this poem, originally found pasted in O (Anonymous) *Scrapbook,* Vol. 2, Saint John Free Library, 75.

5 For Shives's list of agents for the distribution of *The Amaranth* outside of Saint John, see *The Amaranth* 2, no. 5, 128. The periodical was available to readers in Fredericton, Hampton, Sussex Vale, Sheffield, Bathurst, Miramichi, and Shediac in New Brunswick, and Amherst, Bridgetown, Digby, and Westport in Nova Scotia. *The Halifax Morning Post, And Parliamentary Reporter: A Tri-Weekly Newspaper*, edited by John H. Crosskill, regularly reported on the contents of *The Amaranth*. Shives's personal economic situation, not a dearth of material, seems to have brought *The Amaranth* to an end early in 1843.

6 *Argimou*. In addition to exploring the loss of autonomy by Indigenous peoples in eighteenth-century New Brunswick, *Argimou. A Legend of the Micmac* describes the dislocation of Acadian civilians caught up in war prior to the 1755 deportation of over 11,000 Acadians from what are now the Maritime provinces. One of the earliest Canadian novels to depict the situation of the Acadians in 1755, *Argimou. A Legend of the Micmac* was serialized in *The Amaranth* (Saint John N.B.), May–September 1842. It was republished in book form by *The Morning Courier* office, Halifax, 1847. It was serialized in *The Saint John Albion* in 1860 and was reputed to have been issued in novel form in the United States (see W.G. MacFarlane 46). It was republished in book form by the R.P. Bell Library, Mount Allison University, 1977 and 1979, with an introduction by Gwendolyn Davies.

CHAPTER 2

EMERGENT ACADIAN NATIONALISM, 1864–1955

Chantal Richard

While the aim of this chapter is to explore the forces and events that shaped early Acadian literature, it is useful first to situate those forces within political, social, and cultural parameters. As a linguistic and cultural minority that barely survived planned erasure, the Acadians who survived the Expulsions of the mid-eighteenth century had almost no social structures in place 100 years later. While they had somehow maintained a separate language and identity, they lacked formal education and were denied access to political and social power. A small group began to try to remedy this situation in the middle of the nineteenth century by first defining and then celebrating Acadian identity. That process was largely shaped by elements found in the only cultural reference they knew: old France.

In her apposite work, Anne-Marie Thiesse suggests that the conditions for the emergence of a national literature in eighteenth-century Europe include founding ancestors; a storyline that establishes the continuity of the nation through the vicissitudes of history; a gallery of heroes; a language; cultural and historical monuments; places embedded in collective memory; and shared experiences of landscape, folklore, costumes, food, and symbols (52). Beyond those elements, she asserts, a national literature emerges when there is sufficient motivation to mount a literary movement and when there exists the means to do so. Until those basic conditions are met, national or identity-specific literature cannot materialize.

With regard to the first set of conditions—the presence of a national identity through ancestry, language, and shared experiences—it must be pointed out that, compared to many other world cultures, Acadie is a relatively recent cultural construct characterized by an unusual set of circumstances. Until psychological separation from the mother country occurred, those living in the colony of New France (founded in 1604) could not have felt the need to develop a distinct culture, since, as colonials, they were still part of the long cultural and literary tradition of France. And while it seems impossible to determine when the concept of *Acadie* first emerged in the minds of individual Acadians, it is reasonable to assert that Acadian identity was documented collectively for the first time during what is now considered the Acadian Renaissance[1] of the mid-nineteenth century (D. Bourque, "Représentations"). The first condition for the creation of a national literature, then, was only met at that time when, ironically, Acadie no longer existed in any official way. The second condition for a national literature to materialize—the desire to mount a literary movement—depends largely on the establishment of common historical tropes. In the case of Acadie, these tropes came from the Renaissance movement itself and, more specifically, from its recurring themes of a traumatic past. Finally, the third condition—the means to produce a literature—was also not met until the 1860s, when access to post-secondary education became available (1864) and *Le Moniteur Acadien* was founded (1867). As a result, literacy rose sharply at that time, and a French-language press provided a publication venue that did not exist previously.

It was only when all three conditions were met in the middle and late nineteenth century that Acadian literature as a construct and reflection of identity began. With it came consistencies in style, thematic choices, and ideological intent—and a written culture principally inspired by collective memory.

It must also be noted, however, that as much as the social conditions of the mid-nineteenth-century Acadian Renaissance were instrumental in creating the conditions for a literary ferment, a few key authors were also essential to cultivating the ground. In what was a reciprocal relationship between society and literature, the first literary models came from outside Acadie, eventually becoming incorporated into the ideology of Acadian nationalism. In that sense, this period was one of coalescing of social and literary forces—indeed, of literary ferment—that had been slowly gathering strength over centuries.

Many of the pre-Renaissance authors who marked the Acadian imagination can be found in Marguerite Maillet's seminal works *Anthologie de textes littéraires acadiens 1606–1975* (Maillet, LeBlanc, and Émont 1979) and *Histoire de la littérature acadienne: De rêve en rêve* (1983). Despite the fact that each book provides little more than a glimpse of the periods studied, both works are significant for laying the groundwork for understanding the Renaissance and pre-Renaissance periods. In *Anthologie de textes littéraires acadiens 1606–1975*, co-authored with Gérard LeBlanc and Bernard Émont, the beginnings of Acadian literature are traced to a time designated as "pré-acadienne," when Marc Lescarbot wrote his nautical play, *Le Théâtre de Neptune* (1606), to relieve boredom among the French soldiers. Other than this play, the first ever written in New France, Lescarbot also wrote idealized poetic descriptions in *Les Muses de la Nouvelle France* and the first history of the area, *Histoire de la Nouvelle France*, both published in 1609. These were part of an attempt to convince the King of France and Lescarbot's compatriots to invest in the colony. As a result, the author chose to accentuate its positive aspects—vast spaces to be conquered, an abundance of resources and riches—and omitted some of the less appealing details. In the same vein, in 1672 Nicolas Denys described a land so plentiful that he called the river that ran through it "Cocagne," meaning "land of plenty" (qtd. in Maillet, LeBlanc, and Émont 50). Here, according to Denys, the fish and game were so abundant that even the dogs lay on top of carcasses, unable to eat another bite. These hyperbolic descriptions undoubtedly fed the imaginations of many authors to come, including Longfellow when he described Evangeline's paradise lost. Pre-Renaissance work, then, contributed importantly to the creation of a golden-age myth in Acadian literature (M. Maillet 17). Though the literary value of these early texts is certainly questionable, they set the stage for what would become a romanticized Acadian storyline: an Edenic period, followed by a fall, and eventually a resurrection in the form of the Acadian Renaissance (Chantal Richard, "La deportation" 69).

DEMOGRAPHICS AND LITERACY BEFORE AND AFTER THE EXPULSION
To understand the impetus behind the rebirth of Acadie in the second half of the nineteenth century, it is useful to summarize the demographic changes in the colony, which evolved in a climate of political instability. The most important of these were the deportations of 1755–1758. Roughly 11,000 Acadians out of a population of 14,000 were deported between 1755 and 1762 (S.A. White 56), and only about 8,400 survivors and their descendants could still be found in the Maritimes by 1803 (Muriel Roy 143). Although these events marked the darkest chapter of Acadian history, the century and a half of silence and isolation actually began much earlier, when the colony was officially ceded to England in 1713. Being cut off from France and other francophone populations from 1713 to 1763 had the effect of severely

impairing Acadie's social, economic, political, and cultural growth (Maillet, LeBlanc, and Émont 10; A. Maillet, *Rabelais* 5). However, once allowed to return in 1763, and with the encouragement of the Roman Catholic Church (principally led by French-Canadian clergy), Acadians living in the Maritimes experienced a significant resurgence in population over the next century. By 1871, their absolute numbers had increased more than tenfold, to about 99,740 out of a total of 285,594 New Brunswickers, thus making up roughly one-third of the population (Statistics Canada, 1871 census). As a percentage of the provincial population, Acadian numbers had also risen as 76,000 people, mostly anglophones, left New Brunswick for the United States between 1880 and 1900. As historians have surmised, Acadians were "more reluctant than anglophones to leave the region" (Conrad and Hiller 150). Despite this significant population boom, Acadians remained far behind their anglophone counterparts in the areas of education and political power, and they were severely under-represented in the religious hierarchy of the Maritime provinces.

Indeed, despite their large numbers, Acadians were not active participants in the power structures of the early nineteenth century (Doucet 247, 249). This was largely due to the fact that their access to education had been cut off in the early eighteenth century, and the resulting illiteracy relegated them to manual labour occupations. Yet the lack of formal schooling was not inherent to Acadian society since records show that formal and informal French-Catholic primary schools for boys and girls existed in most Acadian centres (Port-Royal, Beaubassin, and Grand-Pré) in 1700, but were closed when the colony fell under British rule in 1713 (Dugas 119–20). And, although literacy levels of Acadians living in those centres in the early eighteenth century matched those of their European French counterparts at around 20% (Dugas 65, 97), the levels began to drop after 1713 and fell to 0% by the mid-1700s. These literacy levels, brought about by British rule, would remain low for quite some time after the Expulsion.

Acadians were permitted to return to their homeland officially in 1763, but they returned slowly and cautiously, as any traumatized population would. Some had been surviving in the forests of central and northern New Brunswick for years, decimated and destitute. In their absence, their lands had been allocated to British soldiers and Loyalists, so Acadians settled quietly on whatever unoccupied lands they could find, where they began rebuilding—literally and figuratively. As their numbers grew and French-Canadian priests arrived to provide religious guidance, it became apparent that education was conspicuously absent. From 1763 to the mid-nineteenth century, the only evidence of Acadian efforts to acquire instruction was the existence of "maîtres ambulants"—roaming teachers (Dugas 47). These travelling teachers lodged in private residences and were paid by local families, but this form of informal teaching did not provide more than very basic literacy in a sporadic manner. And policy forbade little else, as Martin S. Spigelman points out: "The Colonial governments successfully sought to isolate the Acadians by refusing them any place in the administration or educational systems of the Maritime provinces" (qtd. in Doucet 244). Spigelman was referring to the fact that, in New Brunswick, a law passed in 1755 stipulated that "no popish person should be so presumptive as to set up any school in the province" (qtd. in Doucet 244). It would take nearly a century after the Expulsion for a more standardized and widespread French-language school system to take shape (T. Roy 75). The first six French-Catholic primary schools opened between 1826 and 1857 in northern New Brunswick, and basic education could once again be provided to Acadian children in their own language (Dugas 47).

Low levels of literacy and a century of isolation from other French colonies meant that, until the second half of the nineteenth century, Acadians could not access white-collar professions that would put them in positions of power, nor could they have any say in the affairs of state. In comparison, the anglophone population of New Brunswick had had access to post-secondary education since 1787, only a few years after the arrival of the Loyalists. Furthermore, and partially as a result of the lack of access to education, Acadians had internalized prejudices coming from a dominant class that regarded them as "half-breeds" (A. Bourque 6). This was accentuated by a discourse of "cultural uniformity" that had been adopted by a group of Protestant anglophone New Brunswickers. Herman H. Pitts, editor of the *New Brunswick Reporter and Fredericton Advertiser*, launched a campaign in 1890 to "end 'concessions' to Roman Catholics and Francophones and to promote an evangelical Protestant reform agenda" (Conrad and Hiller 151). In other words, the climate was less than welcoming for a rising Acadian elite. In the numerous battles Acadians fought to achieve political and social equality—such as the demand for an Acadian bishop—negative stereotypes surfaced frequently.

Until the early twentieth century, the Catholic Church in New Brunswick and, in fact, the Maritimes, was dominated and controlled entirely by Irish clergy who were unsympathetic to the needs of Acadians. As the pressure mounted for Acadians to be represented in the Church, an article was published in the *Saint John Freeman* of 23 November 1901 that condescendingly claimed it would be impossible to appoint an Acadian bishop since there was a "lack of episcopal timber among our Acadian friends" (qtd. by Poirier and Belliveau in *L'Évangéline*, 30 January 1902, 2). Comments such as this fed an inferiority complex that, along with educational, economic, and political disadvantages, discouraged Acadians from participating in commerce and industry, and kept them impoverished for an extended period of time (Poirier, *Le Père Lefebvre* 309). At the same time, however, it also provoked a strong reaction in a handful of Acadian leaders who were beginning to gather strength and conviction.

Accordingly, a small number of Acadians and their supporters developed a three-part plan to improve the position of Acadians in New Brunswick and contest the privilege of the anglophone majority. This plan included the provision of French-Catholic education, the strengthening of national pride through national symbols, and the emergence of a national narrative that promoted Acadian identity and ensured social cohesion. To achieve these objectives, a slowly emerging but dedicated Acadian elite would have to radically question the power structures of the time and convince the downtrodden and humiliated Acadian population that their cultural identity could be a source of pride.

ADVANCES IN EDUCATION AND LITERACY

When allowed to return to the Atlantic provinces in 1763, Acadians were encouraged to assimilate into the anglophone population. However, as had been the case in the past, they refused to give up their language, culture, and religion, desiring to maintain a separate identity. In fact, in their public discourse during the Acadian Renaissance, Acadians rarely defined their identity in relation to the anglophones around them, except to claim equal rights under Confederation. Rather, their cultural reference points were France and French-Canada. This unwillingness to participate in the culture of the dominant society certainly had a detrimental effect on their access to education and other social programs, but it was also that persistence that ensured the survival of an identity that remains relatively intact to this day. Known for their desire to remain neutral, but also for their unwillingness to compromise their beliefs, post-Expulsion Acadians faced the difficult task of organizing a French-Catholic school system under a hostile British government, knowing, through the struggles, that without education they had no hope of fully participating in society.

New France, a society still based on Old World social configurations, was organized around the notion that Church and State were one; therefore, in North America, it was considered the responsibility of the clergy to provide education to the expansive territory that was Acadie (Ouellet 19). It was a very daunting task and required a level of dedication possible only in a segment of the population that considered self-abnegation a virtue. These religious figures were essential to implementing French-Catholic education in Acadie, and the fact that they came from France and Québec had a significant influence in shaping the first real Acadian elite, for the values they inculcated were those of the *Ultramontains*: values that twinned Catholicism and traditional French-Canadian nationalism. The young Acadians who went to Québec to pursue their studies in French beyond primary school were steeped in these values. If they were gifted, these young students were taken in at the Grand Séminaire at little or no cost, since few Acadian families could afford such an expense. Often, the price to be paid was giving their lives back to the Church, which some did by returning to Acadie to take on religious duties and provide basic education.

It soon became apparent that a post-secondary institution in Acadian territory would open higher education to many more Acadians, and thus open pathways to positions of power in New Brunswick. Father François-Xavier LaFrance, who had been transferred to the parish of Memramcook in 1852, shared this ambition, and on 15 November 1854 he opened the Séminaire Saint-Thomas in Memramcook (Basque and Giroux 9). Initially, local Acadians did not recognize the value of further education and were not keen on losing farm labour to academic pursuits. However, support for the idea of higher education slowly grew within the community and promising students in primary school were encouraged by Father LaFrance to pursue their studies (Basque and Giroux 9).

Father LaFrance soon solicited the help of his brother, Charles-Édouard LaFrance, who was a teacher in Shippagan, and, in the second year of the college, he also hired an Acadian from Caraquet, Juste Haché. Unfortunately, funding proved difficult to secure, and by 1862 the college was in such dire financial straits that it had to be closed. In 1864 a new priest was sent to Memramcook to continue what Father LaFrance had begun. That new priest, Father Lefebvre, opened the doors of the newly renamed Collège Saint-Joseph in June, soon after his arrival. Situated on the same grounds, this bilingual school would become the most influential academic institution of the Acadian Renaissance (Bourque and Richard 5).

On 10 October 1864, Collège Saint-Joseph began to offer classes to about thirty students in the same building used to house Father LaFrance's seminary (Catta 634). Of those thirty students, nineteen were boarders who lived at the college, and a dozen were externals who lived close enough to the college to be able to return to their homes at the end of the school day (Poirier, *Le Père Lefebvre* 115). By the end of the first year, the total number had risen to forty-two and ten years later, in 1874, the tiny college was bursting at the seams with a total of 140 students (Catta 805). The goal was to make all graduates of Collège Saint-Joseph fluent in both languages, which suggests an early recognition of the advantages of bilingualism, a recognition that allowed young Acadians to learn and function in the language of the majority while maintaining a strong sense of linguistic and cultural identity.

Father Lefebvre's attitude and determination earned him an almost legendary reputation among his students and parishioners, as many anecdotes suggest. He was reputed to be a mighty figure who worked tirelessly in austere conditions to build the college. For example, he built a wind-powered wood mill for the college (Chamard et al. 64–65), and when provisions of heating wood became insufficient, he led some of his older students out onto the land to cut wood in the middle of winter. Parishioners were said to have been so embarrassed by this sight that they resolved to keep his woodpiles well stocked thereafter (Poirier, *Le Père Lefebvre* 119). Such acts undoubtedly inspired the students of the college, but the historical accuracy of these anecdotes is less significant than the legendary status attributed to Lefebvre by students and Acadians generally. In idealizing Father Lefebvre Acadians gave themselves a role model and highlighted qualities they valued in a leader, both important features in building a culture of identity.

As generous as he was hard working, Lefebvre also had the reputation of never refusing a student, a practice that often resulted in financial difficulties. The accounts of the college confirm that parents paid or bartered what they could (Catta 796; Chamard et al. 61). Students whose families lived in Memramcook could also attend as externals, thereby eliminating the cost of boarding—this probably accounts for the fact that many students were from the immediate area. But Lefebvre could not finance the college alone, and, within the next few years, Collège Saint-Joseph would require significant expansion of its limited infrastructure. By September 1866, the college seemed to have a promising future with more than $2,500 in its accounts, thanks to revenue from the parish and from provincial government subsidies allocated to educational institutions. Over the next few years, donors also helped fund the college, starting with its predecessor's founder, Father LaFrance, who left the college $800 upon his death in 1867 (Chamard et al. 71). Collège Saint-Joseph was not without its financial hardships, but each hurdle was eventually overcome, and in 1963, under the Louis J. Robichaud Liberal government of New Brunswick, the old college became l'Université de Moncton, an institution that would cement Acadian aims for a new generation.

Father Lefebvre's efforts in the early years of the college were rewarded, and the first generation of graduates of Collège Saint-Joseph became the major figures in the Acadian Renaissance movement.[2] Many played a leading role in organizing the Conventions Nationales Acadiennes[3] (CNA, 1881–1890), which laid the groundwork for a new Acadian identity. In fact, almost half of the twenty-three speakers at the first three CNA were alumni of the college (Bourque and Richard 324–54).

Perhaps the most successful and influential of Collège Saint-Joseph graduates was Pascal Poirier. The son of a farmer who became a senator, Poirier authored the first known play by an Acadian, *Les Acadiens à Philadelphie*, staged in Ottawa in 1875 (Gérin 1993), and the first lexicological study of Acadian French, *Le Parler franco-acadien et ses origines* (1928). He also wrote *Le Glossaire Acadien*, published posthumously in 1977 and again as a scholarly edition in 1993. Many of his publications were meant to rehabilitate the language spoken by Acadians, all too often viewed as an inferior, bastardized version of European or French-Canadian French mixed with some First Nations languages. In the preface to *Le Parler franco-acadien*, for example, Poirier recounts his experience as a student humiliated for using an Acadian locution, "par les petits" (little by little, gradually) (Poirier, *Le Parler* 7). Seeking vindication, he began collecting idioms and researching the sources of Acadian French, tracing it back to regions of France with the explicit intention of showing that the language of his forefathers had been imported directly from seventeenth-century France and had remained largely untouched since then. He was the first of many linguists and writers who emphasized the importance and value of Acadian French—not as the half-breed distant cousin of a Parisian aristocrat, but as an historically accurate language with a deeply rooted etymology.

By the time of the first CNA, which was held on the grounds of the Collège Saint-Joseph in 1881, the status of the college and its Acadian students was no longer in question. Even *The Morning Freeman* of 23 July 1881 remarked that "[t]he Acadians have made great strides in the path of progress in this province within these past few years, thanks chiefly to the great educational work done at St. Joseph College" (qtd. in Catta 990).

Regrettably, not all efforts to provide Acadians with post-secondary institutions were as successful as Collège Saint-Joseph. Father Marcel-François Richard, another Acadian Renaissance pioneer, founded a bilingual college in Saint-Louis in 1874 (Bourque and Richard 351). Perhaps because of its proximity to the Irish-Catholic parish of Miramichi, the presence of French in this college was a source of contention within the diocese. On 5 July 1882, Father Richard's superior, Bishop Rogers, had been invited to attend an oratorical presentation at Collège Saint-Louis. On that particular day, a young Irish student by the name of O'Leary read a play in French, and his performance was immediately followed by a speech from an agitated Bishop Rogers, who accused Father Richard of insisting too much on the acquisition of the French language. The college superior replied by stating that Acadians spoke English as well as this young student spoke French, and that he did not see any harm in teaching French in an institution situated within a largely francophone community (Catta 996–97). A few months later the college was closed by the diocesan authorities. Moreover, Father Richard's superiors refused to allow him to attend the CNA of 1890, further punishing and humiliating him (Bourque and Richard 58). The failure of Collège Saint-Louis illustrates the importance of Acadians having positions of power in the Catholic Church so that their causes would be not only be heard by religious superiors, but also understood.

The education of young Acadian girls, though not entirely neglected, did not coalesce as quickly as it did for boys. Where institutions for girls existed, the few girls who had access to them were not taught in French, but in English. Father LaFrance, who had founded the Séminaire Saint-Thomas on the grounds of Collège Saint-Joseph, hired a female schoolteacher of Irish descent to provide education to both girls and boys, but in separate rooms (Catta 435). In 1848 he appealed to his superior, Bishop Connolly, to bring the francophone Dames de la Congrégation de Montréal to his college, but he was told to make do with the English-speaking Sisters of Charity from Saint John (Catta 443). Father Lefebvre fared slightly better, managing to erect a small school for girls in 1868, and recruiting teachers who had some knowledge of French (Catta 886). This state of affairs seems to have been maintained at least until the early twentieth century, according to an article published in *L'Impartial* on 15 January 1903 by Pascal Poirier. In it Poirier claimed the anglophone Sisters of Charity had a complete monopoly over the education of young girls in the Saint John diocese, which, at this time, included much of southeastern New Brunswick's Westmorland County. Poirier publicly deplored the fact that young girls were being told that speaking French was "vulgar," and he went as far as to say that the best way to kill the French language was to attack it within the home, a method already practised by the Sisters of Charity.[4]

The establishment of a network of French-Catholic schools for young Acadian children and the founding of two post-secondary colleges in southeast New Brunswick and Nova Scotia greatly enhanced education and literacy for Acadians during the Renaissance period. Although a largely illiterate population in the early eighteenth century, by the late nineteenth century Acadians could become lawyers, doctors, politicians, and writers—and could do so in French. Young women did not yet have access to the professions, but they were beginning to improve their literacy levels in schools and convents. This led to the formation of the first educated Acadian elite, which, in turn, gave New Brunswick's Acadians the means to mount a cultural and literary renaissance.

A NATIONAL REAWAKENING

Although newly founded post-secondary institutions would produce the first educated Acadian elite, the first suggestions of an autonomous Acadie would come from outsiders such as Rameau de Saint-Père, author of *La France aux colonies*, published in 1859 (Allain et al. 344). In chapter seven of that book, Rameau provided a clear program for the rebirth of Acadie. That program was taken so seriously that it was followed nearly to the letter by artisans of the Acadian Renaissance. Rameau's first recommendation was that education should become more accessible in Acadie: "Il est donc très nécessaire qu'une instruction plus répandue vienne aider les plus intelligents d'entre eux, à s'élever à des professions libérales ou commerciales" (114).

Secondly, he proposed that Acadians should adopt a symbol and rallying cry that would resuscitate their nationality (115–16). He also suggested the creation of French-language newspapers, a patron saint, and a patriotic society to promote pride in Acadian identity (116–17), a role eventually fulfilled by the Société Nationale l'Assomption created in 1890 (Bourque and Richard 56). Finally, he recommended the adoption of an Acadian national holiday: "ils auraient comme les Canadiens leur fête nationale, jour d'allégresse où chaque homme sait que tous les coeurs sortis de la meme race batte à l'unisson du sien" (117). So influential was he that the very vocabulary of Acadian rebirth may well have come directly from him, for his call to action used terms like "réveil" (114), "ralliement" (115), "résurrection," "progrès," "action commune," and "tradition renaissante" (116). Rameau's influence was also felt in his regular correspondence with a number of key figures in the Acadian Renaissance, including Israël Landry, founder of *Le Moniteur Acadien* in 1867, Father Camille Lefebvre, Father Marcel-François

Richard, Placide Gaudet, and Pascal Poirier, among others.[5] Archival records show how Acadians in key positions kept Rameau informed of developments, as well as financial and political needs in Acadie. In turn, he gave advice and helped organize fundraising, especially for Collège Saint-Joseph.

As proposed by Rameau, an important step in achieving Acadian rebirth was to organize the Conventions Nationales Acadiennes. The format for the CNAS was inspired by a congress in Québec in 1880 attended by an Acadian delegation. This small group, which included Pascal Poirier and Pierre-Amand Landry, resolved to hold a national gathering the following year under the banner "Convention nationale acadienne" (Bourque and Richard 5). Five commissions were created to study issues of pressing importance: choosing and adopting a national holiday; education; agriculture; colonization and emigration; and a French-language press and means of promoting it. The event was hosted in the summer of 1881 by the Collège Saint-Joseph in Memramcook, and was attended by about 5,000 Acadians (Bourque and Richard 11–12). It was a celebratory occasion during which speakers, in emotional, sometimes dramatic tones, marvelled at the very survival of Acadie. Concern for the future was a common theme, but, overall, the momentum was undeniably optimistic and the determination to move forward was unwavering.

Organizers and delegates quickly turned their attention to the most important issue of the three-day event: the choice of a national holiday. Though this consideration may not at first appear to be related to creating the conditions for the emergence of Acadian literature, the choice of a national holiday elicited a list of characteristics that delegates argued defined the Acadian people. Those characteristics, they contended, had been carved out by a distinct history that successive speakers expanded upon at length, often quoting Longfellow as evidence. In doing so, they attributed significant importance to Longfellow's text as a founding myth for Acadie, while also maintaining a strong sense of identity linked to the past, to language, and to religion. These three aspects would eventually provide the basis for a nascent Acadian Renaissance literature.

Two options for a national holiday were proposed: either adopt the 24 June date of Saint-Jean-Baptiste Day and join the ranks of French-Canadian brothers and sisters, or choose 15 August (l'Assomption) and maintain a distinct Acadian identity. Pascal Poirier and Marcel-François Richard spoke in favour of adopting l'Assomption. They warned of the dangers of being assimilated by a Québécois mythology and, as diplomatically as possible, reminded delegates that Acadie was a colony of France, not Québec. They convincingly argued that Acadie had not survived the Expulsion just to be dissolved into Québec and that Acadie had its own powerful and tragic history worth preserving through a distinct identity. In the end, the eloquence of Poirier and Richard won over the audience and l'Assomption was adopted, much to the chagrin of prominent French-Canadians present at the event (Bourque and Richard 22–36). The debate had been lengthy and not without controversy, but it was through this process that a new Acadian identity was defined for the first time in a collective, public way. That identity was further solidified when the speeches were published at length in *Le Moniteur Acadien*.

As significantly, that choice of a national holiday triggered a number of other decisions at the next CNA in 1884, not the least of which were a national flag, a national hymn, and an ensign. The national hymn was *Ave Maris Stella*—the hymn to the Virgin Mary whose Assumption had been selected as the national holiday—and the flag, proposed by Father Marcel-François Richard, was the French *tricolore* decorated simply with a yellow star.

To reinforce that new "public" identity, an identity important enough to have been the topic of a celebrated epic poem, Longfellow was quoted frequently at the CNAs, which indicates that at least some of the speakers had read *Evangeline* in its original, untranslated English. The lines between history and literature were, at this time, blurry at best, and Longfellow was regarded as a credible witness of a pure and virtuous pre-Expulsion Acadie (Bourque and Richard 68–69). Therefore, beyond their practical function of providing Acadians with a social organization and national symbols, the CNAs were a forum in which a national narrative was expressed for the first time, and as such, provided the motivation for an entire generation of authors to produce the first Acadian literature.

MOUNTING A LITERARY TRADITION: IMPORTED MODELS AND INNOVATIVE PRACTICES

Although a largely illiterate population cannot produce a national literature in print, this did not prevent Acadians before and after the Expulsion from preserving an oral tradition that would eventually be documented by many ethnographers and folklorists. Probably the most well-known Acadian author, Antonine Maillet, documented this phenomenon extensively in her Ph.D. thesis, *Rabelais et les traditions populaires en Acadie*. She shows how storytelling was a popular pastime for Acadian families and communities, and how drama as a collective event enacted the participation of players and an audience, making it a form of entertainment that was enjoyed by communities in which literacy levels varied greatly.

Indeed, almost immediately after the founding of Collège Saint-Joseph in 1864, a series of "séances publiques" were organized by professors and students. These were comprised of speeches, plays, and sometimes music, and were well attended by parents and members of the community. (Collège Sainte-Anne, founded in Nova Scotia in 1890, followed suit, paralleling its sister institution by placing literary experience at the heart of the college.) In 1866, only two years after its foundation, students of Collège Saint-Joseph started the Société Littéraire Saint-Jean-Baptiste, the first literary society of its kind in Acadie (*L'Album souvenir* 6). The literary society highlighted five main objectives in its constitution:

1. De former ses membres à la littérature française et à l'éloquence
2. de leur fournir un motif de réunion académique et l'occasion de fraterniser
3. de cimenter l'union qui doit exister entre les membres d'une même famille
4. de promouvoir par toutes les voies, les intérêts littéraires et scientifiques de la population écolière française du Collège et des membres de l'association en particulier
5. enfin, d'engager toux ceux qui en font partie à pratiquer mutuellement tout ce que l'honneur et la fraternité prescrivent aux enfants d'une même famille et d'une même patrie. (*L'Album-souvenir* 51)

The emphasis on family and fraternal relationships, so crucial in the early days of the Acadian Renaissance, found a parallel in the strong bonds created among members of these literary societies.[6] This loyalty to individuals and to a greater political cause likely provided the foundation for securing subsequent victories in the political and social arenas. Indeed, in a letter from Philéas Belliveau to Pascal Poirier dated 12 March 1900, there is mention of an "inner circle," and other letters opaquely refer to "delicate" and "confidential" matters.[7] These references suggest the existence of informal networks of educated and activist Acadians working behind the scenes to promote Acadian causes, and also the increasing awareness that together they could accomplish what was individually impossible.

Beyond creating a fraternal society, the more practical mission of the Société Littéraire Saint-Jean Baptiste was to hold literary events to develop and promote "eloquence," either in closed sessions or ones open to the public, as was the case on special occasions. These could be religious holidays or graduation ceremonies, when parents and members of the public were eager to attend so they could take pride in an institution that they had collectively built.

The oratorical skills acquired by these sons of farmers and fishermen had been modeled by the priests who spoke eloquently during their sermons, and who represented a certain status and potential mobility in society. Moreover, the practise of oratory skills among members of the Société Littéraire Saint-Jean-Baptiste prepared the first generation of the Acadian elite coming out of Collège Saint-Joseph. Thanks to this training, many of the student orators would later take the podium at the CNAS (1881 to 1937) and participate as articulate speakers in nurturing the sense of collective identity in Acadians.

Not to be outdone, the Irish students of Collège Saint-Joseph founded their own literary society, called Saint-Patrick's Academy, in 1874, which provided "literary and dramatic development of its members, while furnishing, at the same time, entertainment for the student body and friends of the college" (*Album historique* 35). Both societies encouraged their members not only to read literature, but also to write original texts. To provide a forum in which to publish their efforts, members of the Société Saint-Jean-Baptiste founded a literary journal called *Acadèmica* in 1883 (*L'Album souvenir* 40–41). This student paper had a fifty-year lifespan.[8] Modest in appearance, *Acadèmica* enabled students to situate themselves more realistically by, among other things, inserting local places in their stories. As such, the journal became a means to a more self-reifying literature in Acadie.

Similarly, in 1892, just two years after the founding of Collège Sainte-Anne in Pointe-de-l'Église, Nova Scotia, the St. Patrick Literary and Dramatic Society was created, followed by the Société Littéraire Saint-Joseph in 1893. Both literary societies held eloquence exercises and oratory debates, much like their sister societies at Collège Saint-Joseph in Memramcook. At both colleges there were sometimes joint meetings where the francophone and anglophone literary societies contributed to the entertainment (*Collège Sainte-Anne* 48).

The existence of these active literary societies is evidence that literature had an important place in early Acadian post-secondary education, for they further exposed young students to written literature. That being said, most of the literature read by Acadian students of the period was strictly controlled by the Roman Catholic Church's *Index Librorium Prohibitorum*, created in 1559. Reading a book from the *Index* brought on internal damnation, though exceptions could be made by applying to Rome for special reading exemptions.

A relevant example of this reactive censorship can be observed in the Acadian newspaper, *L'Évangéline*, which began printing a serial novel, *Les Intrigues de Sabine*, in the fall of 1890. After printing several chapters over the course of a few weeks, the editor-in-chief pulled the *roman-feuilleton* for inappropriate content. The editor apologized for the immoral behaviour of Sabine, which, luckily, had not yet been printed. The passage deemed inappropriate described a young woman who preferred to enjoy the pleasures of life for as long as possible rather than embrace the suffering that came with motherhood (qtd. in Haché 205). Clearly, this challenged the religious ideology that promoted large Acadian families, and could not be tolerated by the Church. This also sent the message to authors that, to be published and read, they would have to comply with the ideological constraints of an all-powerful religion. Religious censorship, then, was central to the many forces that shaped Acadian Renaissance literature.

A list of the forbidden French authors contained in the *Index* includes names such as François-Marie Arouet *dit* Voltaire, René Descartes, Jean-Jacques Rousseau, Jean de La Fontaine, Denis Diderot, Blaise Pascal, Pierre Larousse, Henri Beyle *dit* Stendhal, Victor Hugo, Alexandre Dumas (*père et fils*), Gustave Flaubert, Émile Zola, André Gide, and, much later, Jean-Paul Sartre and Simone de Beauvoir ("Milles Vies"). In other words, most great authors since the Enlightenment were deemed too controversial to be read, either because of allegations of heresy, immorality, sexual content, or political subversion. The fact that young Acadian scholars were discouraged—if not entirely prevented—from reading contemporary authors explains why their first attempts at writing tended to imitate outdated models. Since they were not reading the prominent authors of their time, it is worth exploring what young Acadians were reading. Authors on the approved reading list in the early years of Collège Saint-Joseph included French authors François Fénélon (late 17th century), Jacques Delille (18th century), François-René de Chateaubriand (18th century), Alphonse de Lamartine (18th–19th century), Félicité Robert de Lamennais (18th–19th century), Jacques-Bénigne de Bossuet (17th–18th century), and Blaise Pascal (17th century) (P., F., *Notions élémentaires* 12, 13, 73), as well as patriotic French-Canadian authors Pamphile LeMay, Adolphe-Basile Routhier, and Henri-Raymond Casgrain (12). There is a clear preference, then, for *ancien régime* France in the selection of texts (Haché 17). Although Voltaire and La Fontaine are also mentioned in a textbook written explicitly for the students of Collège

Saint-Joseph in 1889 (P., F., *Notions élémentaires* 25, 30), they are included because they have not yet been added to the *Index* by Rome.

Because of this prescriptiveness, it would take some time for Acadians to reject the rigidity of Catholic hegemony. And if the forms they chose (or were, by circumstance, allowed) seem primitive in comparison with their francophone counterparts in France and, to some extent, in Québec, the real contribution of Acadian Renaissance literature was the gradual insertion of a local and historical consciousness in literary texts, a consciousness that had so far been hampered by the absence of the Acadian experience in the materials they were allowed to read. The slow emergence of this reactionary consciousness was political and identity forming, and it opened the door for other literary movements that would follow in Acadie.

This nascent localism of history and place began to circulate widely among the population due in large part to an unprecedented explosion in French-language newspapers. Between 1867 and 1895 four Acadian papers were created: *Le Moniteur Acadien, Le Courrier des Provinces Maritimes, L'Impartial*, and *L'Évangéline*. Along with the establishment of an educational infrastructure, the creation of a French-language press was crucial to the ferment that produced the first Acadian literature. Again, Rameau de Saint-Père had wisely included this condition in his program for an Acadian Renaissance, highlighting the role an Acadian press would have in reviving Acadian pride: "On lirait ces pages dans les veillées, les anciens en commenteraient la lecture par leurs souvenirs, et mille récits revenant à leur mémoire ranimeraient l'ardeur de la jeunesse par les relations du courage et des malheurs de leurs aïeux; c'est ainsi qu'au foyer domestique la tradition renaissante viendrait se joindre à l'enseignement du présent pour préparer le développement de l'avenir" (115). Rameau had predicted correctly, for these papers provided essential narrative content to families on long winter evenings, replacing mostly nonexistent home libraries (Haché ii). Significantly, the French-language press served to twin the rich oral tradition with the printed means to concretize an Acadian discourse, thus further stirring the embers of Acadian nationalism.

Censored and sometimes even controlled by Church authorities, these papers nevertheless had a very significant impact on what the majority of Acadians read. The authors who were published in their pages—both literary and journalistic—endorsed the dominant Acadian ideology of the time, since dissension would have been considered immoral and intolerable. If these exclusionary constraints did not encourage innovative literary practices, they nonetheless ensured the coalescence of a strong common narrative, and equally strong social cohesion, at a time when both were needed in a minority literary context.

Through a francophone press, literature written in French began to enter Acadian homes in 1867 with the founding of *Le Moniteur Acadien*, the first French-language paper published in Acadie. The newspaper introduced the literary on many levels: for example, it published lists of Church-approved books so Acadians could choose their readings judiciously. Most of the books were historical and patriotic titles such as *La Tragédie d'un peuple* by Émile Lauvrière. As was the case in Europe and elsewhere in the world, serialized novels were also published quite regularly in *Le Moniteur Acadien*'s pages, a practice that kept readers hooked for months and boosted sales. It was through this mass circulation that the figure of Evangeline made her appearance in most Acadian homes for the first time; she arrived in the translation of Longfellow's original poem by Pamphile LeMay in 1867.

Few literary texts published by or about Acadians after 1867 escaped *Evangeline*'s influence, despite the fact that Longfellow never set foot in Acadie and considered its inhabitants gone forever. It is difficult to say how much direct influence the original may have had on Acadians, however, since it is unknown whether the English version was widely read. But what is known is that its numerous translations and rewrites were published frequently in French-language newspapers and were appropriated by the elite. What is also clear is that the romantic tale was woven into the national narrative of a population whose traumatic experience of forced exile (some have argued genocide)[9] was being validated by outside authorities. Though later criticized as too virginal and devout, even submissive, the character of Evangeline embodied the great sorrow and loss that were still profoundly felt by a large portion of the population.

In Acadie, Evangeline's submissiveness was often rewritten, tuning the tale to serve a growing mythology of resistance. In fact, the translated version of the epic poem that circulated widely in Acadian homes is not entirely faithful to the original: Le May's version is significantly longer than Longfellow's and is considered by many critics to be a rewriting rather than a translation of the original:

> More engaged and more aggressive, Le May insists on the brutality of the expulsion: the Acadian characters in the translated version are chained (1865a 41; 1870a 85), even though this was not the case in Longfellow's version.... Longfellow portrays the expulsion as a departure—to him, the Acadians are "farmers forever departed" (verse 12)

[.] Le May considers that they were driven away ("ont été chassés") (1865a 2).... The behavior exhibited by the British soldiers is presented as more barbaric in this version. (Bourque and Merkle 129, *my translation*)[10]

In his initial version of the poem, Le May went as far as to show Évangéline (the accents denoting the French heroine) dying, but after Longfellow expressed his displeasure with Le May, the translator-cum-author changed the ending in his rewriting of the poem in 1870.

Other translations of *Evangeline* were published, but Le May's version was most effective at capturing the Acadian imagination (Bourque and Merkle 126–27, 131). Perhaps this is due to the fact that it was the first version of the poem published in French in a French-language newspaper, and also because it contained the key elements that would serve the Acadian elite so well during the Renaissance: heroism, religious devotion, patriotism, and tragedy. In other words, by fulfilling the conditions for the creation of a national identity, this narrative was the perfect symbolic model for an emergent Acadie.

Another literary work that used the Expulsion as a central theme was *Jacques et Marie* (1867) by Napoléon Bourassa, also published as a serial novel in *Le Moniteur Acadien* in the same year as Le May's translation. Like Longfellow, Bourassa had never been to Acadie and was, in fact, using Longfellow's romantic story to promote French-Canadian nationalism among the youth of Québec (Viau, "L'épée" 54–55). Notwithstanding the author's intent, his novel was read repeatedly by Acadians and published twice in *Le Moniteur Acadien* and twice in *L'Évangéline* between 1867 and 1933. According to Acadian genealogist Placide Gaudet, "other than the names LaFrance and Lefebvre, not a single [French-]Canadian name is more known or more loved among Acadians as that of the author of 'Jacques et Marie'" (14).[11]

This strong endorsement by the Acadian readership of a love story as metaphor for a tragically lost Acadie inspired Collège Saint-Joseph students and professors to re-utilize certain elements of Longfellow's storyline when they began writing original plays. Those plays often left out the Romantic features, foregrounding instead the historical backdrop of the Expulsion while minimizing the love story and descriptions of nature. They did this to preserve modesty and to focus on the narrative of displacement, loss, and exile, sometimes even embellishing that narrative to add elements of the tragic. Pascal Poirier observed that there was a pronounced penchant for tragic homicidal plays at the all-male Collège Saint-Joseph (Poirier, *Le Père Lefebvre* 187).

The original repertoire for those students—plays by Shakespeare and Molière, stripped of their female characters (Poirier, *Le Père Lefebvre* 186)—did little to reinforce an Acadian identity grounded in local events and geography. However, when that limited classical repertoire of plays was exhausted, students and professors improvised. Albeit awkwardly at first, they imitated the classical models they had learned while also adding their own history partly borrowed from Longfellow's Romantic model. The result was an unusual form of hybridization.

Poirier provides an example of this fusion between tragic and Romantic models when he describes a play written by a young Irish ecclesiastic about the Expulsion of Acadians: "Rien de plus douloureux à voir et surtout à entendre! Le sang coulait à flots, dès le premier acte. Au quatrième, tous les personnages français avaient péri sous le poignard ou par l'épée; et, quand le rideau tomba sur la scène finale, il ne restait plus assez de vivants pour enterrer les morts" (*Le Père Lefebvre* 187).

The last expression—translated as "there were not enough survivors to bury the dead"—is perhaps more tragically symbolic than hyperbolic, and was also used by Poirier to describe one of his own unpublished plays. Poirier further claimed that almost every student of rhetoric at the college at that time had written a tragic play, though most were hidden in desks and would never see the light of day (*Le Père Lefebvre* 187).

The tragic classical form and the Romantic sensibility imposed by religious authorities in the colleges had been the default models for literature in these early years, but a distinct shift occurred at the thematic level when Acadian history and geography started to become integrated into these models. The first significant effort to substitute the local for the global was undertaken by Pascal Poirier in his play *Les Acadiens à Philadelphie,* staged in Ottawa in 1875. No longer a timid student, Poirier was then postmaster of the Dominion Parliament, and, as such, was bolder and less constrained in his writing. The play's action unfolds entirely in Philadelphia, one of the locations where Acadian exiles were treated with great cruelty. It develops ideas of resistance as deported Acadians who are about to be sold as slaves rebel, turning the work's ending into a bloodbath (Bourque and Merkle 136). In a significant political gesture, Poirier insisted that the profits of the play be donated to the rioters of Caraquet who were protesting the Schools Act of 1871, an act that withdrew provincial support from denominational schools. What is considered the first truly Acadian play, then, was doubly anchored in the historical and political context of Acadians (D. Bourque, "Le nationalisme" 53).

Starting from an oral tradition, Acadians in the early Renaissance period were initiated into imported literary models that they embraced, sometimes awkwardly, given their anachronistic detachments from the local. Nonetheless, the historical backdrop of one of those foreign texts—Longfellow's *Evangeline*—resonated for many Acadians. Through literary and dramatic societies, and within the pages of new French-language newspapers in Acadian territory, Acadians began expressing a more local perspective connected to their experiences and cultural identity. This development in the first Acadian literature was coloured by Acadian history and a consciousness of place, both of which appealed to collective memory and reached back to the oral tradition of their ancestors.

LATE-RENAISSANCE PERIOD

The beginnings of the Acadian Renaissance are clearly aligned with the founding of Collège Saint-Joseph in 1864 and the creation of a French-language press in the same decade. A generation later, emergent Acadian nationalism reached its peak during the first three CNAs of 1881 to 1890. The considerable strength of this movement, coupled with the persistent challenges faced by Acadians, meant that the Acadian nationalism created by the Renaissance patriots would be felt for several decades, right up to the celebrations surrounding the bicentennial of the Expulsion in 1955. Similarly, from a literary point of view, Acadians would not begin to move away from traditional forms and content until the middle of the twentieth century. Therefore the first half of that century continued to produce literature inspired by the ideology of the Renaissance, but with slight modifications, most notably in the form of more pronounced narratives of resistance.

One such example is found in the work of James Branch, a student at Collège Sacré-Cœur de Bathurst, who wrote a series of plays that were inspired by current events and issues concerning Acadians. In *L'Émigrant acadien* (1929), he raised a problem of grave concern to the Acadian elite: the outmigration of Acadians to the United States. In *Jusqu'à la mort! Pour nos écoles* and *Vivent nos écoles catholiques! Ou la résistance de Caraquet*, both published in 1929, he further defended those who were struggling to keep French-Catholic schools open. The latter play was Branch's most popular and went on tour in 1932 (M. Maillet, *Histoire de la littérature* 138–41).

After the first wave of original plays in the new century came a number of novels, often published in weekly instalments in the newspapers. Most of those were somewhat didactic and were presented under the banner of youth literature, seemingly in an effort to promote national ideology to a young generation of readers. A commission on publications in Acadie since 1921 at the CNA of 1927 was explicit in that regard: that it was absolutely crucial to share the history of Acadie with the youth to inspire them with their own national heroes. That commission likely accounts for the recurrence of themes and emphases in the literature of the time:

> Les accents maintes fois répétés de ces discours tomberont toujours pour la première fois sur de jeunes oreilles, car les enfants se joignent à leurs aînés dans la célébration de la fête nationale. Ils se souviendront longtemps de ce qu'ils y entendent. C'est une raison de plus pour laquelle on doit raconter souvent à nos réunions nationales notre belle histoire.
>
> On ne cesse de nous exhorter à demeurer catholiques et français, à imiter nos aïeux. Afin de suivre l'exemple de ceux qui ont tout sacrifié pour que nous conservions leur foi et leur parler, il faut être au courant de ce qu'ils étaient, de leur vie, de leurs vertus et de leurs épreuves. C'est l'histoire qui nous en fera part. Enseignons donc l'histoire partout où l'occasion s'en présente. Toute race a besoin de s'inspirer de ses héros disparus. La nôtre doit aussi être consciente de sa noblesse d'origine pour entretenir de hautes aspirations. (Robichaud 11)

Among those who participated in this sudden upsurge of youth literature was Antoine Léger, first president of La Société Mutuelle l'Assomption,[12] who published two novels for young readers: *Elle et Lui. Tragique idylle du peuple acadien* (1940) and *Une fleur d'Acadie. Un épisode du grand dérangement* (1946). Similarly, Laurent Albert, a Québécois sympathetic to Acadians, published an adventure novel, *Les Splendides Têtus. Roman acadien* in *Le Supplément à l'Action paroissiale* (1939). Eugène Achard, also from Québec, published four books in the 1940s, placing the Acadian Expulsion at the heart of each: *La douloureuse aventure d'Évangéline, Les exilés acadiens, La touchante Odyssée d'Évangéline,* and *Trois villes martyres: Port-Royal, Grand-Pré, Louisbourg*.

The trend in this youth literature was to repeat and synthesize the collective narrative so that the elements most useful for national ideology would be retained. As a result, heroes and heroines subscribe to a narrative of resistance rather than to Evangeline's model of passive submission. For the purposes of the late Acadian Renaissance, it seemed increasingly necessary to create proactive characters who wilfully contributed to rebuilding a nation.

Despite the fact that many of the works of the early twentieth century continue the practice of aligning theme with the goal of social cohesion, there are also in evidence a number of innovative techniques that carry the literature forward. In *Une Fleur d'Acadie*, for example, Acadian author Antoine Léger listed a number of Acadian place names from before the Expulsion and linked them to the new names adopted under British imperialism. Place names thereafter remain an important component of the literature of the latter part of the twentieth century. Léger's female character, Hélène, is also noteworthy. Separated from her fiancé by the Deportation, she embodies resistance as a strong warrior figure, visibly distinct from a more passive Evangeline: "Elle a exigé et a obtenu une paire de bottes hautes, une large ceinture à laquelle elle a suspendu un couteau, une hache légère au manche court, une carabine, de la poudre et des balles. Ainsi accoutrée, elle n'a pas peur pour elle-même car, plus d'une fois déjà, elle a fait preuve d'audace au-dessus de son âge et de son sexe" (Léger, *Une Fleur* 56). In addition, in an unusual juxtaposition of the virtues of compassion and authority, Hélène looks after the sick in Petitcodiac (as did her fictional predecessor Evangeline), but also commands her charges with the confidence of a general: "Hélène, avec l'autorité d'un général, commande aux habitants d'abandonner leurs maisons pour habiter les lisières de la forêt où l'ennemi ne pourra les surprendre; puis de semer, près des grands bois, le peu de froment et de grains qu'il [sic] ont pu sauver, et de planter les légumes qu'ils ont soigneusement conservés. Elle dirige et surveille ce travail avec l'œil d'un grand capitaine qui passe devant ses troupes, distribuant le blâme ou l'éloge" (74).

Many late-Renaissance authors employed an abundance of such figures of resistance and authority, thus contesting the docility of Longfellow's representations (Bourque and Merkle 132). At a time when Acadians were repositioning (and reasserting) themselves within a dominantly anglophone society, these models served an obvious function: under many layers of diplomacy and *bonne-entente*, they were a call to action for the entire Acadian population.

By the middle of the twentieth century—and coincident with the new literary figures who begin to emerge, such as Antonine Maillet and Ronald Després—the last murmurs of traditional nationalism can still be found in the poetry of Napoléon Landry. Landry published his second book of poetry, *Poèmes Acadiens*, in the year of the Acadian Expulsion's bicentennial, 1955, which marks an important turning point for Acadian society in general.

The cathartic celebrations around the bicentennial were held in every Acadian village, and included Évangéline parades and the very first Tintamarre.[13] In a special issue dedicated to the bicentennial, the newspaper *L'Évangéline*[14] provided a forum for photos and messages of survival and optimism to Acadian parishes and various organizations. The celebrations were widespread, reaching the population in a way that no commemorative event had ever done. As such, those celebrations ushered in a new era of modernity in Acadie, serving as a point of transition between the past and the future (Hautecoeur, *L'Acadie* 30). The traditional nationalist ideology promoted by the Société Nationale L'Assomption, which, significantly, changes its name to Société Nationale des Acadiens in 1957, began to wane as many of the Acadian founding patriots were replaced by a new generation. The last CNA took place in 1937—fittingly in Memramcook—and Clément Cormier calls it the swan's song, "le chant du cygne" (qtd. in Hautecoeur, *L'Acadie* 96), of these patriotic gatherings.[15]

CONCLUSION

The first efforts to create an Acadian literature were timid and fraught with obstacles, some historical, others institutional. Nonetheless, the Acadian nationalism of the late nineteenth and early twentieth centuries was instrumental in providing a framework within which Acadian society could begin to move forward collectively. That framework was rigid and exclusionary because the first Acadian elite felt that their grasp of collective identity was tenuous and fraught with risk. As a minority culture without a territorial claim or political power, they clung to the only type of nationalism they had known: a nationalism attached to old France. That the authors of the Acadian Renaissance were selected and sanctioned by a small Acadian and Québécois elite largely explains their reliance on ideological themes set out in pan-French nationalism. The founding of two colleges, a French-language press, and a national narrative in Acadie, however, created the conditions wherein a national *Acadian* literature could emerge. Although the discourse that emerged at that time imposed a mindset that has been criticized as limiting creative expression (Cogswell, "Modern Acadian Poetry" 63–68), it gave direction and focus to a small group of young, idealistic Acadian authors who needed a road map. The road map became too rigid and new trails would eventually have to be blazed, but the nascent literature served clear social and political functions that made it historically valuable and personally fulfilling. Literature was perceived by the recently educated elite as a powerful tool to propagate pride in Acadian identity and elevate Acadians to a status equal to that of other cultures.

In just a few decades, Acadian literature developed from oral storytelling to hybridized classical theatre to a romanticized version of the Expulsion myth, each stage getting closer to expressing the lived experience of Acadians. Having gained familiarity with the European literary canon in the colleges, Acadians increasingly recognized the need to tell their own stories. This initiated a shift in the literature they produced, and eventually would lead to a rejection of classical models altogether.

Perhaps more importantly for future generations of Acadian authors, a move to localism (often characterized by naming places) emerged, especially in the works of Acadian-born authors like Pascal Poirier, Antoine Léger, and James Branch. This localizing via place names represented more than just a desire to situate imaginative work geographically; rather, it represented an act of political resistance as well as a commemorative monument of collective mourning that functioned as a testimonial to the loss of home and community. To name was to assert presence, but also to mark and remember absence. This clearly emerges in the interregnum between the nineteenth and late-twentieth-century periods of Acadian nationalism, specifically in the poetry of Napoléon Landry who, in 1949 and 1955, published *Poèmes de mon pays* and *Poèmes Acadiens*. In those collections, and through his regular publications in francophone newspapers in the 1930s and 1940s, he continued the re-appropriation of Acadian territory, but with more resonant symbolic effect. In poems containing names like "Baie Française" (now Fundy Bay), "Cap des Beaumonts" (now Lower Cape), and "Chébouctou" (now Halifax), as well as in poems of epic battles, Landry memorialized collective memory by daring to insert Acadie into its own narrative (Chantal Richard, "*Poèmes Acadiens*" 59–64).

The importance of such commemorative projects is underlined by Gilbert, Bock, and Thériault, who agree that for francophone minorities outside of Québec, naming the local is as eminently political as it is sustaining (4). To name, they suggest, is not only to emplace but also to endow place with dimension and significance: "Dire un lieu, on le sait, est le moyen par lequel ce lieu voit son existence confirmée. La toponymie crée donc la mémoire, tandis que la cartographie la confirme et lui assure une certaine pérennité. La littérature et les autres formes d'art sont aussi des moyens par lesquels le lieu de mémoire naît et se transforme. C'est ainsi que le discours, la narration, font partie intégrante de l'édification du lieu de mémoire" (9).

Inserting the place names of an historical Acadie in the cultural agenda was one of the conditions for the emergence of a self-actualizing Acadian literature. That action was not just a turning point for Acadian literature and Acadian nationalism, but also the link that reconciled pre-Expulsion Acadie with the newly reborn Acadie of the twentieth century.

Linking pre- and post-Expulsion Acadie through place ensured the preservation and perpetuation of collective memory, cementing memory in the written record, but even more importantly liberating memory from the past through a process of collective mourning. According to Gilbert et al. memory is freed when it is re-appropriated and consecrated in writing. Acadian authors and ideologists could once again focus on the future without giving up the past (25). Place names, especially in the form of lists like the one at the beginning of Antoine Léger's *Une Fleur d'Acadie*, are likewise striking monuments to fallen places.

In that sense, the gradual localization of theme and place during the nineteenth century Acadian Renaissance effectively decolonized collective memory through literature. Rooted in but moving beyond the inflexible forms imposed by the religious elite, Acadian nationalism emerged from the speeches of the CNAs, which, though perpetuating a linear storyline that narrowly cast Acadian history in a rigid myth, also attributed a social and political role to literature that was compelling to students and a broader Acadian readership alike. Without its dual pedagogical and ideological functions, then, literature would not have had as central a role in the rebirth of Acadie. The emerging literature of the early Renaissance period was just as essential as the rejection of that same literature would be for the next generation of Acadian authors that emerged in the 1970s. What would remain as most relevant among the next generation of authors was the early nationalists' self-determination and re-appropriation of place and collective memory. In many ways, the next generation of literary nationalists would simply repeat and make anew what the previous generation had also sought to achieve.

NOTES

1 For the purposes of this chapter, the expression "Acadian Renaissance" denotes the period that started in the 1860s with the founding of Collège Saint-Joseph (1864) and the creation of the first French-language Acadian newspaper, *Le Moniteur Acadien* (1867). There has been confusion among scholars regarding the designation "Acadian Renaissance" and some have used it to refer to the more recent emergence of an autonomous Acadian literature in the 1970s, a

movement marked by the establishment of Acadian publishers and the rise of poets Guy Arsenault, Herménégilde Chiasson, Rose Desprès, Gérald Leblanc, Raymond Guy LeBlanc, Dyane Léger, and others. For purposes of clarity, however, it is preferable to differentiate the two periods and reserve the expression "Acadian Renaissance" for the period of intense social activity starting in the 1860s, as a number of prominent scholars have done before me (Godin and Basque 2007; Camille Richard 1960).

2 A list of the graduates of Collège Saint-Joseph during the first phase of its existence from 1864 to 1880 (*L'Annuaire* 9–16) proves the point: Pierre-Amand Landry (1846–1916) became the first Acadian to be admitted to the New Brunswick bar in 1871 and the first Acadian judge in 1890; Pascal Poirier (1852–1933) became the first Acadian to be named to the Canadian Senate; Placide Gaudet (1850–1930) was the first and most prolific Acadian genealogist and authored *Le Grand Dérangement* (1921); François-Xavier Cormier (1846–1906) was the first Memramcook-born priest and was named as a member of the committee tasked to choose the national Acadian holiday at the first Conventions Nationales Acadiennes (CNA) in 1881; Philéas-Frédéric Bourgeois (1855–1913) authored *L'école aux apparitions mystérieuses* (1896) and many historical and pedagogical textbooks; Fidèle Belliveau (1845–1891) was a speaker at the first CNA (1881); Lucien-Joseph (1861–1911) became first mayor of Shediac; Philippe-Louis Bellivau (1861–1933) spoke at six of the ten CNAs; André D. Cormier (1854–1930) became the college's accountant and brought electricity, running water, and a gymnasium to the institution; Gilbert-Anselme Girouard (1846–1885) became a prominent provincial politician; and Valentin Augustin Landry (1844–1919) founded *Le Courrier des Provinces Maritimes* in 1885 and one of the longest-standing francophone newspapers in the Maritimes, *L'Évangéline*, in 1887.

3 Hereafter CNA, CNAS.

4 "Le seul moyen efficace de tuer la langue française, en Acadie, c'est de l'atteindre au foyer domestique; et ce moyen est tout trouvé déjà et pratiqué." See Poirier in *L'Impartial*.

5 All correspondence comes from: Fonds Rameau de Saint-Père, Letters from Rameau de Saint-Père to Israël Landry, 2.1-8; to Father Lefebvre, 2.1-7, 12, 14, 30; to Father Marcel-François Richard, 2.1-18, 20, 23, 25; to Placide Gaudet, 2.1-24, 25, 27, 31, 34; and to Pascal Poirier, 2.1-14, 15, 16, 17, 19, 23, 26, 27, 29, 30, 31, 33, 35, Centre d'Études Acadiennes Anselme-Chiasson (CEAAC).

6 Fonds Pascal Poirier, 6.1, CEAAC; Fonds Pierre A. Landry, 5.1, CEAAC.

7 Fonds Pascal Poirier, 6, CEAAC. 1–5.

8 For extant issues from the 1920s and 1930s, see CEAAC: Pl. 5620.01, Pl. 5620.02.

9 See, for example, John Mack Faragher, *A Great and Noble Scheme*, 470–71.

10 The original text reads: « Plus engagé et plus agressif, Le May insiste sur la brutalité de la déportation : les personnages acadiens évoqués dans la traduction sont enchaînés (1865a 41; 1870a 85), alors que ceux de Longfellow ne le sont pas. [...] Si Longfellow voit la déportation comme un départ—pour lui les Acadiens sont des « *farmers forever departed* » (vers 12), pour Le May les Acadiens « ont été chassés » (1865a 2). [...] Le comportement des soldats britanniques est présenté comme plus barbare. » (Bourque and Merkle 129).

11 The original text reads: « À l'exception des noms de l'abbé Lafrance et du Père Lefebvre, pas un seul nom canadien n'est mieux connu et plus aimé chez les Acadiens que celui de l'auteur de 'Jacques et Marie.' »

12 Unlike la *Société Nationale L'Assomption*, which was a patriotic organization, la *Société Mutuelle L'Assomption* was a cooperative association that provided insurance and scholarships to Acadians, and, as such, played a significant role in the economic recovery of Acadians. The similarity in their names has often created confusion, but it is important to recognize that they were distinct entities fulfilling distinct roles.

13 As part of the celebrations around the bicentennial of the Expulsion, Acadians marched in the streets of Moncton, making noise with improvised instruments to affirm their presence, vitality, and to reclaim their space. Subsequently, the concept was embraced in many other Acadian regions, most notably in the town of Caraquet, which holds the largest Tintamarre in New Brunswick each year on 15 August. For more on this important Acadian tradition, see Labelle, "Tintamarre."

14 *L'Évangéline - numéro du Bicentenaire*, 15 August 1955, 81 pp.

15 For more on these commemorative events, see Ronald Rudin, *Remembering and Forgetting in Acadie*.

CHAPTER 3

THE FREDERICTON CONFEDERATION AWAKENING, 1843–1900

Thomas Hodd

No discussion about the history of Canadian literature can take place without recognizing the importance of two major figures in its formation: Charles G.D. Roberts and Bliss Carman. First cousins on their mothers' side, these two late-nineteenth-century writers, along with others of their generation, carved a literary space in the new Dominion that scholars have since dubbed "The Confederation Period" of Canadian literature. But this landmark group of poets did not spring full-blown from the head of Zeus. On the contrary, they developed in cities and from a provincial milieu that fostered their imaginations. For Archibald Lampman, Duncan Campbell Scott, and William Wilfred Campbell, Ottawa, Ontario was the place that would cultivate their aspirations; for Roberts and Carman, it was Fredericton, a quiet aristocratic town on the bank of the St. John River that served as the province's legislative and, for much of the nineteenth century, intellectual centre. Roberts in particular recalls that "the Fredericton of those days was a good place for a poet to be. The lovely little city of the Loyalists, bosomed in her elms and half encircled by the sweep of her majestic river, was stirring with a strange aesthetic ferment" ("Bliss Carman" 416). Understandably, then, much scholarship has been produced over the last century about Roberts, Carman, and their respective oeuvres. But the small New Brunswick city was more than the birthplace of two poets: it was the focal point of a significant period of cultural activity that spawned a community of writers and laid the literary groundwork for future generations of New Brunswick authors.

Scholarly criticism on the cultural milieu into which Roberts and Carman were born reveals that environment is just as important to understanding the writer as the analysis of the work itself. Alfred G. Bailey ("Creative Moments"), Malcolm Ross ("A Strange Aesthetic Ferment"), and more recently, D.M.R. Bentley (*The Confederation Group of Canadian Poets*) have identified some of the factors that influenced the work of Fredericton's late Victorian writers, notably the figuring of Bishop Medley in the shaping of the city's future fortunes; the presence of influential role models such as George R. Parkin, who taught both Roberts and Carman and helped cultivate their love of literature; and the significant part played by the University of New Brunswick in the flowering of these young authors.[1] Such convincing critical commentary, supported by Muriel Miller's biography of Bliss Carman (*Bliss Carman: Quest and Revolt*), as well as Elsie Pomeroy's and John Coldwell Adams's respective biographies of Charles G.D. Roberts (*Sir Charles G.D. Roberts*; *Sir Charles God Damn*), show that extratextual factors in the development of a literary community warrant more serious attention from scholars and that critical engagement with such social conditions can generate new matrices of knowledge regarding the relationship between writers and their milieu. The ensuing chapter, then, is concerned not so much with the literary history of individual poets in New Brunswick but with the conditions that played a role in shaping Fredericton's literary community during the latter half of the nineteenth century.

These "sites of influence," as I call them, are the physical and intellectual spaces that the city's writers would have witnessed and experienced during their formative years, creative markers that would have had an influential effect on their individual and collective imaginative psyches in the 1860s and 1870s. What's more, it was as if the province and its capital had prepared the creative soil for their arrival. Until the 1820s much of New Brunswick consisted of small communities, largely Protestant and Loyalist in ancestry, with Saint John as the commercial heart of the province and Fredericton as the legislative centre. But as W.S. MacNutt argues, in the early 1820s "[a] new New Brunswick, a turbulent, expansive society, was taking form" (*New Brunswick* 185), fuelled in part by an expansion in population from less than 25,000 at the turn of the century to more than 74,000 in 1824 (162). Even more significant, an influx of mostly Irish immigrants over the succeeding twenty years more than doubled the province's population to 200,000 by the 1840s (MacNutt, *New Brunswick* 277). Such a dramatic rise in population over the early decades of the nineteenth century, particularly in Saint John, led to increased social diversity, calls for educational reform, and a growing chorus that challenged the policies and executive appointments by

Loyalist Anglican elites in Fredericton that had dominated the province's affairs for several decades.

A TRUE CAPITAL TAKES SHAPE

Ironically, the result of such demands led, not to a more influential role for Saint John in the administration of the province, but instead to a reshaping of Fredericton as the province's educational and intellectual leader as well as a reasserting of its rightful title as the provincial capital. Although Fredericton had been designated the provincial capital back in 1785, up until the early decades of the nineteenth century it did not display the kind of architectural, intellectual, or cultural status typically associated with other international capitals, such as London and Paris. In fact, during the middle part of the nineteenth century Fredericton had a much smaller population than that of Saint John: the port city boasted a robust citizenry numbering around 42,000 by the 1860s, whereas Fredericton's population during this period was slightly less than 6,000.[2] Moreover, as a result of its sizeable port accessed via the Bay of Fundy, Saint John was more easily navigable than the narrow St. John River route to Fredericton, and so not surprisingly it became a prime destination point for immigration as well as a centre for trade in the province. Judith Fingard notes that during the 1820s, "the central element in the colony's development was the economy of Saint John," a "leading urban-mercantile centre in the region [and] the first to establish corporate institutions for finance, insurance, resource development, and trade" (279); and by the early 1850s Saint John had become "the biggest shipbuilding centre in the Maritime region and one of the leading ship owning ports in the world" (Robertson 337).

By contrast, Fredericton's position as the provincial capital made it a natural gathering point for the province's political elite and, since 1785, the place for higher learning for the province's young male aristocracy, and so whereas Saint John evolved into a centre for the merchant class, Fredericton increasingly became a destination for the province's intelligentsia. Put another way, what Fredericton lacked in growth of numbers, it made up for through growth in status: from the early 1840s to 1860s Fredericton underwent a transformation of sorts, a period marked by significant changes to its intellectual, ecclesiastical, and cultural landscape that would mold it into New Brunswick's "Celestial City" and prepare it to receive the province's future literary leaders.[3]

One illustrative case in point was the change to the administration and direction of the University of New Brunswick during this period. Begun in 1785 as a preparatory school teaching the liberal arts and sciences, the

Collegiate School was originally "patronized by the official and well-to-do classes of Fredericton" (MacNutt, *New Brunswick* 199). In 1800 Thomas Carleton granted a charter to the College of New Brunswick, which was followed by Sir Howard Douglas's petitioning for a Royal Charter and the opening of King's College in 1829. This new college enabled young New Brunswick men to stay home for their education rather than go abroad to the United States or to Windsor, Nova Scotia. Controversial from the start, though, was the Royal Charter's stipulation that, even though students could be of any denomination, "the members of the college council should be Anglicans and that the president and vice-president should be Anglican clergymen" (MacNutt, *New Brunswick* 201). Moreover, the new vice-president chosen to manage the college, Dr. Edwin Jacob, "brought from Oxford the clear conviction that classical literature and moral philosophy were essential subjects of study in new countries" (201).

For the less than well-to-do, such liberal arts education offered little to the young men hoping to achieve success in the province's successful timber trade, agriculture, or commerce. Not surprisingly, then, during the 1830s and 1840s the College suffered from considerable criticism (and even threats to burn it down) for a curriculum that, in many people's view, was not serving the needs of either Fredericton or the province (see Firth 22–32). Bowing to pressure, in 1845 "the majority of members of the assembly still professed to be members of the Church of England ... but they readily agreed ... to a bill that seriously limited the position of the Church in King's College" (MacNutt, *New Brunswick* 306). The result was that the bill "substituted the lieutenant-governor for the bishop as Visitor, made the office of president no longer the possession of the archdeacon of the province and, most important of all, reorganized the college council by expelling from it Principal Jacob and the professors, making it open to persons not members of the Church ... the college [thus] became considerably more public and less exclusive" (306). A decade later Saint John politician John Hamilton Gray, who had recently chaired a commission of inquiry into the activities at King's College, "voiced the great vision of the age—a provincial university beyond denominational control that should be open to all on equal terms" (370). His commission's report led to the 1859 act that reformed the college from a largely Anglican preparatory college into a secular, provincial university, a change in charter that effectively broadened the University of New Brunswick's mandate and helped expand its program offerings. The net result was that the school's reputation during the latter part of the nineteenth century shifted from a negative, elitist one to that of a leading provincial intellectual institution whose singular purpose was to cultivate the minds of its best young citizens, regardless of religious affiliation. In so doing, the university fostered a new kind of inspiring and more democratic environment that, less than two decades later, would begin to welcome through its doors a generation of New Brunswick writers ready to embrace their intellectual and creative destiny in a place of shared purpose.

Another factor in this 1840s sea change was the 1845 arrival in Fredericton of Church of England clergyman John Medley and the building of Christ Church Cathedral. Born in Chelsea, England and Oxford-educated, Medley was sent to the then colony "to heal the divisions in the New Brunswick church and to proclaim a comprehensiveness wide enough to embrace low churchman, high churchman, or ritualist" (Ross, "Medley, John"). He was responsible for creating the Anglican Diocese of Fredericton and was appointed Bishop of Fredericton in 1845. Later that year he laid the cornerstone for the new Christ Church Cathedral, amid controversy and much to the displeasure of the Anglican clergy in Saint John who, as William Christian notes, "naturally expected him to establish his seat there rather than in Fredericton … [because] under English ecclesiastical law, the bishop's seat had to be a city" (11). Officially opened in 1853, the cathedral is considered "one of the best and earliest examples of Gothic Revival architecture in Canada" (Wallace-Casey 46) and at the time of consecration its spire would have towered over much of Fredericton's skyline. What's more, not only did the cathedral change the physical landscape of the town, but the granting of Fredericton status as a cathedral city also had an impact on Church of England worshippers. As the Right Reverend Horatio Southgate pointed out at the consecration of the cathedral: "[t]his Church has a peculiar use and purpose in being the Cathedral Church of the Diocese. It is the seat of your Bishop, the Centre of your ecclesiastical unity, the source whence the most potent influences will extend themselves, like concentric circles on a lake, throughout your Province" (18). In short, this impressive and inspiring building affirmed for local Anglicans that their home town was worthy of becoming the ecclesiastical capital of the province.

Three years after Medley laid the cornerstone for Christ Church Cathedral, Fredericton received its City Charter, a new municipal status that would manifest itself in the construction of several new buildings over the next three decades. One of the city's architectural achievements was the Exhibition Palace, which opened in 1864. This impressive building on the southwest side of the city was influenced by the Crystal Palace of the Great Exhibition of 1851, held in London. Like its British counterpart, the

Exhibition Palace was meant to symbolize the capital city's new era of progress. As such, the Palace served as a focal point for celebrating the city's and province's achievements in industry; it also aimed to inspire its agriculture and manufacturing. The building burned down in 1877, but as Lorna Williams convincingly argues, during its short tenure the Exhibition Palace and other provincial exhibitions served as important meeting places for agriculturalists ("From Agricultural Improvement"), a sentiment best summed up by the *New Brunswick Reporter and Fredericton Advertiser* in August 1870: "The advantages to be derived from these exhibitions are so numerous that the point needs no enlargement; where there is a concentration of talent and skill, discovered as it were by a single glance, there must be a vast diffusion of information, and where knowledge grows prosperity increases" ("Fourth Great Provincial Exhibition" 2). Other key municipal initiatives in the latter half of the nineteenth century were the construction of the Fredericton Branch Railway, completed in 1869, which connected Fredericton with other coastal parts of the province; the opening of a new red-brick City Hall in 1877; and the completion of the new legislative building in 1882, the height of which, in relation to its much shorter predecessor, made it a towering and impressive structure that complemented in stature the Christ Church Cathedral located less than a kilometre away. Undoubtedly, these new buildings instilled a collective feeling among Frederictonians that this was no longer a quaint river town, but represented a prosperous provincial capital within a new nation, a capital worthy of cultivating and sustaining creative talent.

A third factor in the shaping of Fredericton's literary community was the role of three influential newspapers in the capital during the 1840s and 1850s, all of which promoted literature in their respective journals. The first to appear on the scene was Thomas Hill's *Loyalist and Conservative Advocate*, in the spring of 1843. Originally begun a year earlier in Saint John as the *Loyalist*, Hill and his partner James Doak decided to move the newspaper to Fredericton where it remained in circulation for three years before they returned the newspaper to Saint John.[4] Hill was also a poet and playwright, and during his short tenure in Fredericton he published *The Constitutional Lyrist: a Collection of National Songs, Original and Adapted to the Use of the Loyalists of New Brunswick* (1845), as well as the controversial play *Provincial Association: or, taxing each other* (1845). More importantly, it appears that Hill's move from the commercial city of Saint John to the more aristocratic town of Fredericton meant he had to address the cultural tastes of a new readership, for, as Edward Mullaly notes in

"Thomas Hill: The Fredericton Years," once the paper moved to Fredericton "the paper's literary content increased, as the editors began using its front page to serialize stories and novels written anonymously" (192). Likewise, the changing face of Fredericton obviously had an effect on Hill's own creative and literary aspirations, since "it would be difficult to imagine that [the fiction appearing in the *Loyalist*], with its New Brunswick settings, its narrative blended with original poetry and songs, and its strongly loyalist plots and themes, was written by anyone other than Hill" (192). Worth noting here is that Hill not only exposed Fredericton readers to more kinds of literature, but also encouraged them to recognize the creative potential of their local landscape by setting his own stories in New Brunswick.[5]

A year after Hill began publishing the *Loyalist and Conservative Advocate*, James Hogg, an Irish ex-pat, launched the *New Brunswick Reporter and Advertiser*. Purportedly the first New Brunswicker to publish a book of poetry in 1825, he was an avid supporter of "responsible government," but also championed arts and culture, devoting "much attention to literature, and his paper was enriched by original poems and stories. He endeavoured to make 'the Reporter' a power in letters as well as politics" (W.G. MacFarlane 44). Indeed, as Cassandra Inch points out, Hogg published work by local writers like Peter John Allan and Julia Catherine Hart, along with "reprinted essays and poems from various international papers (from Philadelphia, Boston, New York, and Belfast)" ("New Brunswick Reporter"). Equally important, C.M. Wallace notes that Hogg used his press to print a number of journals during the 1840s and 1850s, including the *Young Aspirant*, a magazine for children; the *Journal of the New Brunswick Society for the Encouragement of Agriculture, Home Manufactures, and Commerce*; as well as Bishop John Medley's *New Brunswick Churchman* ("Hogg, James"). His achievements, however, were short-lived: he died from an accidental shooting in 1866. But over two decades he had succeeded in providing local readers with increased exposure to local and international literature as well as "moderately responsible journalism during a period of extremes," thus making the *New Brunswick Reporter* "the most successful weekly in the province" for its time (Wallace, "Hogg, James").

The third newspaper to help shape Fredericton's literary community during mid-century was *The Head Quarters*. First published in 1843, *The Head Quarters*—like the *Reporter*—included poetry as well as a "Literature" column, both of which appeared regularly on the front page of the weekly paper. The "Literature" column in particular became a space for poems, short stories, and non-fiction pieces, as well summaries of public lectures.

First published by James Phillips, the journal's original long-time editor was William Grigor. But in the spring of 1854, the editorship of *The Head Quarters* changed hands, moving to King's College professor Marshall d'Avray. Future chief superintendent of education for New Brunswick, d'Avray arrived at the capital in 1848 to found the province's first training school for teachers. Soon after he also assumed the position of professor of modern languages at King's College, where he would teach English and French literature for the next twenty-three years, counting among his students George R. Parkin, future headmaster of the Collegiate School, and Canon George Roberts, Charles G.D. Roberts's father (Bailey, "d'Avray, Marshall de Brett Maréchal"). Moreover, after becoming editor of *The Head Quarters*, d'Avray continued the newspaper's literary tradition by including poetry, fiction, and dramatic sketches in his newspaper, as well as commentaries on the literature of the day. Significantly, one of d'Avray's early editorials in 1854 reveals much about his sense of duty in promoting and reviewing only the best books: "We do not think that a great demand for and a rapid sale of works ... be any proof of intellectual superiority, and we will be glad to do our part to restrain their profusion in this Province by calling attention to whatever may be really worthy of perusal" (Bailey, "d'Avray, Marshall de Brett Maréchal"). d'Avray also used his position to defend the value of a liberal arts education, writing in the mid-1850s "a series of witty editorials which exposed to ridicule the arguments of the attackers of the University" (Firth 28). In short, although he spent just a few years as editor, d'Avray succeeded in bringing an intellectual perspective to the newspaper that was meant to challenge rather than pander to the newspaper's readership. The *New Brunswick Reporter* and *The Head Quarters* were thus instrumental in encouraging cultural literacy in Fredericton during this period.

A GROWING DESTINATION FOR LOCAL TALENT

The net result of such multifaceted changes in the city's fortunes and self-image is that Fredericton became a destination for members of the cultural, ecclesiastic, and intellectual classes in the 1850s and 1860s. Three significant figures came to Fredericton during this period of change, two of whom had a direct influence on the city's future writers. The first to arrive was Margaret Catharine Gill Currie. A teacher originally from Springhill, New Brunswick, she had received her Class 1 license in January 1861 from the Normal School in Saint John, which enabled her to practise in St. Mary's Parish, located just across the river from the capital. She began teaching there in 1861 and for the next several years moved between St. Mary's and Kingsclear Parish, before settling in Fredericton sometime after 1869 (Davies, "Currie, Margaret Catharine Gill"). What is significant about Currie, however, is her first book of verse, *Gabriel West, and Other Poems* (1866), published by Fredericton printer Henry Cropley. More specifically, Davies notes "Currie's strong patriotic feelings for the province" in *Gabriel West* as well as her engagement with her Loyalist roots ("Currie, Margaret Catharine"); indeed, Currie dedicates her book "To the descendants of the Loyalists ... by one of their number" (n.p.). Moreover, Currie explains in her preface that "it has often been observed that something should be done to preserve the memory of the LOYALISTS from oblivion. I have felt the force of the remark, and determined to contribute my mite for that purpose" (n.p.). In short, Currie's publication signalled a new kind of local patriotism, in which one's personal cultural landscape served as the chief inspiration for the work. More importantly, although there is no evidence to suggest her book directly influenced Roberts, Carman, Straton, or any of the other future Fredericton poets of the late nineteenth century, it is telling that her embracing of the local was a theme echoed in all of their work.

The second figure to arrive in the capital was George R. Parkin, a native of Salisbury, located a few miles outside Moncton. Displaying promise as a scholar, he enrolled at the University of New Brunswick in 1864 where he took both his B.A. and M.A. before taking a post at the Bathurst Grammar School from 1867 to 1871. In the autumn of 1871, though, he moved to Fredericton and the following year began his duties as the new headmaster of the Fredericton Collegiate School, taking over from Charles G.D. Roberts's grandfather. More importantly, he soon found himself under the mentorship of Bishop Medley, who not only encouraged him to take a leave of absence to study for a year at Oxford, but also helped finance the trip (Christian 25). There he immersed himself in the study of Greek and Latin, as well as attending John Ruskin's lectures on art, among others, gaining valuable experience and ideas from the latest philosophical and literary movements in Britain that he could bring back to New Brunswick to enrich his teaching.[6] What's more, Parkin's return to Fredericton in September 1874 came at a precipitous moment, for his first cohort after such an intense immersion in the best of British culture included Charles G.D. Roberts and Bliss Carman, closely followed by other members of the Roberts clan as well as Francis Sherman a few years later. Parkin stayed in the position at the Collegiate School for the next fourteen years, teaching a generation of future Fredericton writers the classics as well as Romantic and Victorian authors, imparting to them a love for the written word and the value of the minutiae in poetry. As Bliss Carman recalls in a touching tribute to his old mentor: "He was a fascinating teacher, this intense and magnetic personality. There was never a dull moment in his classroom or in his society.... In the classics ... much of it had to be learned by heart, and all of it minutely mastered, with a thorough knowledge of grammar and construction, and an understanding of all the poetic and mythological references" ("Sir George R. Parkin"). Equally important, Parkin represented for these students the emerging figure of domestic achievement: that is, New Brunswick's educational system was shifting away from foreign-born, foreign-educated teachers during this period to hiring more native-born instructors. Parkin was a fellow young New Brunswicker who had achieved international educational success, and so, in addition to exposing Roberts, Carman, and others to international literary currents, he served as an inspiring local model of their own future literary and intellectual potential.

No event had more of a direct influence on the city's future literary community, though, than the arrival in 1873 of George Goodridge Roberts. Although born in Saint John, Roberts had moved to Fredericton when he was young and was a graduate of the city's renowned Collegiate School as well as King's College, completing his B.A. in 1852 and his M.A. in 1854. In June 1857 he married Emma Wetmore Bliss, Carman's maternal aunt; later that year, he was ordained an Anglican priest by Bishop Medley, then assigned to the Parish of Douglas, just north of city. However, in 1860 he left Douglas to take over St. Ann's Parish in Westcock, near Sackville, and there the family stayed for more than a decade until Medley recalled him to Fredericton to serve as pastor of Christ Church Parish Church at the corner of George and Westmorland (Boone, "Roberts, George Goodridge"). Roberts's move to Fredericton, then, was more of a return than a new destination; having been brought up and educated in the city, his return symbolized a story of local intellectual and ecclesiastical success which rivalled that of Parkin. While there he also home-schooled his eldest son, Charles, teaching him Latin, algebra, and arithmetic, as well as instilling in him an early love of literature and a fondness for the outdoors (Whalen, "Lorne Pierce's 1927 Interview"). He helped shepherd the Anglican community for the next thirty years, as well as serving as examiner for degree candidates at the University of New Brunswick and as secretary of the Fredericton Institution for the Education of the Deaf and Dumb. Equally important, Roberts brought back with him a daughter, Elizabeth, as well as his son Charles, who would both help solidify Fredericton as the future "Poets' Corner of Canada."

NATIONALIST FERVOUR

The other event to have an impact on Fredericton and its future literary community was Confederation. Hotly contested by the province's politicians, the prospect of union with Canada was viewed with suspicion by many New Brunswick citizens, only garnering sufficient support after a shift in public opinion in the latter part of 1865 (MacNutt, *New Brunswick* 439). But the shift in opinion was not a full embrace of revolutionary ideas. Instead, it was "with reluctance that the majority of the New Brunswick population were turning to accept Confederation. Resignation prevailed.... Union with Canada appeared to be the only prospect open; there was no exhilaration" (MacNutt, *New Brunswick* 443). That is not to say all parties felt threatened by Confederation. Among the merchant class, particularly those outside Fredericton, opinion was not as easy to gauge: Alfred G. Bailey points out that "[t]he cleavage of opinion seems not to have followed either occupational or class lines. The manufacturing interests were divided, some strongly favouring union" ("Basis and Persistence of Opposition" 379–80). The Fredericton *Head Quarters*, however, was unequivocal in its opposition: in its 3 October 1866 issue, for instance, the newspaper employed a sardonic and somewhat vociferous tone in what is an obvious anti-Confederation editorial rant, referring to the "so called constitutional lawyer, Mr. Fisher" and how it is "somewhat amusing and gratifying to see how those demagogues [the pro-Confederates] who use Her Majesty's name for political purposes, are treated by the constitutional press of England" ("Everybody remembers" 2). Even more poignant is *The Head Quarters*' description of the mood among citizens just two days after New Brunswick officially entered into Confederation: "The future may be full of hope, and it may give birth to great opportunities, but it is useless to shut one's eyes to the fact that in New Brunswick there is discontent and indignation smouldering in many places" ("First of July" 2).

Although the first wave of Fredericton's Confederation writers—Charles G.D. Roberts, Bliss Carman, Barry Straton, and Elizabeth Roberts—would have been too young to understand fully the implications of the period of political change they were born into, they would have heard and experienced the intellectual and emotionally charged language and ideas of Confederation that swirled around their supper-tables. After all, each of their fathers was a part of New Brunswick's educated class: Charles and Elizabeth's father was a parish priest, Carman's father was a barrister, and Barry Straton's father was a lawyer as well as clerk of the Executive Council.

In fact, as Muriel Miller recounts, on the day that Carman and Roberts met, "their parents had discussed the new Canadian Confederation and the promised Intercolonial railway" (4); consequently, Roberts and Carman became so "well versed on the matter of the 'Inter-Colonial Railway' that they later attempted to create their own version of the railway on the lawn with logs from the woodshed—a moment of youthful imagination that served to destroy much of the grass and anger Carman's mother" (4–5).

Worth noting is that Roberts's experience of the mood of Confederation in the rural community of Westcock, just outside Sackville, was much different from that described in *The Head Quarters*. In an interview with Lorne Pierce in 1927, for instance, he recalls hearing "both [Sir Charles] Tupper and [Sir Leonard] Tilley" who were "friends of my father and mother" (qtd. in Whalen). Given these friendships, during those years he would have been surrounded at the supper-table and in the parlour by men who passionately believed in the benefits of Confederation. Equally important to Roberts's thinking about Confederation was his father: Roberts's biographer Elsie Pomeroy recounts that "from the first suggestion of Confederation his father had been an ardent supporter of the idea, and had talked about it to his young son. Never did the boy forget his father's enthusiasm when the Union was about to be achieved" (10). Roberts would confirm in an interview, "I owe the emotion that I felt for the confederation of Canada to my father" (qtd. in Whalen). The future Confederation poets, then, were aware that something important was happening to their community, and that they were living in a period of profound change within their home province.

With its literary spirit, ecclesiastical guidance, socio-political union, and educational vision finally in place, Fredericton was ready to nurture the young people who would spend their formative years in the capital city, living, reading, and learning to create. Not surprisingly, a remarkable number of writers emerged from Fredericton during the 1870s and 1880s. The majority, of course, are already known to scholars: Charles G.D. Roberts, Bliss Carman, Francis Sherman, Barry Straton, Elizabeth Roberts, Theodore Roberts, and William Carman Roberts. This group formed the nucleus of a literary community that Charles G.D. Roberts would attempt to replicate over a thirty-year period, first in Windsor, Nova Scotia, then in New York City, before he and other key members went to seek their individual literary fortunes elsewhere in the early part of the twentieth century. Several, of course, were cousins, but the Carman, Straton, and Roberts families were more than just blood relatives: they were also linked by religion and geographic proximity. In addition to being members of the Church of England, they all lived within a stone's throw of one another. As Lilian Maxwell points out, the Roberts lived "on George Street, the Stratons a block away [from] the Rectory on Brunswick Street, and the Carmans half a block away on the corner of George and Church Streets" (50), while Francis Sherman's home was only four blocks from the Rectory (Roberts, "Francis Sherman" 420). Moreover, the Collegiate School that they would all attend was just down the street from the Rectory and located on the same grounds as Christ Church Cathedral. In short, during their formative years, the group's church, school, and friends were all located within a four-block radius, creating an almost self-contained community within Fredericton itself.

THE RECTORY

It is within this microcommunity that the province's Confederation poets came in contact with a number of key New Brunswick people and sites of influence that would help shape their individual creativity into a sense of local literary belonging. Chief among those sites was the Rectory. Arguably the most significant literary landmark in Fredericton, the Rectory on George Street was more than just the Roberts family home: it was a focal point for community gatherings, both in terms of entertainment and for literary fostering. Charles's son, Lloyd, recalls in *The Book of Roberts*: "It is any day, any month of the year—for what are seasons among friends, or hot and cold to those whose hearts blow always warm?—when word goes round among the clan that the Rectory is entertaining" (L. Roberts 93). C.F. Fraser corroborates the Rectory's importance by recounting that "of winter evenings the favourite gathering place was about the great centre table in the sitting-room, where the young people were wont to read aloud for each other's amusement the rhymes or stories which the day had called forth" (qtd. in Hale 92). In their younger days, Roberts and his cousin, Bliss Carman, would have participated often in these gatherings; their cousins, the Stratons, would have also visited for some of these events. Tammy Armstrong notes that Francis Sherman was also invited to the Rectory on several occasions in the late 1880s and early 1890s: "It was during these years that Sherman was invited to Canon George Goodridge Roberts's rectory on George Street, where Carman and Roberts met for poetry readings and debate" ("Francis Joseph Sherman").

It must be said that the mothers of these literary children played an important role in fostering their imaginations. The three Bliss sisters (Sophia, Bliss Carman's mother; Emma, Charles's mother; and Sarah, Barry Straton's mother) undoubtedly encouraged their children to be creative. Maxwell notes that "a niece of the three sisters ... told the writer that the sisters, when they corresponded, did so in verse" (50). Likewise, Helen Mowat states that "Mrs. Straton ... used to write for the amusement to her friends but never published" (7). Sophia was a diarist: included among the William F. Ganong Papers are her diaries from the 1870s and 1880s, each spanning several months. As for Emma Bliss, according to the *Canadian Magazine* she instilled in the Roberts children a love of reading as well as poetry: "Mrs. Roberts read aloud to her children a great deal. She read beautifully, and the smallest baby sat spellbound listening to her voice, even though the words were unintelligible. During the time when the little Roberts's [sic] were too small to listen to reading, she used to recite the most wonderful rhymes, gradually educating them to Longfellow and Tennyson, with the result that at the age of six, Elizabeth Roberts Macdonald could repeat 'The Lady of Shalott' without 'ever having learned it,' as she says" ("The Mother of the Roberts" 343).

There is also the example of the Roberts family amusing themselves at the Rectory with homespun publishing ventures. In 1879, the first number of the "Attic Portfolio" magazine was issued "in manuscript, from the Attic of the Fredericton Rectory by the Attic Club" (Mowat 7). More importantly, as Mowat points out, "every member of the household from the head of the house down to the babies of two and four, had to contribute an original article and not even the busy house-mother was exempt except on rare occasions" (7). Will, Theodore, and Charles contributed to the magazine, while Jane—then just thirteen years old—served at times as editor; moreover, among the people outside the family to contribute to the paper were "Bessie Jack, then a child staying at the Rectory, and Jean Murray Carman, a first cousin and sister to Bliss Carman" (7). In short, the Rectory served as one of the community's centres for intellectual and literary discussion, as a nurturing point for the love of literature, and as a space for early creative expression among the Roberts clan.

THE COLLEGIATE SCHOOL

The second site of influence for the future Fredericton writers was the Collegiate School. Originally conceived as a preparatory school for King's College, the Collegiate School was initially meant to include a Grammar School, as well as an English School. The English master was to teach reading, writing, and English grammar, as well as geography and history, among other subjects (MacNaughton 52). Barry Straton was the first of the future writers to attend the Collegiate School, graduating around 1869 or 1870.

The first of the Roberts siblings to attend the Collegiate School was Charles, beginning in 1874, followed a few years later by Elizabeth and the others; Lloyd, too, would eventually attend Fredericton Collegiate. Bliss Carman attended Collegiate at the same time as Charles, and Francis Sherman would follow in their footsteps a few years later.

With the exception of Straton, the majority of Fredericton's Confederation poets who went to the Collegiate School fell under the tutelage of George Parkin before his departure in 1888. Alfred G. Bailey ("Creative Moments"), Desmond Pacey ("Sir Charles G.D. Roberts"), and Malcolm Ross ("A Strange Aesthetic Ferment") have all commented on the role Parkin played in the nurturing of Roberts and Carman. Roberts himself later admitted that "Parkin's return to the school was an event which stamped itself ineffaceably on our lives. The influence of that stimulating contact was never afterwards quite to fade away" ("Bliss Carman" 413). Likewise, nearly fifty years after graduating from the Collegiate School, Carman recalled how Parkin inspired in them a love of poetry:

> One of the class would be sent running to Mr. Parkin's rooms to fetch a book; Tennyson, perhaps, or Rossetti, or Arnold, or another, and we might listen to his poem on the subject. These were wonderful hours of growth, though we never dreamed of our incomparable good fortune, so rare a tutor. I can hear now that ringing voice in many lines of English poetry, as he read them to us, feeling all their glorious beauty. Small wonder if some of us became infected with the rhythms of the muses, all unconsciously, and must be haunted forever by the cadence of golden words. ("Sir George R. Parkin")

Indeed, Parkin's true gift to his students was his ability to instill in them a love of literature; and for Roberts, Carman, and a few others, Parkin made them feel that they were in the literary motherland, witnessing the cutting edge of poetry. As Roberts recounts, Parkin exposed them to the "new music, the new colour [of] the new raptures of Swinburne and Rossetti" and he "would take us [on long hikes] as comrades, not as pupils; and his talk would weave magic for us till the austere fir-clad slopes would transform before us into the soft green Cumnor Hills, and the roofs and spires of Fredericton, far below, embowered in her rich elms, would seem to us the ivied towers of Oxford" ("Bliss Carman" 413). In short, Parkin sparked their literary imaginations, taught them to dream of themselves as writers, as future men and women of letters.

But the Collegiate School as a place for cultivating young minds cast a wider net over the future literary community than just Parkin's specific role as headmaster. It must also be remembered that Roberts's grandfather was headmaster of the Collegiate School before Parkin, and that Roberts's father had also taught there—and so the school was not just a family tradition in terms of attending as student, but equally represented for the Roberts clan a tradition of educational leadership. It is little wonder, then, that besides becoming a writer Charles worked as principal of Chatham Grammar School, then later as professor of English and French literature at King's College in Windsor, Nova Scotia. Similarly, Carman taught for a short period at the Collegiate School after attending the University of Edinburgh in the early 1880s, counting among his pupils Francis Sherman. More generally, leadership was not unfamiliar to this first wave of Fredericton poets: Charles G.D. Roberts, Bliss Carman, Barry Straton and Francis Sherman were all the oldest siblings in their respective families, while Elizabeth was the eldest female in the Roberts household, and as previously mentioned, their parents were leading members of society in Fredericton during this period. The idea of them becoming future leaders in the community—literary or otherwise—was therefore something expected of them from a young age given their privileged social status. This concept of leadership also informed the philosophy of the Collegiate School: as David and Robert Murray note, part of the school's function was to prepare students "for success in university and leadership in society ... through a rigorous training in classics with an accompanying program in character-building" (16).

Another aspect of the Collegiate School that helped promote and maintain a sense of community among the future Fredericton writers was the "Old Boys Society of the Collegiate School." Serving as a kind of social club for current students, faculty, and alumni, the objective of this body was to encourage Collegiate students to seek higher education by offering prizes for essays, speeches, and debating. The society's "Minutes Book" reveals that members also frequently discussed the kinds of books that they felt were important for students to read and should be purchased for the school. Parkin and Reverend Roberts were prominent members of the group, and Carman also served frequently on the board. Although he had left Fredericton by then, Roberts made several appearances at their meetings, usually as a guest speaker or to present awards; at one meeting he gave a talk on the importance of students studying history. The society even received local newspaper coverage for its activities: *The Capital*, for instance, devotes a whole column to the society's 1881 annual meeting, publishing the full remarks of the prize presenter, alumnus George W. Allen, along with the name of the winner and details of that year's prize—a five-volume edition of Shakespeare ("The Old Boys' Society" 4).

Above all, the Collegiate School was the formative meeting place for a group of young people with similar life circumstances or, as Roberts described it, a "coterie of schoolboy intimates bound together by like tastes and pursuits" ("Bliss Carman" 411). It was in such an environment that this future generation of writers met, read, dreamt, explored, and even attempted to mimic the cultural activities occurring around them. Of particular note is the significantly titled, but ill-fated journal *Progress*, which was the brainchild of a secret group of school-chums from the Collegiate School in the mid-1870s, whose members included Roberts, Carman, and two of the Straton boys (although not Barry, as he had already graduated). As Pomeroy recounts, it was a bold, but less than successful venture:

> The club early decided to bring out a paper which they named *Progress*. Naturally Roberts was greatly interested in the venture but, although he was very active in its promotion, he never attempted to write for it. He and Douglas Hazen had the audacity to apply to the Lieutenant-Governor and other prominent men for support and secured sufficient subscriptions to buy a hand-press. Although they worked desperately hard, they failed dismally in the handling of their precious press and never succeeded in bringing out the magazine. Two copies were afterwards printed by a local newspaper and then poor *Progress* faded away. (16)

Such publishing collaborations would re-emerge in later years in different forms, notably in the Roberts family "Attic Portfolio" magazine, Bliss Carman's co-publications with Richard Hovey in their *Songs from Vagabondia* and the collaborative anthology *Northland Lyrics*, which included work by the Roberts siblings (William Carman, Theodore, and Elizabeth) that was selected and arranged by Charles. Also of note is the short-lived partnership between Roberts and Barry Straton, who in 1878 "collected their poems together in a single manuscript which they bundled off to a New York publisher. It was promptly rejected, and the disappointed poets dissolved their partnership" (Pomeroy 19). And so, while at the Collegiate School the students not only kindled their love of literature, but also their taste for publishing, both of which fed the growing sense of competency that the young writers felt. In other words, the publishing experiments that began at the Collegiate School and continued at the Rectory were hardly the products of prescribed school assignments: they were inspired imitations of a burgeoning local literary scene around them, facilitated by a growing reading culture that literate newspapermen like Thomas Hill and Marshall d'Avray had cultivated in Fredericton just decades before.

THE KINDRED WILDERNESS

The other important activity of this group, afforded partly by their social status as well as encouragement from instructors, was its exploration of the wild. In addition to their hikes with Parkin, the schoolmates were fond of canoeing, a fact that would have important implications for their literary work, reflecting their love of place and their view of the New Brunswick landscape as something they now owned as citizens of a new Dominion. As Pomeroy notes, "another project of the T.O.E. club was an annual camping expedition.... They went camping for the two succeeding summers when Roberts was fifteen and sixteen, and also the following summer after he and some other members of the club had entered the University" (16). Moreover, "at intervals during the summer [Andy] Straton, Carman, and Roberts and others of the group would go on brief camping expeditions to Savage Island, an uninhabited island about six miles north of Fredericton. There they 'camped' in an old, ruined stone house" (18). Such outings were, in essence, an outcropping of the long-held tradition of summer voyages that the Roberts clan took to Savage Island—now Eqpahak—approximately seven kilometres northwest of Fredericton along the St. John River, in which they set up tents and stayed for a few days together, engaging in song, as well as literary and dramatic performances. It was a tradition Charles would attempt to replicate many years later in Windsor, Nova Scotia, when family and friends would come to Kingscroft during the summer and pitch tents on the lawn.

Also of note is a particularly long camping and fishing trip that members of the group took in the summer of 1877, in which they travelled by rail to Edmundston, in New Brunswick's northwest, then "set out in three birch canoes" (Pomeroy 24). Not only was the experience enjoyable for the group, it also proved inspirational, since the trip formed the basis of *Around the Campfire*, Roberts's first full-length prose work (24). Moreover, their launching-off point for many of those adventures was Sherman's Wharf, another key location in their four-block microcommunity, which was owned by Francis Sherman's father before he died. As Roberts recounts, "This massive old structure, since fallen to decay and removed, lay along the riverside in front of the Cathedral and Parliament Buildings, only a couple of hundred yards from the Collegiate School; and throughout the spring, summer and autumn it was the very centre of our schoolboy activities, our favourite resort. Around it, under the shelter of the high bank, we swam, we launched our birch canoes, we explored for spruce gum the great log-rafts sometimes tied up below it" ("Francis Sherman" 420).

Equally significant is the fact that Sherman's Wharf reminded the young men of the history of the area each time they cast off in their canoes: "Close at hand the white arches of a bridge denote the mouth of the Nashwaak River, opposite Sherman's wharf. There is the birth-place of the history of this spot. To that low point from behind which rolls out the Nashwaak, Villebon, true hero and leader of men, in 1692 betook himself from the Gemsec, to be still further secure from invasion, and to be nearer his Melicite [sic] allies" (Roberts, "New Brunswick" 767). Likewise linked to canoeing and their collective love of the wilds was the ever-present St. John River. Not only could the Fredericton group see the river from the Collegiate School, but it was also the catalyst for many of their travels, as well as the place where they would witness commercial exploits. Far from being a dangerous waterway for young outdoorsmen, "an easy and charming canoe-trip may be taken from Fredericton down the river to St. John, an indolent voyage, with no fishing or hard paddling to do" (Roberts, *The Canadian Guide-Book* 150–51). In short, to the young, inspired students of George Parkin, the St. John River was their Thames.

It was here, then, in the wild of the local landscape, that the Fredericton Confederation poets discovered topics and images worthy of creative expression, a fact that did not escape Alfred G. Bailey: "the most distinctive thing about the new poetry was the intimation of spiritual renewal that its authors caught from the wooded valleys and seascapes of the land where they were born" ("Creative Moments" 56–57). In short, the Fredericton group laid claim to landscapes that until 1867 were not fully embraced by the non-Indigenous citizens of New Brunswick: their collective love for this outdoor living would find fruition in such works as Barry Straton's *Hunter's Handbook* and in Roberts's travel guides—a tradition of nature writing in New Brunswick that would continue with the accounts of other outdoor enthusiasts, such as Tappan Adney's canoe voyages up the St. John River in the 1880s. In other words, the New Brunswick group soundly rejected the notion of the "garrison mentality" that Northrop Frye has argued informs much of early Canadian literature in its depiction of closely defined communities that are "confronted with a huge, unthinking, menacing, and formidable physical setting" (227). Instead, these New Brunswick writers defined themselves by the ease with which they entered into the wilderness and embraced it as Self rather than Other. Roberts's comments on such a relationship with the wild are instructive: "The present writer, having spent most of his boyhood on the fringes of the forest, with few interests save those which the forest afforded, may claim to have the intimacies of the wilderness as it were thrust upon him. The earliest enthusiasms which he can recollect are connected with some of the furred or feathered kindred" (Prefatory Note viii). The wild, then, aided rather than abetted New Brunswick's Confederation group in articulating their reality of a new Dominion, since their extensive explorations of the local landscape were rooted in a love, rather than a fear, of place.

Closely linked to this idea of a kindred wilderness and a new-found sense of history following Confederation was the social proximity in the Fredericton area between settler populations and the Maliseet and Mi'kmaq Nations. For Roberts and Carman particularly, the presence of Indigenous peoples along the St. John River helped reinforce their desire to connect with the land from a young age. It is unlikely that the educated Roberts clan, for instance, was unaware that their place of summer gatherings, Eqpahak, had until 1764 been the area's main Maliseet village (Nicholas, "Acquin, Gabriel"). Given that St. Mary's First Nation was directly across the river from Fredericton, and was officially recognized during the year of Confederation, the young canoeists would have also regularly witnessed and likely passed by Maliseet canoes on their outings. Nor was it uncommon for non-Indigenous outdoorsmen in New Brunswick to make use of Maliseet guides in the province: Roberts himself describes in his entry for *Picturesque Canada* that, upon arrival at the village of Andover, "[w]e had little difficulty in securing three trusty Melicites [*sic*], with their still more trusty canoes—a canoe and an Indian for each of our party" ("New Brunswick" 768). Equally telling is Roberts's dedication in his 1902 novel, *Red Fox*, to famous New Brunswick guide Henry Braithwaithe, who was himself mentored from a young age by legendary Maliseet guide Gabriel Acquin (Hamilton, "Braithwaite, Henry").

One major consequence of this exposure to First Nations and their place in the province's history and local landscape is that Carman and Roberts, in searching for ways to articulate their local experience within a new nation, took inspiration from the Maliseet and Mi'kmaq in some of their early work. One of Carman's earliest publications, for instance, was an 1884 review of Charles G. Leland's *The Algonquin Legends of New England* in the University of New Brunswick (UNB) student newspaper, *The University*

Monthly. Furthermore, D.M.R. Bentley posits that Roberts may have been exposed to Mi'kmaq stories during the early 1880s via articles in the Fredericton and Chatham newspapers ("Charles G.D. Roberts" 21), and that they, along with other sources, informed Roberts's decision to employ First Nations mythology for mid-1880s poems such as "The Departing of Gluskap" and "The Quelling of the Moose." Also, in his 1886 essay "The Outlook for Literature: Acadia's Field for Poetry, History and Romance" Roberts suggests two sources for future cultural work: Acadian history and mythology as well as Mi'kmaq legends. More importantly, he suggests in his article that writers could use Mi'kmaq legends as an "indirect" source for inspiration and cultivation, which Roberts himself went on to do in his later work. Evidence suggests, then, that although the Mi'kmaq-inspired work by Roberts was not published until after he left Fredericton, he encountered the initial sources for that inspiration—both material and literary—while he was still living in the provincial capital.

FREDERICTON'S INTELLECTUAL SUMMIT

In the fall of 1876, after winning the Classics Medal, Charles G.D. Roberts made his way up the hill to the next site of influence for the majority of the Confederation group: the University of New Brunswick. It was the same path that Carman, Francis Sherman, and the rest of the Roberts siblings would follow a few years later.[7]

There is no question that the University of New Brunswick looms large in the literary history of the province during the latter part of the nineteenth century. Alfred G. Bailey was one of the first scholars to offer a compelling argument about the university's shaping of Roberts and Carman, noting that "the education of its members and in the formation of their literary standards and tastes the University in Fredericton played a part that can hardly be exaggerated" ("Creative Moments" 54). A year later Desmond Pacey expanded upon Bailey's comments in the *University of New Brunswick Memorial Volume*, identifying some of the individual professors who played a role in moulding members of the Fredericton group. Declarative in tone, his statements are poignant and illuminating:

> Why was it, for example, that the university during these decades produced writers such as Charles Roberts and Bliss Carman, Francis Sherman and Theodore Roberts? Most biographies of these writers play down the influence of the university and give credit to George R. Parkin of the Collegiate School. But Parkin himself was a product

of the university, and as he himself testifies, it was Marshall d'Avray, professor of English and French from 1848 to 1871, who stimulated his interest in literature. Thus at the very least the university had an important indirect part to play in moulding these men. But I believe there was a direct influence also. When Carman and Roberts were students, Dr. Harrison was professor of English and philosophy, and he must have exercised great influence upon them. Certainly he was thoroughly versed in the English poets: we are told by his students that even his later mathematical lectures were sprinkled with apt quotations from poetry. The classical background is very important in the early poetry of Charles Roberts—and the professor of classics during Roberts' undergraduate days was none other than George E. Foster, one of the greatest statesmen and orators Canada has ever produced. Can we doubt that Foster inspired Roberts with his own sense of "the glory that was Greece and the grandeur that was Rome"? (Pacey, "The Humanist Tradition" 64–65)

As Pacey rightly argues, there were key individuals at the institution who helped continue the work of George Parkin in influencing the Fredericton group's future literary direction. Thomas Harrison, in particular, had a significant impact on Roberts. John Coldwell Adams points out that "Roberts' favourite professor was Thomas Harrison" (17), a truth reflected in the fact that Roberts's degree upon graduation in 1879 included "Honours in Mental and Moral Philosophy," one of Harrison's specialty subjects. What's more, many years later Roberts admitted that he modeled his own style of teaching poetry after his mentor: "Dr. Harrison did not formalize his teaching of English. He would read the poems and commend them to his students, telling them to live with them, associate with them and draw them into themselves. He gave no biographical details and no analyses. I followed this same method—which seems to me the true method of teaching literature—with my own classes later in King's College [in Windsor]" (qtd. in Whalen, "Lorne Pierce's 1927 Interview"). It is also worth noting that, like Parkin, Harrison was New Brunswick-born (Sheffield, east of Fredericton), was internationally educated (Trinity College, Dublin), and returned to his native province after his studies to become an educator.

A second seldom-mentioned influence on the Confederation group was Professor William F.S. Stockley, another member of the English department. Although Armstrong notes that Sherman "worked under George Foster" while there, Lorne Pierce notes that Stockley "later became an intimate friend" of Sherman and "under his inspiring mentorship Sherman broadened out from his early passion for [the English adventure novelist] Rider Haggard" (4), a move which undoubtedly helped influence Sherman's future literary output. Annie Harvie (Ross) Foster, a contemporary of Sherman and fellow future New Brunswick writer, likewise credits Stockley with fostering her love for literature (MacCallum, "Foster, Annie Harvie (Ross)").

Equally important as the professors' mentorship was the creative environment that the University of New Brunswick afforded the young Fredericton writers. Pomeroy for instance, notes that "[i]t was during his first year at the college that Roberts began writing in earnest" (26) and that "several of the short poems which were published in *Orion, and Other Poems* were written in the classroom behind the safe seclusion of black glasses which he was obliged to wear" (29). Nor can we ignore one of the group's main creative outlets, located just inside the walls of the university: *The University Monthly*, UNB's newspaper. Originally founded in 1867, the newspaper's first incarnation was short-lived, but it was revived in 1882 and flourished thereafter. Although little scholarship has been produced regarding its role in fostering the literary lives of Roberts, Carman, Sherman, Straton, and others, it certainly played a significant role in furthering their publishing experience as well as bolstering their dreams as future authors. For instance, both Roberts and Carman served for a time as corresponding editors. More importantly, all four had works appear in its pages. Roberts had the most contributions: several of his poems from *Orion, and Other Poems* were reprinted in the late 1882 and early 1883 editions of the paper; also, his important Alumni Address at the university's May 1883 graduation ceremony, "The Beginnings of Canadian Literature," was printed in the June 1883 issue. He also had first appearances of poems such as "On Reading the Poems of Sidney Lanier" and "To Bliss Carman, with a Copy of Lang's 'Helen of Troy,'" which ran in the April 1885 issue. Appearing, too, in installments from April 1882 to March 1883 was Roberts's translation of a 1793 article, "Ye Truie and Faithfulle Hystorie of Ye Squattyckke Tripp." Carman's review of Charles G. Leland's *The Algonquin Legends of New England* was published in the November 1884 edition, while his review of John Burroughs's *Winter Sunshine* appeared in the May 1885 issue. Barry Straton and Francis Sherman also published several poems in the *University Monthly*. Notably, Sherman's four sonnets, which appeared in the newspaper's April 1897 edition, were later published as part of his collection, *The Deserted City*, in 1899. Martin Ware notes that many of Theodore Goodridge Roberts's early poems also appeared in *The University Monthly* (xviii).

Roberts also achieved the Confederation group's first publishing milestone: in 1880, J.B. Lippincott of Philadelphia published *Orion, and other Poems*, financed partly by Roberts's future father-in-law George Fenety, Queen's Printer for New Brunswick and future mayor of Fredericton (Pomeroy 28). Money aside, the symbolic value of Roberts's book cannot be understated. Receiving positive reviews in both Canada and the United States, the *Canadian Monthly and National Review* rhetorically asked: "[Does] not the publication of such a book by this Mr. Roberts, of New Brunswick, justify us in arguing good things of the spread of a genuine literary spirit in Canada?" (qtd. in Hall 313). While many scholars have commented on the book's impact on a young Ottawa poet named Archibald Lampman, *Orion, and Other Poems* also played a role in spreading "genuine literary spirit" in New Brunswick, for it signalled the beginning of a flourish of publishing activities by Fredericton writers that would continue over the next two decades. In 1884 a trio of first books appeared: Elizabeth Roberts's *Poems*, Jean Nealis's *Drift*, and Barry Straton's *Lays of Love*. Jean Nealis (1842–1910) was a contemporary of Margaret Currie and grew up on Waterloo Row, just down the street from Bliss Carman. Like the Roberts clan, she too was of Loyalist stock, on her mother's side, as well as an Anglican by birth and upbringing. Significantly, she served for a time as organist in Christ Church Cathedral before eloping and marrying Hugh Nealis, a Roman Catholic (Maxwell 45). Although she wrote her poetry and published her book long after leaving Fredericton, there is clear evidence that Nealis's literary sensibility was equally shaped by this transformative period in the capital's cultural history.

Straton fared even better than Nealis in terms of publishing credits. A year after *Lays of Love* appeared he published his only non-fiction book, *The Hunter's Handbook*. Then in 1887 he published *The Building of the Bridge, an Idyl of the River Saint John*. Although he published little after this intensely creative period, it is worth noting that four of Straton's poems appeared in William D. Lighthall's *Songs of the Great Dominion*, several less than Roberts (who had twelve included), but only one less than Bliss Carman. Roberts published his second collection, *Later Poems*, in 1881, followed by *In Divers Tones* in 1886. What's more, the overall success of the group's literary efforts in the 1880s was followed by a second period of publishing activity in the 1890s. Carman's first book, *Low Tide on Grand Pré*, appeared in 1893; Sherman's first collections, *Matins* and *In Memorabilia Mortis*, appeared in 1896; and Roberts's first animal stories and novels were published during this time. The year 1899 would also signal the start of a long and successful publishing career for Theodore Goodridge Roberts, who appeared in the Roberts anthology, *Northland Lyrics*, along with Elizabeth and William Carman. For her part, Elizabeth Carman went on to publish an additional collection of poetry, *Dream Verses*, in 1906, as well as a children's book, *Our Canadian Cousin*, in 1904. Echoing Straton's short publishing career is that of Sherman—intense but all too brief; he published five collections of poetry between 1896 and 1900.

One of the reasons for such a lengthy and sustained period of publication by the Fredericton group was the indefatigable spirit of Charles G.D. Roberts, for after he left Fredericton in 1885 to begin his duties as professor of English and French literature at King's College, Windsor, Nova Scotia, he assumed the role of unofficial leader of the New Brunswick writing community. Leading by example, he constantly published in a variety of genres. He also used his position to facilitate the publication of others in the community, for instance offering the names of Carman, Straton, and Elizabeth Carman to William Douw Lighthall for inclusion in *Songs of the Great Dominion* (*The Collected Letters of Sir Charles G.D. Roberts* 83–85), as well as agreeing to select and introduce the anthology of his siblings' work, *Northland Lyrics*. Likewise, in his correspondence with Carman he constantly encouraged his cousin to write, offering criticism of Carman's work and providing an environment for them to work on their craft. More specifically, for several years Carman spent a number of weeks at Roberts's house in Windsor, Nova Scotia where they, along with Richard Hovey and others, would write, as Charles's son Lloyd recounts in *The Book of Roberts*: "It was summer-time and the big wooden college on the other side of the Cricket Field was closed. So, 'Bliss scribbled, Dick [Richard Hovey] scribbled, we scribbled all three,' as Browning might have phrased it" (L. Roberts 37). After his brief return to Fredericton in 1895, Roberts also met with Sherman and no doubt encouraged him to publish his work, particularly since he found him "most congenial, not only in his devotion to poetry, in which our tastes consistently agreed, but also in his passion for canoes and for the life of the wilds" ("Francis Sherman" 421). Roberts also invited his brothers, Theodore and William Carman, to New York and helped find them literary employment there. In short, the leadership shown to Roberts during his younger years by figures such as Parkin, George E. Foster, Thomas Harrison, and others became internalized and he went on to embrace his role as mentor of the next generation of Fredericton's literary community. Without Roberts's leadership, it is unlikely that the literary roots of Fredericton would have grown so deep.

In 1825, New Brunswick-born Oliver Goldsmith published *The Rising Village*, a book-length poem about the progress of civilization in the North American colonies. Written in heroic couplets, the poem praises not only the successes of Acadia and imperial Britain, but equally warns against the vices that might impede their progress. In particular, he warns the reader against the peril of idleness:

> Yet, tho' these simple pleasures crown the year,
> Relieve its cares, and every bosom cheer,
> As life's gay scenes in quick succession rise,
> To lure the heart and captivate the eyes;
> Soon vice steals on, in thoughtless pleasure's train,
> And spreads her miseries o'er the village plain.
> (*The Rising Village*, 1989 285–90)

So begins the tragic love story of Albert and Flora, Goldsmith's moral exemplum meant to warn the younger generation to guard against leisure time. But what Goldsmith, a descendent of Loyalists and the Church of England tradition, could not have anticipated is that fifty years later his cultural kin in Fredericton would turn that same vice of leisure into a virtue of literary success. Barry Straton, Charles G.D. Roberts, Bliss Carman, Elizabeth Roberts, and Francis Sherman, all born during one of the most transformative periods in Fredericton's history, were exposed to a burgeoning intellectual and cultural environment that Goldsmith believed was a threat to the colony's future prosperity. Indeed, as A.J.M. Smith pronounced in "The Fredericton Poets," his Founders' Day Address at the University of New Brunswick, "the spirit which finds expression in this poetry is an essence skimmed only from the dominating classes of the New Brunswick social system.... The lucky artist who is nurtured in such a culture is set free to deal with what is universal, with the fundamental emotions of the human heart, and with the adventures of the soul" (71–72).

This is not to say there was no literary activity or no writers in Fredericton before Confederation. But from the 1840s to the 1860s, Fredericton underwent a period of substantial change that saw it transform from a sleepy, small, aristocratic town into a vibrant capital city whose new architecture, home-grown educational leaders, and increasingly sophisticated literary tastes made it a stimulating environment for inspiring young minds. Moreover, unlike previous generations, the young men and women who grew up in the provincial capital in the 1870s were not so much individuals as they were, for the first time, parts of a creative collective that developed within the new Dominion of Canada. They lived within a four-block microcommunity near the edge of the St. John River, brought together by family ties as well as similar social circumstances. More importantly, they were exposed from an early age to vibrant, local cultural publications, and were encouraged to experiment as well as imitate some of those magazines. They also fell under the tutelage of New Brunswick–born teachers whose ideas about culture and literature were informed by international educational experiences, yet simultaneously grounded in local pride for landscape, heritage, and history. In short, had this confluence of social, educational, and literary circumstances not come together when it did, an influential New Brunswick group would have not been able to embrace its "simple pleasures," and the upward progress of what has become a definable Canadian literary tradition would have been that much harder to achieve.

NOTES

1. Also worth noting was their common Anglican upbringing: as D.M.R. Bentley notes, Roberts and Carman—not to mention the other members of the Confederation group of poets—"were born and raised in environments in which Christianity in its Anglican and moderate forms was a continual and formative presence" (*The Confederation Group of Canadian Poets* 204).

2. According to Alexander Monro's *History, Geography, and Statistics of British North America*, the population of Fredericton "in 1840 was 4,002; in 1851, 4,438; and in 1861 it was 5,652" (292).

3. Although employed sardonically by the citizens of Saint John, the nickname "Celestial City" has long been a source of pride for Frederictonians. The term has been in use since at least the mid-1850s—see Robert Cooney's *Autobiography of a Wesleyan Methodist Missionary*—and later used as a marketing element in promoting the city as a tourist destination. See, for instance, Frank Risteen's *Fredericton, the Celestial City and the River St. John* as well as Katherine Hale's chapter on the "Celestial City" in her *Canadian Cities of Romance*.

4. Although I have found no published explanation for the newspaper's move to Fredericton, one likely reason is that Hill wished to be closer to the discussions surrounding responsible government. As Eric Swanick notes in his biography of Hill, "under Hill's editorship the *Loyalist* was an outspoken champion of the imperial connection and Orangeism, and an opponent of responsible government" ("Hill, Thomas"). In fact, Doak and Hill were found guilty of libel in 1844 for an editorial attack on Lemuel Allan Wilmot, one of the legislature's leading proponents of responsible government (Swanick).

5 Although Hill originally spent only three years in Fredericton, the city had a lasting impact on him, for he returned in the early 1850s and served on the editorial board of *The Head Quarters* until his death in 1860.
6 Medley also encouraged Parkin to visit other parts of England while overseas, and to expose himself to the cultural riches the country had to offer (see Christian 30–31).
7 Barry Straton, the eldest of the New Brunswick Confederation poets, was the only member of the group not to attend the University of New Brunswick. After graduating from the Collegiate School, he worked briefly in a law office before turning to farming as his main occupation (see Maxwell 51).

CHAPTER 4

MID-CENTURY EMERGENT MODERNISM, 1935–1955

Tony Tremblay

Similar to previous periods of heightened literary activity in New Brunswick, the period of twentieth-century emergent modernism knew no fixed temporal frame, or at least no clear beginning. By the turn of the century, the key literary practitioners of the Confederation era were already growing weary of the antimodernist tones that had won them such wide appeal in the largely conservative milieu of still-colonial Canada. Bliss Carman, for example, had caught the eye of Decadent poet Arthur Symons, who saw in his work something akin to the daring of the French Symbolists whom he had popularized. So convinced was Symons of Carman's avant-garde aesthetic in *Songs from Vagabondia* (1894) and *Behind the Arras* (1895) that he took Carman to visit W.B. Yeats in 1896, desiring that the leading fin-de-siècle spiritualists should meet. Symons wrote a short time later that Carman was to be admired for "fresh, new, and unspoilt [forms]." Here was a poet, said Symons, who was "trying to express more than he at present knows how to express" (qtd. in T. Ware 101), an acknowledgement of Carman's grasp at modernism that Ezra Pound, too, found compelling. Pound would follow Symons's lead by famously declaring that "among contemporary North American poets Bliss Carman was 'about the only one of the lot that wouldn't improve by drowning'" (qtd. in Carpenter 150), a statement Pound made a few months after arriving in New York in 1910.

In *The Birth of Modernism*, Leon Surette would qualify the interest in Carman by pointing out that "to be 'modern' ... is to have transcended history, to have climbed out of history into an unmediated, incorrigible realm of knowledge" (4), which Carman certainly did in hastening poetry's transition from the Walter Pater school of classical beauty to the more effectual realms of the intellectual and esoteric. That modernism "is more continuous with late nineteenth-century aesthetic practice than the ... New Critics permitted" ("Ezra Pound" 66), is Surette's larger argument, an argument that places one of New Brunswick's (supposedly) pre-eminent antimodernists squarely at the scene of twentieth-century modernism's beginnings.

To propose a date, however, when one era ended and a new era began is to miss the extent to which literary modernism as we know it today—as distemper, renovation, and formal experimentation—was already taking shape in the work and thinking of earlier writers. Perhaps it is better to say that, by the second decade of the new century, the integrative naturalism, high seriousness, and lofty rhetoric of the Roberts-Carman generation was largely over. George Parkin, uncompromising imperialist and mentor to the Fredericton poets, would soon be dead (1922); Francis Sherman had long ceased writing poetry and would also soon die (1926); Carman was entering his final years, having moved from the avant-garde mysticism that Pound once admired to the quackery of the domestic popular occult; and Charles G.D. Roberts was soon to make his final tour of Canada (1925), returning after almost thirty years in exile to a country that welcomed him as a curiosity as much as a serious artist. When he toured the country as president of the Canadian Authors Association in 1927, he did so as an elder statesman, as a remnant (albeit respected) of a post-Swinburne literary aristocracy. He seemed to know that he was soon to become folklore (Adams 158).

The last of his generation to survive, Roberts's final tour of his once-fawning nation was unceremoniously footnoted by F.R. Scott's poem "The Canadian Authors Meet" (1927), a biting satire of literary peerage and puffery. "The cakes are sweet," wrote Scott, "but sweeter is the feeling / That one is mixing with the *literati*" (70; emphasis in original). The poem not only signalled the end of Roberts's reign—and with it a rejection of the nineteenth-century Arnoldian belief in art as moral uplift—but also the relocation of Canadian literature from New Brunswick and the East, where it began, to the urban and cosmopolitan centres of Canada, first Montreal and then Toronto. For writers and cultural workers in New Brunswick, that relocation was felt as a *dislocation*, and it would have profound implications for how later movements in the province expressed their sense of identity, struggle, and reformist animus. Not only had the centre moved, but it had been dislodged by the jeering sarcasm of the urban elite. New Brunswick's literary class would thereafter demarcate and defend positions on an aggrieved periphery of the nation.

An uneasy interregnum followed from this centralist-abetted demotion, an unease characterized, not surprisingly, by literary styles that sought to emulate and even resuscitate those of the past. The work of H.A. Cody is typical, its muscular Christianity turning common farmers and loggers into nobles who, by a sort of Loyalist predestination, resist change to pursue "happiness unalloyed" (280). Even an aged Bliss Carman considered Cody's fictions anachronistic, saying in a 1928 letter to Rufus Hathaway that he would like to expunge Cody from the national record (*Letters of Bliss Carman* 363). When imaginative energies of more identifiably modernist concern ignited again, they did so in Saint John, New Brunswick's oldest and most consciously working-class city. In this chapter I describe those energies and the institutional apparatus for cultural production that accompanied the formation of the post–World War Two New Brunswick state. Beginning in the port city among a miscellany of intellectuals and artists associated with Ted Campbell's studio (among whose number were A.G. Bailey, P.K. Page, Kay Smith, and John Sutherland), those energies moved north to Fredericton where Bailey recruited figures such as Desmond Pacey, Fred Cogswell, and Elizabeth Brewster to radically localize cultural expression. The results included *The Fiddlehead*, Brunswick Press, and a series of other developments, from new academic departments and library expansions to, most importantly, the realization that New Brunswick, though culturally isolated, could also participate in larger aesthetic movements while meeting its own needs for self-expression.

INCUBATING A CULTURE OF ALIENATION, ACTIVISM, AND INVENTION

To understand the context within which cultural modernism transitioned from aesthetic fancy (evidenced in Carman's avant-garde spiritualism) to reformist, working-class practice in New Brunswick (evidenced in the mid-century poetry of Smith and Bailey), it is essential to consider the overarching economic narrative of the Maritime region in the early decades of the new century.

By the close of the 1920s, the decade that was witness to the dissolution of the Carman-Roberts mystique, the region's provinces had been reduced to "supplicants," to use political scientist Hugh Thorburn's term (16). Not only had the economic promises of Confederation proven false, but the macroeconomic retrofit that had radically altered trade patterns from vertical (north–south with the Americas) to horizontal (east–west with Quebec and

Ontario) had also strengthened the centre of the country at the expense of the East. As early as 1891, Goldwin Smith had sounded this warning, stating in *Canada and the Canadian Question* that Prime Minister John A. Macdonald's National Policy was "unnatural, forced and profitless" (166).

The case of the Intercolonial Railway provides the best example of what Smith identified as the relationship between structural intervention (the creation of an artificial economy) and reversing fortunes. Though the railway was indeed operational and moving Maritime goods westward in the early years of the new century, freight rates had become crippling, rising "between 140 and 216 per cent" between 1916 and 1920 (Forbes, *Challenging* 103). The irony of those increases was not lost on the Maritime merchant class: the region had, under duress, entered Confederation on the condition of a rail line to the west, that railway had been built, yet access to it (and, more importantly, to the only protected markets for manufactured goods on the continent) was financially prohibitive. Distance to Quebec and Ontario markets made rail necessary, in other words, but the costs of that infrastructure, and thus of interprovincial trade, made it very difficult to sell Maritime goods in the rest of Canada at competitive prices. Yet, despite this structural disadvantage, Maritime manufacturers had few options: they could sell at a loss in an uneven Canadian market; return to the high-tariff, post-Reciprocity American market; or not sell at all. The unsettling truth about Confederation, observed economist Donald Savoie, was that "economic protectionism and the National Policy *forced* producers in the Maritimes to ship their goods on expensive rail routes to central Canada" (emphasis added), thus stifling profits and leading to rapid reductions in manufacturing capacity (*Visiting Grandchildren* 28). Professor Savoie's evidence is compelling: "relative to Canada, the Maritimes accounted for 14 per cent of goods produced in 1880, only 9 per cent in 1911, and 5 per cent in 1939" (31). And along with that decline, he notes, came a corresponding loss of political power, "from 43 [House of Commons] seats in the 1870s to 31 in 1921" (29). Maritime historian John Reid punctuates the point with brio: "In the years between 1920 and 1926, some 42 percent of the manufacturing jobs in the region simply disappeared" (*Six Crucial Decades* 164–65).

In opening trade to central Canada and the West, the new country had, in effect, defied the logic of 100 years of economic history, and its wager on the Laurentian corridor was as bold as it was disruptive. The result was both material and symbolic: materially, the slow collapse of a once self-sufficient Maritime region; symbolically, a series of narrative changes affecting how the region was perceived in the new nation. That the region's economic collapse occurred when affinities were shifting from European to continental did not help. J.M.S. Careless described that larger context, and the corresponding decline in North American Toryism, as one of the defining features of the 1920s, the decade during which the imperial phase of Canadian history was reverting to the environmental. By that decade, he noted, the Loyalism that had built "a second community in North America outside the American republic"—a Tory Loyalism that had privileged the entitlement compacts of the East—was transitioning to a more utilitarian frontier mythology "emblematic of native democratic progress" ("Frontierism" 68). In the narrative of the young country, the symbolic consequences were devastating for the Maritimes. What developed were changes in attitudes that altered both the region's sense of agency and the new country's sense of the region's robustness.

In a complex cultural operation that became embroiled with the trope of an innovative and fiercely self-reliant American frontier—a frontier characterized by "restless, nervous energy" and "that buoyancy and exuberance which comes with freedom" (Turner 22)—an economically slumping and stubbornly Tory Maritime region was quite deliberately pitted against the dynamism of a liberal West. The political strategy that emerged to capitalize on this circumstance, wrote E.R. Forbes, invested the West with "the progressive dynamic animating Canada in the late nineteenth and early twentieth centuries" while using the Maritimes "as a foil against which to demonstrate the [opposite]." The logic that followed "suggested that, if the frontier encouraged progressive, egalitarian and democratic attitudes, then that part of the country furthest removed from the frontier stage [the Maritimes] must be conservative, socially stratified and unprogressive" (*Challenging* 50–51). The narrative sleight of hand worked best if subjectivity was substituted for social circumstance—that is, if economic want was anthropomorphized so that it was understood to be the *creation* of people living in its midst. If the gambit worked, a collective Maritime malaise would be perceived as the cause of a scarcity of jobs and manufacturing capacity. How else could one explain the relative dynamism of one part of a country and the rapid decline of another? It was by that symbolic operation—an operation that masked macroeconomic gerrymandering while also forgetting responsible government and other progressive Tory innovations—that infirmity was mapped onto an entire region of the country. In short, to hide the truth of the manufacture of economic inequity, the Maritime region had to be made to appear deficient, transformed from the quaint and quiescent (J. Reid, *Six Crucial Decades* 185) to the feeble. And thus did the region become, to quote historian T.W. Acheson, "a 'problem' of interest primarily to social scientists whose function was to prescribe an appropriate cure for the ailing patient" (8). The Duncan Commission of 1926 (more accurately referred to as the Royal Commission on Maritime Claims) was the first of many federal tribunals to study and diagnose the patient with the hope of finding a cure for the Maritime malaise.

Coincident with the popularization of this new narrative of infirmity was the Maritime Rights Movement of 1919–1927, a regional protest movement that Forbes described as "a spontaneous expression of the economic and social frustrations of the Maritime people" (*Maritime Rights* viii). Though that movement focused largely on economic adjustments—reducing freight rates, restoring the primacy of Maritime ports, dampening inflation, adopting equalizing tariffs and subsidies, and increasing immigration quotas—it *did* galvanize the Maritime imagination around the problem of unevenness, thus in ironic ways affirming the larger narrative being shaped about infirmity. Along with a spike in social gospel activism in pulpits and parishes across the region, including work by James Tompkins at St. Francis Xavier University to bring adult education to seasonal labourers in the region, the reversal of economic fortunes and the corresponding rise of secular and religious protest pointed to an irrefutable truth: that the region had become isolated, indigent, and powerless. Not only was it on the wrong side of history, but it was also being mocked for lacking a gumption that other regions of the country had in abundance, or so said the fiction that had been created. It is within that context that historian George Rawlyk observed that "according to the high priests of the so-called Upper Canadian historical and political tradition, the main thrust of Canadian development has owed little, if anything, to events or persons in the four Atlantic provinces." Moreover, Rawlyk added, "for many Canadians the Atlantic region remains an anachronistic backwater of political, social, and cultural despair" (30).

The business class in New Brunswick responded to this characterization of the Maritimes in the pages of *The Busy East*, a monthly magazine that began circulating out of Saint John in 1910 and enjoyed a wide regional readership in the 1920s and 30s. One of the most strenuous arguments advanced in its pages concerned the uneven landscape for interprovincial trade. In what became the drumbeat of the magazine, H.J. Logan wrote in 1924 that "if it is denied that the Intercolonial Railway is to be operated for national purposes and for the creation and carrying on of interprovincial trade, then the assent of the people of the Maritime Provinces in 1867 was secured under false pretenses" (23). Though the language was strong, it reflected the region's palpable sense of abandonment and treachery.

What made *The Busy East* unique, however, and especially relevant to this study, was how its rhetoric grew beyond grievance. In editorial after editorial, fervent encouragement and bold initiative rallied Maritime readers. Reminders of steadfastness and hope were frequently in evidence, as were challenges to the assumptions of Upper Canadian superiority. And while these injunctions may have indirectly condoned the social-eugenic narratives of Maritime backwardness and despair being circulated in popular media, they also served to revolutionize a population that felt stereotyped and neglected. Penned by leading figures in the region, these calls to action were the seeds of a new narrative, an antithesis of Maritime malaise. "To lose our optimism," wrote New Brunswick premier Walter Foster in one such editorial, "is to lose our faith and our courage and the visions of prosperity" (12). This liberalizing tendency became a hallmark of the magazine's editorial politics. Manifest in a vehement opposition to Tory traditions and politicians in New Brunswick and Nova Scotia, it recollected powerful regional symbols and motifs, frequently "the faith of Sam Slick" ("The Faith" 3). The objective was clear: Maritimers had to define their own place in Confederation, even if that meant defying Tory traditions and looking south for models and corridors of enterprise. If central Canada was going to look after its own interests, as the last twenty-five years had shown, then the Maritime region must do the same.

In the latter half of the 1920s, this renewed self-reliance started to ferment. In 1929 a Maritime Provinces Trade Commission was set up in Toronto to boost tourism and trade, the outreach continuing a practice that had begun a few years earlier when the region sent speakers and delegations to central Canada to plead for reductions in freight rates (J. Reid, *Six Crucial Decades* 171–72). A few years later in Saint John (1932), The Maritime Confederation League began to encourage greater Maritime cooperation. When the provincial Liberals won office in Nova Scotia in 1933, Premier Angus L. MacDonald established the Jones Commission to examine how the legislative Act of Confederation could be used to legally impel the federal government to address disparities. If the federally mandated Duncan Commission's recommendations were going to be ignored—a full seven years after they were tabled no significant action had been taken, the exercise clearly a move by Mackenzie King to turn "Maritime rehabilitation into a plan for Maritime pacification" (Forbes, *Maritime* 176)—MacDonald would set up his own commission to get to the root of federalist problems.

The 1932–1933 period, of course, was also the time during which the CCF party was founded in Alberta to address many of the same problems that Maritimers were experiencing. And though Depression-era conditions were more directly at the root of that political movement, the problem of federal authority in matters of trade, finance, and resource management was a central feature of the CCF's Regina Manifesto, and thus as relevant in industrial Cape Breton or Minto, New Brunswick as in agricultural Saskatchewan. On both sides of the country, then, power was being reorganized in ever-smaller increments: in regional rather than national terms and in community-based rather than centralized forms. "The Frosting on the Cake," wrote *The Busy East*'s "Literary Chef," was when a man "start[ed] at the A.B.C. of things" and faced the "old world [that] handles us so roughly" with the independence of mind and action "that breathes in every line of [Kipling's] 'If'" ("The Frosting" 42). The centralized federalist collective—that bold Tory experiment that hybridized British parliamentary controls to keep the republicans at bay—was showing cracks.

It was within that environment of broken federalist promises, structural economic disadvantage, and the circulation of counternarratives of self-reliance and geographic isolation that an artistic group in New Brunswick emerged from the shadows of Roberts and Carman to assert a new kind of socio-cultural expression, an expression born of the twin forces of alienation and invention.

TED CAMPBELL'S STUDIO AND EARLY REPUBLICAN MODERNISM

The group began in Saint John, a city of eruptive political energies rooted in religious and class divisions between patricians and plebeians; that is, between the founding British Loyalists of the 1780s and a large influx of Catholic Irish of the 1840s. Not only was Saint John the first city to be incorporated in Canada (1785) and the locus of important advances in trade unionism (as well as labour riots), but, by the beginning of the 1920s, it was also being recognized as home to Dr. W.F. Roberts, the first Minister of Health (1918) in both New Brunswick and the British Empire. The city, then, was progressive, diverse, and politically charged, its long history of waterfront commerce and newspaper wars having created an environment of working-class pride, militancy, and partisanship. Having rebuilt itself after a devastating fire in June 1877, it was a city ideally suited to the revisionist poetics of Daniel Edwin (Ted) Campbell and his fellow artists.

That revisionist poetics manifested itself in an aesthetic that grew from and later reshaped the preoccupation with landscape that New Brunswick artists had embraced under the influence of John Hammond, the province's most important art educator of the nineteenth century. Appointed principal of Owens Art School in Saint John in 1884, Hammond was an acknowledged master of the seascape ("Fisherman Repairing Nets," "Misty Morning, Saint John Harbour"), a style well suited to Saint John's seafaring history. And though Hammond would leave the port city for Sackville when the art school and gallery were sold in 1893, his depictions of the shores of southern New Brunswick had, by that time, been widely circulated and popularly received. When the Saint John Art Club opened in 1912, Hammond's name and aesthetic held powerful sway and seemed to find parallel a few years later in the "wilderness nationalism" (R. Wright 45–50) of the Algonquin group, later known as the Group of Seven. The difference between Hammond's aesthetic and that of the Algonquin group would prove important, however, in the development of modernism in New Brunswick. Hammond's work renounced the Post-Impressionism of Tom Thomson and Arthur Lismer, whose styles were thought to distort form for expressive effect ("The Art Exhibition" 3). Following, instead, the method of the Boston Museum School of Art, Hammond and subsequent Saint John Art Club teachers chafed against Post-Impressionism, insisting that New Brunswick artists apprentice in classical approaches, namely "good drawing [and] meticulous rendering of form" (Pinsky 157). With an emphasis on draftsmanship (Bradley 75), the teaching of those classical forms became the signature of the Art Club's most influential teacher, Elizabeth Russell Holt, who counted among her pupils Ted Campbell and Miller Brittain (Herring 24). Classical rendering aimed at clarity of form, Holt insisted, was the only means by which art could be communicated across classes, an outcome particularly important in a city of such marked class divisions.

Most of New Brunswick's leading artists of the 1920s and 30s apprenticed at the Art Club and later found their way to the art department of the Saint John Vocational School, which opened in 1926. The "who's who" of provincial artists trained there included Jack Humphrey, Julia Crawford, Fred Ross, Violet Gillett, Norman Cody, and Betty Sutherland, in addition to Brittain and Campbell. By 1935, north Saint John–born Ted Campbell had become a galvanizing force of the group, opening a large studio loft at 147 Prince William Street. Spacious enough to accommodate 100 people, its "back wall was practically all windows looking out on the harbour," recalled poet Kay Smith, "and at night it was magical with all the lights" (qtd. in "An Unlikely Time" 44). It became the Saturday evening gathering spot for artists of all media and styles, and Campbell became "the fulcrum in the birth of New Brunswick regional art of the 1930s" (Larocque 40). Kjeld and Erica Deichmann, the Danish potters, were frequent visitors to the studio, as were playwright Phil Golding, musician Kelsey Jones (the first conductor of the Saint John Symphony), art curator Avery Shaw, and the worldly Kathleen Shackleton, younger sister of the Antarctic explorer, Sir Ernest (Sweet 34–35). Eastern Canada's pioneering literary modernists—P.K. Page, Kay Smith, A.G. Bailey, "Thede" Roberts (younger brother of Charles G.D.), and John Sutherland—also met there with varying degrees of frequency, absorbing the peculiar energies of eclecticism and continental art theory. Decorated with artwork, two grand pianos, and bric-a-brac from Campbell's international travels, and modelled after the cultured salons of Europe where John Hammond had socialized with James Whistler and Jean-François Millet, Campbell's studio was a "place of stimulation, exchange, and dissemination of artistic, social, [and] political ideas" (Herring 100). It was, to say the least, not typical of New Brunswick: a locus of bohemianism, spontaneous antics, puppet shows (Campbell had studied puppetry in Chicago), and interactions among writers, actors, musicians, and craftspeople. Most important for the creative personalities that met there, it was a place sheltered from the scorn normally directed at the artistic sensibility in utilitarian New Brunswick. Said artist Fred Ross, "[Campbell] gave one the feeling that it was possible to be an artist, which probably wouldn't have occurred to most of us, considering our economic background" (qtd. in "An Unlikely Time" 42).

One of the vigorous discussions that recurred at the studio was Campbell's well-known post-Confederation critique. Resisting the east–west tide of nation building, he openly advocated the importance of maintaining the earlier north–south routes of cultural commerce that had existed during New Brunswick's golden age. Though he publicly proclaimed the logic of proximity to support this view—arguing that he and his group were mostly American-trained (he at the Art Institute of Chicago; Humphrey and Brittain in New York; many of the others in Boston) and that the art centres of Boston and New York were but $11–13 away by bus (Hill 40)—he said privately that the real reason for southward loyalty was a desire to expose artists to internationalism in order to enhance their provincial perspectives (Herring 142). He championed the local, even insisting in his classes that it be foregrounded, but cautioned that this localism must be schooled in the latest European and American art theory. This view put Campbell and the Saint John artists in conflict with the direction the National Gallery had embraced under the leadership of Assistant Director H.O. McCurry. Though supportive of experimental practice, McCurry was working with the Carnegie Corporation at the time to centralize Canadian art (see Brison, *Rockefeller*) and was not yet ready to embrace the post-national expression that Campbell's radical (and humanist) localism entailed. The National Gallery's intention to nationalize the style and reputations of the Group of Seven alienated Campbell's group at a time when such alienation was rife in the region. To the New Brunswick artists who were following the styles of American portrait painters like Charles Webster Hawthorne and the regionalists of the Cape Cod School and Boston Painters Workshop, the Algonquin group appeared merely to be adding hyper-realistic touches to the pastoralism of the earlier Confederation artists. The human figure was missing, a class ethic was missing, regional difference was missing, and, perhaps most importantly, the larger democracy that twinned art with social reality was missing. The real Canada, said Montreal artist John Lyman in sympathy with Campbell's Saint John group, "takes place in the sensibility and imagination of the individual," not in and around "the Arctic circle" (qtd. in D. Reid 196).

The lukewarm support at the centre, coupled with material and aesthetic ties to the United States, led the Saint John artists to an activism outside the Canadian mainstream, an important characteristic of which was foregrounding the human figure in its social milieu, something foreign to the Group of Seven painters. This focus, of course, hearkened back to Whistler and Hammond and Holt—and, in a literary context, anticipated the social registers of two generations of New Brunswick *literary* modernists, from Kay Smith's poems of women and children in *Footnote to the Lord's Prayer* (1951) and Fred Cogswell's portraits of valley folk in *The Stunted Strong* (1954) to Alden Nowlan's poignant vignettes of rural New Brunswickers at the crossroads of socio-economic change.

The New Brunswick modernism (literary and cultural) that took shape in Ted Campbell's Saint John studio starting in 1934 was therefore a human-centric modernism of social concern. Though theoretically informed, it differed significantly from the high intellectualism being espoused by central Canadian figures such as A.J.M. Smith, which, following T.S. Eliot and the New Critics, depoliticized and decontextualized expression. It also differed considerably from the work of Manitoba abstract painter Bertram Brooker, an especially progressive modernist of the Canadian Group of Painters that had ties to the Maritimes. (Brooker was close to Fredericton artist Pegi Nicol MacLeod.) Brooker's work, however, especially his portraits, resembled those of Marcel Duchamp and Wassily Kandinsky in their cubist angles and machine-like modelling, thus transforming the human figure from a social to an ideological entity, a being defined by law and authority rather than by the domesticities of community, work, and family. By contrast, what strikes one about the New Brunswick aesthetic, observed Fred Cogswell, "is the way in which it expresses primarily a personal reaction, and only secondarily ... a doctrinaire or dogmatic conviction" ("Modern Acadian Poetry" 64). Jack Humphrey, the most influential and accomplished of the artists in Ted Campbell's group, corroborated Cogswell's characterization when describing his own experiments with colour, used, he said, "for representing character, movement ... and for emotional overtones" (qtd. in Herring 56). In her description of Miller Brittain, the second most well known of Campbell's confrères, Pegi Nicol MacLeod, focused on a similar integration of the individual and the social: "Man moving and acting; persons by shape and form, by personality and feeling, juxtaposed against each other. This sort of painting has been decidedly missing from Canadian art" (14). MacLeod's comment about Canadian art was not without authority. "While the majority of painters were religiously hiking north," wrote *Saturday Night* magazine art critic Graham McInnes, MacLeod resisted, preferring what she saw from her back window: "an immediate, interesting activity of people, and significant formal relationships" (qtd. in J. Murray 32). For Avery Shaw, art curator of the New Brunswick Museum, it was those formal relationships that Ted Campbell's artists turned into "socially conscious art," art that deliberately contested the apolitical work of the Group of Seven while also avoiding the liberalizing utility of America's New Deal artists of the 1930s (n.p.).

The aesthetic incubated in Campbell's studio, agree McInnes and Shaw, is found in how its attentions to form, colour, and address enact an ethic of the personal, an ethic immediately apparent in Humphrey's portraits of citizens going about their daily business (either dancing or waiting for a streetcar) or in Brittain's sketches of longshoreman and the Saint John slums. The mural work of the group was apropos of this interest in the personal and quotidian. The larger the canvas the more it was thought to accommodate the broad perspective of lived reality. Brittain's decision to serve as a bombardier rather than a war artist is especially illustrative of this ethic. At a farewell party given in his honour, he told one of Campbell's guests: "I have to get into it. I've studied the First World War art, and the only painters who caught the real feeling of war were those who had been part of it" (qtd. in Sweet 34). Participation was the route to understanding—and understanding the only means to communicating the essential domesticity of lived reality.

MID-CENTURY EMERGENT MODERNISM, 1935–1955

Acadia University fine arts professor Walter Abell, who considered the Saint John group to be a model of the integration of art and civic engagement, expounded a manifesto of domestic relevance when addressing delegates at the Conference of Canadian Artists in Kingston in 1941. The "democratic usage of art," he explained, "[must] serve the life of the people as a whole; no particular class, no particular individual, but the whole of society served in the fullest, richest possible way, in order the bring about the greatest ... dignity of living through the services of the artists to the community" (qtd. in Niergarth 5). Echoing the popular reconstruction ethic of Franklin D. Roosevelt's 1935 Works Progress Administration initiative, a key aspect of which was the Public Works of Art Project that employed thousands of artists during the Depression, Abell believed that artists committed to a grassroots representational aesthetic, as Campbell's group was, display the highest civic and democratic impulses. Theirs is never an intellectual exercise but a community-building one, never a movement of desiccated rationalism or self-indulgence but one of public engagement (Abell, *Representation* 75–78). Artists must therefore produce work that speaks to and of average citizens. If they do not, Abell argued, not only will their art cease to be relevant (a possibility rather easily avoided in the 1930s as socialist empathies begin to emerge), but the enterprise of art will also accede to the same centralist logic that picks economic winners and losers. This address to the larger national context was what Abell found so compelling about the portraiture and domestic vision of the Saint John artists: their aesthetic was simultaneously humane and "republican" in the classical sense of the term. It existed within, yet was fully conscious of, the broader context of distributed federalism, replete as it was with what Jeffrey Brison would later identify as elitism, centralization, and bureaucracy ("Kingston Conference" 504). The Saint John artists showed that that federalism was an overarching force that imprinted itself on a body politic—and they painted those bodies, the acted-upon, as evidence. What early New Brunswick modernism sought to unsettle, Abell implied, was the presumed neutrality of a benevolent liberal order that was billed as being good for everyone. The Saint John artists and intellectuals of the 1930s knew that to be untrue.

When modernism asserted itself in Saint John in the mid-1930s, it did so in relative isolation, its affiliations and models more closely aligned to Boston, Chicago, and New York than Toronto or Montreal. Decidedly more visual than textual—its dominant media ranging across paint, musical notation, textiles, and pottery—it existed within, while fundamentally opposing, the national art direction of the period. In resisting the National

Gallery's ambitions—ambitions that picked representative styles and subject matters (namely the Group of Seven's)—New Brunswick's first modernist artists had to be self-reliant, a condition reflected in the creation of the Maritime Art Association in 1935; the founding of the *Maritime Art* magazine in 1940, the first such magazine in the country (conceived in a discussion at Ted Campbell's studio ["An Unlikely Time" 46]); and the establishment of a Bachelor of Fine Arts degree at Mount Allison University in 1941, the first degree of its kind to be conferred in Canada (Herring 28). Not far behind this self-actualizing fervour was the editorial echo from the pages of *The Busy East*. New Brunswickers were mobilizing against forces that were pre-determining them.

The extent to which this pioneering visual art activism influenced literary practice in New Brunswick was as much material as ideational. While the visual artists were the better known of the eclectic mix of personalities at Campbell's studio, literary artists were always present, though more in apprenticeship roles than as leading practitioners ("An Unlikely Time" 40). Teacher and recent Mount Allison Ladies College graduate (Speech and Drama) Kay Smith was a frequent guest, as was playwright Phil Golding, both at the start of their careers. As early as 1936 P.K. Page, then twenty, had forged a connection with Campbell's group, her arrival in Saint John a year earlier the result of her military father's transfer to the port city. Smith, Page, and Jean M. Sweet, a reporter and bon vivant in Campbell's circle, formed a writing group that met every few weeks to share work and discuss reading. At the urging of Golding, Page joined the Theatre Guild of Saint John, where Smith was starring as Nora in J.M. Synge's controversial *The Shadow of the Glen* (Deichmann 55). (Page, Smith, and Sweet would later work together to write plays for children and perform in amateur theatre, and Smith, particularly, would develop a reputation as the most important theatre director of her generation in the province.)

John Sutherland, the future editor of Montreal's modernist magazine *First Statement* (1942–1945), was also in Saint John at the time and peripherally attached to Campbell's group through his sister Betty (Cameron 137), soon-to-be wife of Irving Layton. Sutherland had spent his high school years in the city and had returned to convalesce from tuberculosis of the kidney. Alfred G. Bailey, working in Saint John as assistant director of the New Brunswick Museum (and another of Campbell's wider circle), visited Sutherland at the Saint John Tuberculosis Hospital in late 1937, reading to him from T.S. Eliot's *The Waste Land* and effectively introducing him to modern poetry (Whiteman x). Roy Daniells had introduced Bailey to Eliot and the moderns five years earlier when both were studying at the University of Toronto (Lane, "Bailey, Alfred Goldsworthy"). P.K. Page followed Bailey's lead, reading Nietzsche's *Thus Spake Zarathustra* to Sutherland, a book recommended by Campbell regular Kjeld Deichmann (as a grand-nephew of the philosopher Søren Kierkegaard, Deichmann had fashioned himself into an expert in European philosophy). In their correspondence of the time, it is clear that Bailey, Page, Smith, and Sutherland were reading the moderns precociously: Henrik Ibsen, Katherine Mansfield, Virginia Woolf, and D.H. Lawrence, in addition to Eliot, Pound, and Yeats, prominent figures in the copy of Harold Monro's *Twentieth Century Poetry* anthology that changed hands among Page, Smith, and Sweet (Djwa, *Journey* 63–64). Like the visual artists in Campbell's group, the writers were also travelling to Boston and New York to partake of the rich culture, especially the theatre, in both cities.

Campbell's belief in the stimulus of a vibrant network of artists sharing work and ideas was fundamental to the incubation of literary modernism in New Brunswick. That network enabled visual *and* literary artists to, in Page's words, "find each other" when they needed each other (64), thus partaking of a cross-fertilization of ideas and benefiting from contacts that others in the group had. This was never better illustrated than in the cascade of circumstances that brought Page and Smith into contact with poets Anne Marriott and Dorothy Livesay, and eventually Alan Crawley, editor of the important modernist magazine *Contemporary Verse*. The impetus for those circumstances began in Saint John, and only because of an expansion of the Canadian Authors Association into New Brunswick that was abetted by Bailey (P.K. Page 65). Just before she left Saint John for Montreal in 1941, Page sent the poem "Ecce Homo" to Crawley. The poem, writes Sandra Djwa, was unlike Page's work of the pre-Saint John period; it was, instead, boldly modern in "linking the experience of viewing and talking about modern art with the evolution of her own aesthetic consciousness" (*Journey* 67). Page, in other words, had matured in Saint John, as had Bailey and Smith. What had been a tentative verse of mimicry and apprenticeship—evident, in Bailey's case, in the Carmanesque rhythms and imagery of *Tâo* (1930)—had been transformed during her brief but intense period of association with Ted Campbell's group.

When Bailey moved from Saint John to Fredericton in 1938 to begin a professorship in History at the University of New Brunswick—and further advance literary modernism in the province with the Bliss Carman Society and *The Fiddlehead*—he was not practising *modernist* cultural activism in New Brunswick for the first time. Rather, he was transplanting to Fredericton what John Hammond, Elizabeth R. Holt, and Ted Campbell had already established in Saint John as an activist, socially engaged, and place-based modernism, a modernism that was bottom-up (republican) rather than top-down, and that rooted its politics in the local in order to speak against a cultural landscape that was as artificially manufactured and uneven as the economic landscape that had been created by Canada's distributed federalism.

A.G. BAILEY AND THE FIDDLEHEAD SCHOOL

The creative energies that coalesced in Ted Campbell's Saint John studio did not dissipate as much as expand outward during the later years of the 1930s, that expansion precipitated by the disruptions of war. By 1941, the *literary* core of Campbell's group had fragmented. While Kay Smith would remain in Saint John for the duration of her career, John Sutherland and P.K. Page had moved to Montreal, and Bailey to Fredericton. Even Campbell was spending a few days each week in Fredericton, where he was teaching art at the Provincial Normal School. His friend Jackie Good observed that, in typical fashion, he had "transplanted the Saint John art scene, artists and all" to the capital city (qtd. in "An Unlikely Time" 47). The comment was partially true. Campbell did, indeed, bring his enthusiasm for art and many of his peers to Fredericton for lectures and exhibits, but the city was enjoying its own art renaissance in the late 1930s. In 1936 the Fredericton Art Club had been founded with two primary goals: to be a centre of art education and the base from which art could be promoted in the community. The proactive nature of those goals meant that the artists of the Fredericton Club were as socially engaged as their Saint John peers, which would prove to be important for later developments that were to occur in the capital city.

The tenor of art engagement in Fredericton stemmed from the city's particular social makeup. Whereas Saint John was older, larger, and more politically and socially diverse, Fredericton in the late 1930s was still a garrison town of less than 9,000 people. Moreover, it was Loyalist, conservative, bureaucratic, suspect of the avant-garde, and still clinging to the cultural high water mark of the Confederation poets of a generation earlier. If the colonial town had any advantage over Saint John in how it could accommodate a progressive aesthetic movement, that advantage was its provincial university, an infrastructure that offered equal measures of stability and freedom to artists and intellectuals alike. "In Fredericton," wrote Roy Daniells, the conduit of A.G. Bailey's introduction to literary modernism, "the conservation of British values and the preservation of a colonial culture were no deterrents to the acceptance of nineteenth-century liberal ideas" (219). That those liberal ideas would develop most fully in the medium of print rather than paint or textiles was not altogether surprising given the university's rather patrician influence over culture in the community. When the modernist aesthetic seeped into Fredericton in the late 1930s, then, it attached itself to a group of working artists who rapidly forged affiliations with University of New Brunswick (UNB) writers, thereby availing itself of an audience of sympathetic, knowledgeable, and relatively wealthy patrons.

Fredericton photographer and businesswoman Edith Marjorie (Madge) Smith was characteristic of this town-and-gown hybridity. At her art studio on 610 Queen Street, she sold the works of Humphrey, Brittain, and many other Saint John artists and craftspeople, trying to be as relevant to the university community as to the community of local artists. Her studio became central to the capital city's art culture (L. Swanick 35). When nationally known artist Pegi Nicol MacLeod first visited Fredericton from New York in the summer of 1940—that visit celebrated by "Thede's" son Goodridge Roberts, her friend from the École des Beaux-Arts de Montréal—it was Madge Smith's studio and friendship that she sought. Smith's studio was where MacLeod met the Deichmanns (Brandon 120), the Moss Glen potters who were central fixtures in Campbell's Saint John circle. Smith's studio was also where MacLeod reconnected with artist Lucy Jarvis, and where she and Jarvis hatched the plan to visit Margaret MacKenzie, wife of the new president of UNB (1940–1944), Norman MacKenzie. "Out of [that] visit," wrote Laura Brandon, "emerged the Observatory Summer School for the Arts, ... a centre for studying and teaching art and for displaying paintings and drawings and holding concerts" (116). The later-renamed Observatory Art Centre, a university structure built in 1851 to house the instruments that had been used to demarcate the boundary between Maine and New Brunswick (Bailey, "Early Foundations" 16–17), was one of many initiatives that UNB undertook to provide a foundation upon which art and literature could thrive in the capital city (Donaldson 1). Prints on loan from the New Brunswick Museum in Saint John adorned its walls when it opened on 7 July 1941 (J. Murray 165), that exchange illustrating the closeness of the major art communities in the province.

If Madge Smith's studio and the Observatory Art Centre existed at the halfway point between artists and the university, both also inculcated a particular aesthetic in their preference for the themes and styles of the Saint John group. It was an aesthetic that appealed immediately to Pegi MacLeod, who became as central and frenetic a figure in Fredericton (artist, teacher, organizer, activist) as Campbell was in Saint John (J. Murray 45). In a bid to fully enter the New Brunswick aesthetic, MacLeod adopted the localist tenets of American muralist Thomas Hart Benton, who she saw as inspiring the domesticity of Campbell's group. Accordingly, she painted "the streets and sidewalks of Fredericton," the "horses at the experimental farm outside the city," and "the virtues of vocational training as it related to the rural way of life" (Brandon 122, 127). In a September 1941 letter to Madge Smith, who was photographing the same street and market localism, she also proposed the commissioning of a group of hand-woven rugs called "The Fishermen of New Brunswick," the detail of those rugs—"carried out as accurately as possible"—capturing the quotidian realism of Benton and the Saint John painters that she was emulating (qtd. in Murray 167). New Brunswick focused her humanism, observed J. Russell Harper, taking her "beyond the lonely Canadian landscape to use life as a motif" ("Pegi Nicol MacLeod" 49). MacLeod said as much to H.O. McCurry, echoing what was then a familiar aesthetic refrain in New Brunswick: "The artists' duty is to stimulate the cultural life of the community as their contribution to the 'Four Freedoms'" (qtd. in Brandon 139)—the Four Freedoms (of speech and worship; from want and fear) referenced a State of the Union address given by United States President Roosevelt seven months earlier. MacLeod's reference reflected her commitment to the values of cultural democracy that had been foregrounded at the 1941 Kingston Conference, which she, Lucy Jarvis, Jack Humphrey, Miller Brittain, and Walter Abell had attended—and where Thomas Hart Benton delivered one of the keynote addresses. To be an artist in Fredericton, MacLeod learned, was to be touched directly by both the university and the extended family of artists in the province.

Building on the opportunity of those networks, MacLeod and Jarvis began forging associations with UNB writers. MacLeod reached out to Alfred G. Bailey, who had been a classmate of her husband. She and Bailey "shared a common interest in poetry and Canada's First Peoples" (Brandon 121) and often had tea at the Observatory, which became known as the "Tea Pot School" for its hospitality (Bradley 104). The Bliss Carman Society of poets sometimes met at the Observatory, and university readings often took place there. MacLeod also met and tutored Donald Gammon, an art student at the Observatory who would become the first editor of *The Fiddlehead*. Gammon put her in touch with Desmond Pacey, head of the English department, who at the time was looking for illustrations for his children's book, *Hippity Hop*. So central did the Observatory become to life on campus that professors started taking art lessons and "relating their courses to art" (J. Murray 235, 255; Bradley 108). It was at that point of intersection between a provincial art culture re-energizing in Fredericton and a pre-existing institutional capacity at UNB that Bailey's role in defining the next phase of New Brunswick modernism became vital. If Smith, MacLeod, and Jarvis were the dominant figures around whom an activist art enterprise in Fredericton flourished, Bailey was the *literary* flashpoint. He would achieve in Fredericton what John Sutherland may have achieved in Saint John if that city had had the resources that Bailey did at UNB. (Knowing that it didn't, Sutherland had moved to Montreal.)

Much less an extrovert than the visual artists, Bailey nevertheless had an impressive avant-garde pedigree and influence equal to others in galvanizing a community of creative, albeit more conventional, personalities. Born in Quebec in 1905 but with deep New Brunswick roots, he graduated from UNB in 1927, soon after completing M.A. (1929) and Ph.D. (1934) degrees at the University of Toronto, where his modernist and leftist awakenings had occurred under the tutelage of Roy Daniells, Robert Finch, Dorothy Livesay, Frank Underhill, and Earle Birney (Pacey, "A.G. Bailey" 51, 57). After postgraduate work in economics and political science at the University of London, he was awarded a Carnegie fellowship to study museum administration in Britain, that fellowship part of the Carnegie Corporation's philanthropic outreach into Atlantic Canada (see J. Reid, "Health" 69). It was by that credential that Bailey was appointed as "curator trainee" to the Dr. and Mrs. Clarence Webster Collections at the New Brunswick Museum in Saint John in 1935 (Stanley 60)—where he became a participant in Ted Campbell's circle, his entrance into that sphere initiated by Mrs. Webster, whom he had met in London and with whom he worked closely at the Museum. Bailey became deeply involved in the Saint John art scene, acting as president of the Saint John Art Club (1936–1937) and executive member of the Maritime Art Association (1936–1938) (Record of Alfred Goldsworthy Bailey). When UNB President C.C. Jones succeeded in petitioning the government of New Brunswick to fund a chair in history (he solicited Bailey's help to do so after an earlier application to the Carnegie Corporation [1933] had failed), Bailey moved to Fredericton in 1938 to become the first professor of the new history department, and just as importantly, to take his place at a university that bore the imprint of his family's great ancestors, grandfather Loring Woart Bailey and great-grandfather Joseph Marshall, Baron d'Avray. Jones's choice of the third-generation Bailey rested on the prestige of that ancestry and on the library-cataloguing prowess of the young scholar, a prowess that was needed if UNB was to secure the Carnegie funds necessary to expand its library, thus becoming a legitimate university. Pre-eminent provincial historian J.C. Webster, whose collections filled the holdings of the New Brunswick Museum, wrote on Bailey's behalf. "As curator of my Historical Collection ... as well as of the Collection relating to the Fine Arts," Webster said, "[Bailey] has worked hard to make himself thoroughly conversant with the great variety of subjects therein represented." Webster excitedly expressed the view that Bailey would be the ideal candidate "to establish contacts between the University and the Museum" (letter to C.C. Jones, 14 June 1937).

The spirit of Webster's endorsement was clear: Bailey's role at UNB was to align the museum's mandate of provincial custodianship of history and fine art with that of the province's largest university, thus institutionalizing to a greater extent the work the museum had been doing to collect, catalogue, and promote New Brunswick heritage. Webster saw that UNB and Bailey were the most powerful conduits to carry the mandate and to build future research capacity around it. Moreover, Webster's scholarly and philanthropic status in the province was such that effecting a change in UNB's institutional direction—in effect, *defining* its role in the humanities—was entirely reasonable. With Bailey's New Brunswick roots, his intellectual pedigree, his education and professional museum training, and his knowledge of provincial art and history (as well as their practitioners), he was the ideal candidate for a position in British North American history that was envisioned, despite the broad title, as substantially regional.

He was, in effect, being appointed to the first chair in New Brunswick studies at UNB, a fact made clear eight years later by then-President Milton F. Gregg when thanking Bailey for the cultural stewardship he had embarked upon under Norman MacKenzie's presidency. "[Bailey's] conception of the University's obligations to the community," wrote Gregg, "has included an untiring search for source material and the production of a series of monographs on provincial subjects" (n.p.). In a rare moment of personal declaration, Bailey agreed with Gregg, articulating an activist research agenda considerably ahead of its time. The agenda, he explained, used social and cultural history, and Rockefeller Foundation funding, as a means of providing Canadians with maps of "their own national identity," thus yielding "answers to many of the questions that now baffle the student of Canadian society" (Introduction 1). Based theoretically on "the concept of culture as regional" and on the macroeconomic view that "'chronic depression'" is both structural and deterministic (assumptions, again, that were decades ahead of their time), Bailey concluded that the cultural ethnology he was proposing would "create an *intellectual ferment* without which there can be little hope of progress towards the realization of a better life for all" (emphasis added) (Introduction 2). In quite deliberately attempting "to revive the literary tradition of Fredericton and the University of New Brunswick" (qtd. in Toole 5), Bailey, in other words, had set out to do exactly what Webster and Jones had envisioned—and via the activist, republican means that he had been witness to in Toronto and Saint John.

What is essential about this stated objective, however, is the degree to which Bailey moved from both pedigree and inheritance to become his own man. What Michael Ignatieff said of such efforts certainly applies to Bailey: "I have learned," wrote Ignatieff, "that you can inherit loyalties, indignation, a temperament, the line of your cheekbones, but you cannot inherit your self. You make your self with your own hands, here and now, alone or with others. There is no deliverance, no imperative in the blood. You cannot inherit your purposes" (184).

One of Bailey's early strategies to effect such ferment and purpose was to organize a writing group, fashioned, socially, after Lucy Jarvis's Tea Pot gatherings at the Observatory Art Centre, and, practically, after a small group of poets (Roy Daniells, Robert Finch, Earle Birney, and Bailey) that met in Toronto between 1933 and 1934—Bailey, remembered Birney, "the most adventurous technician of us all" (26). In his manifesto for the Fredericton group, which launched as the Bliss Carman Society in December 1940, Bailey quoted T.S. Eliot in acknowledging both a literary tradition and the experimentation needed to keep that tradition alive. "By continuing a tradition is not meant a slavish imitation of past themes and methods," Bailey wrote, "nor does it mean a complete break with the past. To continue a tradition is to develop it to the point of contemporaneity" (Foreword). "The tradition," understood by Eliot and the modernists as the organic presence of the past in the everyday (Eliot 49), became a preoccupation of the Bliss Carman Society's poets. Founding members Dorothy Howe, Robin Bayley, and Linden Peebles (mostly students of Bailey) met monthly at his house not only to preserve New Brunswick's rich literary heritage, but also to follow Eliot's dictum to renovate literary inheritance by practice, workmanship, and focused study of other poets, often in foreign languages. Bailey made it clear that only new modes of versification would be allowed and discussed, and he used his own high-modernist work as model. Influenced first by Eliot and later by the inchoate and startling conceits of Dylan Thomas, Bailey's work followed patterns of what Bailey himself described as "'stimulus diffusion'"—patterns that were "off-beat, incorporative, galloping," and which he used in Jungian fashion to "render elements of the subconscious [and] the primordial" (qtd. in Toole 4). The results were bold and surprising, advancing the work of each member of the Bliss Carman Society. Bailey, who wrote "The Unreturning" and "Northwest Passage" during those sessions, said that the Fredericton writers around him stimulated him "to write more and better than I had ever done" (qtd. in Toole 8). Part of his effort was to evoke in poetry what he had written about in prose: namely, in *The Conflict of European and Eastern Algonkian Cultures, 1504–1700* (1937), the crimes against the country's Indigenous populations. Renewal, he believed, was possible only through an honest accounting of a nation's past. Without that accounting, "the sachem voices ... out of the hills" would forever be angry, and Canada forever colonial ("Miramichi Lightning" 16). Creating new narratives, he told young writers and students alike, began in seeing history differently.

As reports of the group's success spread, the Bliss Carman Society expanded to include figures whose names would soon be associated with *The Fiddlehead*: Elizabeth Brewster, Frances Firth, Margaret Cunningham, Eleanor Belyea, Robert Rogers, Desmond Pacey, and Donald Gammon. When this larger body felt the need for a permanent record of the poems workshopped at their meetings, Bailey proposed the idea of a mimeographed magazine, an idea that first registered when he was an undergraduate student at UNB. In a meeting at Bailey's house on 26 January 1945, a meeting enthusiastically recorded in Elizabeth Brewster's diary (Bailey, "Literary Memories" 3, 15), the Bliss Carman Society agreed to start publishing. Following the recent examples of Alan Crawley's *Contemporary Verse* (1940), Patrick Anderson's *Preview* (1942), and John Sutherland's *First Statement* (1942), Donald Gammon started producing the mimeograph, which featured a cover print of a fiddlehead drawn by the Observatory's Lucy Jarvis. Bailey gave the name "Fiddlehead" to the magazine, and his 1940 Bliss Carman Society "manifesto" was repurposed as the first editorial in the February 1945 inaugural issue. The name and editorial were significant in situating the magazine in a New Brunswick locale and cultural tradition, thus extending the aesthetic that had been central to the Saint John modernists.

On the first page of the first issue, Bailey identified the fiddlehead as "that small plant that grows in the Saint John River valley in the spring, and which is said to be symbolic of the sun" ("The Fiddlehead" 1), linking his cultural project (the instrument of cultural renovation) to the First Peoples of the province and to one of the region's most visible rites of spring. "The Maliseets harvested them and still do," recalled Robert Gibbs, an early member of the group that founded *The Fiddlehead*. "For them, as for us, [fiddleheads] are an apt symbol of the sun's renewal" ("Portents and Promises" 11). Renewal, yes, but also tradition, the second of those twin forces that Eliot insisted was central to the modernist enterprise. It was therefore entirely appropriate that Bailey's earlier manifesto about provincial literary heritage—about Jonathan Odell, James Hogg, Peter John Allan, Roberts, and Carman—would have status equal to that of renewal. Only if his larger objective was to localize radically, which it was, would that heritage matter, which it did. In his powerful desire to politicize the local, including its erasures of the past, Bailey thus followed in the tradition of William Francis Ganong, John Clarence Webster, William O. Raymond, and George Frederick Clarke as one of the pre-eminent historians in the province—and, like them, a provincial custodian of a heritage that was widely defined as literary, cultural, and historical. So highly was Bailey considered in that regard that he was asked by New Brunswick Premier John B. McNair to arrange the state funeral for Charles G.D. Roberts in 1943.

As Bailey's reputation grew, so did the mark of his particular influence: an influence seemingly contradictory in combining a conservative reverence for the past with a modern and activist desire to both localize and repurpose that history. He built a history department whose defining focus continues to be a critical militancy about Atlantic Canada, and he mentored countless scholars and students in similar forms of scholarly practice. One such scholar was Desmond Pacey, who arrived in Fredericton in 1944 to begin a program in creative writing at UNB, which was designed to equip students with the means of their own expression. (Bailey encouraged Pacey's first publications in *Queen's Quarterly* ["The Novel in Canada," 1945] and *The Dalhousie Review* ["The First Canadian Novel," 1946].) Another scholar who came under Bailey's direct influence was William S. MacNutt, invited by Bailey to come to UNB after the war. MacNutt wanted to specialize in Italian history, having recently fought in the Italian campaign, but Bailey dissuaded him: "I told him everybody has written on Italian history but almost nobody has written on New Brunswick history" (qtd. in Lane "Interview" n.p.). Out of that persuasion came MacNutt's *New Brunswick, A History: 1784–1867* (1963), the most comprehensive history of the province to date. Bailey was equally helpful to Elizabeth Brewster, Fred Cogswell, and Robert Gibbs, all students and members of his Bliss Carman Society. Virtually every aspect of UNB's literary community bore his imprint, from the fledgling university archives, headed by his student Frances Firth (her 1945 master's thesis was entitled "The History of Higher Education in New Brunswick"), to the editorial direction of *The Fiddlehead*, and the institutional realization that cultural custodianship was as much the business of universities as it was of governments. Perhaps most importantly, Bailey perceived his cultural work as having social and political benefits for an economically struggling region, as outlined in notes he made for a speech delivered in the mid-1940s. The importance of his thoughts warrants the following long quotation:

> That the Maritimes may be regarded as mere appendages of Ontario and Quebec is due to a fault that rests partly with ourselves. There are those amongst us who say that New Brunswick has become, economically, a mere tributary to central Canada. Now, it is impossible to separate human activities into water-tight compartments, as there is actually, for instance, a very direct relationship between economic status and art. So that I think it is just to say that, as our economic life lagged, the difficulties with which the artist was faced in this province were augmented, so that it has been harder for him to transfix the quintessence of life as it is lived on this Atlantic seacoast, than it was for the central Canadian artist to capture the essential spirit of the wilderness of northern Ontario.... The artist's economic status, and his position in the hierarchy of classes that exist in his community, condition his responses to his environment and his artistic expression to a marked degree.... I believe that in studying the economic, religious, political, and stylistic bias of the artists of New Brunswick a valuable work would be done.... Our task should be to isolate our local differences that give us a distinctive flavour, and to universalize these differences in permanent art forms. ("Address" 1–2)

His conclusion is succinct: "I think we should proceed to discover ourselves" (2). Though seemingly simple, that conclusion, Bailey later admitted, deliberately "ran counter to the 'frontier thesis' of Frederick Jackson Turner because although one could accept the emergence of homespun democracy and democratic individualism in the areas of the west where self-reliance was the only means of survival, conditions to be found there were by no means conducive to creative expression in the arts and to works of the speculative intellect" ("Literary Memories" 21). Bailey was, then, working quite consciously to understand the narratives of federalism and local "quintessence," which were discernable, he felt, in the literary and historical records of each region. That focus would guide the institutional work he undertook when the post–World War Two ferment fully seized New Brunswick in the fall of 1946. In that year he became UNB's first dean of Arts and honorary librarian, overseeing curriculum and library acquisitions at the university. In the years ahead he would work closely with Lord Beaverbrook, the university's chancellor, to manage a substantial library expansion, build an official university archives, and position UNB to become a world leader in graduate research about the Atlantic region, thus fulfilling the earlier wish of J.C. Webster. Though he would write no more manifestos, Bailey's institutional stewardship, as well as the loyalty of his students, many of whom came back to teach at UNB, ensured that his influence continued.

The intellectual climate of the time, though replete with centralist bias, gave larger credence to Bailey's work. Building on the staples theory of Harold Adams Innis and the Laurentian thesis of Donald Creighton, W.L. Morton, another historian, published *The Progressive Party in Canada* in 1950, an account of Western activism and protest—and, seven years later, *Manitoba, A History* (1957). Both books were instrumental, said J.M.S. Careless, for being "benchmark[s] in the study of distinctive regional societies in Canada" (*Frontier* 57). The presumed "rightness" of Canada's federalist manifest destiny was again being troubled, and while the contrivance of nationhood was not new for still-struggling New Brunswickers, it certainly added legitimacy to the work of figures like Bailey who were seeking to further partition the nation into the regions and separate histories that constituted its truer essence. That balkanization was anticolonial in seeking new political spaces, and new identities, between the warring traditions of British triumphalism and American continentalism, thus for the first time establishing a Canada-first perspective that, wrote Careless, "offered a positive, at times ardent, assessment of historical Canadian experience—not at all in the customary vein of self-disparagement" (*Frontier* 6). It was in that new affirmative space that Bailey found traction for his work. Denying provincial and regional identity for national fealty was no longer the price of citizenship. As Bailey and other leading historians illustrated, identity and the cultural expressions that sprang from it were local before they were national, and mature nations were characterized by the amalgam of both.

When the Royal Commission on National Development in the Arts, Sciences and Letters set out to do its work in 1949, it was that view of a fragmented but operative nationalism that prevailed. And with it, the realization of new opportunities for expression that Innis, Bailey's dissertation supervisor, would explore in 1952, specifically with reference to the increasingly decentralized communications environment that opened possibilities for new media such as *The Fiddlehead*. "The conservative power of monopolies of knowledge," Innis observed, "compels the development of technological revolutions in the media of communication in the marginal areas" (78), thus privileging places like New Brunswick as sites of innovation in the new media of little magazines, small presses, and other means of "republican" (bottom-up) activism, all of which occurred in Fredericton under Bailey's gentle but focused guidance. As a student of Innis at the University of Toronto, Bailey was well aware of the socio-cultural dialectic between dominance and invention—and, as the senior administrator of fine arts and humanities at the province's largest university, he was certainly well positioned to foster the conditions that would accomplish those republican (that is, decentralized) aims.

That the first comprehensive critical assessment of Canadian literature—*The Literary History of Canada* (1965)—would be shaped by an advisory committee that included Bailey (along with Northrop Frye, Roy Daniells, and Carl F. Klinck) was not, then, surprising given Bailey's central position in the East, nor was Bailey's warning against the "territorial fallacy" of loading the editorial board and contributors ranks with scholars from "the centre" (qtd. in Djwa, *Giving Canada* 112). Though the others disagreed with him, Bailey eventually prevailed, enlisting his UNB colleagues David Galloway, Desmond Pacey, and Fred Cogswell as contributors to the *Literary History*, thus ensuring that the cultural heritage he had chosen to defend (not just regional but more fundamentally disruptive) would be sufficiently distanced from central Canadian control.

Bailey's position at the forefront of aesthetic change in Canadian and New Brunswick literature has been unacknowledged because it was so unique. He did not employ the editorial bombast of A.J.M. Smith or Louis Dudek, nor embrace the provocations of politics as Dorothy Livesay and Earle Birney did. He did not write, as critic and poet, at the edge of a changing paradigm, nor enjoy the large university and urban canvases of George Woodcock and Northrop Frye. Rather, despite lasting commitments to progressive movements such as the CCF and The League for Social Reconstruction, he chose to effect change through institutional means, preferring not to risk the erasure of the past for benefit of the present. In that regard he was both humanist and modernist, much in the image of Eliot and Gerard Manley Hopkins, and much in the style of Ted Campbell's artists. Connected to the leading modernists of his time, he cultivated an unusual loyalty among colleagues and students, who embraced his ideas and shaped them into their own. *The Fiddlehead* and Fiddlehead Poetry Books became Fred Cogswell's responsibility. Brunswick Press (incorporated as The University Press of New Brunswick in 1950) was funded by Lord Beaverbrook, then-chancellor of UNB, but largely conceived by Bailey. It was "the first publishing house in Canada," said bookseller Margaret Hall, "to publish local authors" (qtd. in Belier n.p.). Each enterprise bore the imprint of Bailey's wish "to discover ourselves," and, by doing so, to free New Brunswick from the usually debilitating narratives of others.

As a social historian, however, and as one, moreover, whose life's work was the study of intellectual movements, Bailey would have observed the fortuitousness of his own formation, which must serve as the final note of this chapter. Linked by blood and fidelity to the great artistic flowerings of the previous two centuries, he was attuned to the high-water marks of New England and New Brunswick literature as few others were. He was also fortunate enough to have had a remarkable education: first at the hands of a poetry-loving father who was taught by Bliss Carman; then by a Toronto peer group consisting of Canada's foremost modernists and intellectuals; and finally by an eclectic group of visual artists whose working-class aesthetic foregrounded action, connection, localism, and humanist commiseration. Finally, he found and assumed positions in the province's most important heritage institutions, the New Brunswick Museum and the provincial university, the latter providing him with the formal means to realize (and to a large extent normalize) his localist aims. That he had established himself at UNB before the postwar expansion, before the country's most significant cultural self-examination (the Massey-Lévesque Commission), and before the McNair government's program of New Brunswick modernization meant that he was well placed to influence and to act on these important developments as they took hold. By birthright, education, timing, and sympathy, he was the hinge on which New Brunswick *literary* modernism turned, a hinge that opened multiple environments in which provincial writers could work. Significantly, his own role as teacher, pioneer, practitioner, and model attests to the biographical pluralism of formation: that is, to the fact that ferment is best understood when widely conceived as being cumulative, as the social interaction of minds and movements rather than the solitary genius of individuals. Bailey certainly was a major enabler of renewal in New Brunswick literature, but he was also the sum of an extraordinary confluence of events in southern New Brunswick in the second quarter of the twentieth century.

CHAPTER 5

MODERNITY AND THE CHALLENGE OF URBANITY IN ACADIAN LITERATURE, 1958–1999

Marie-Linda Lord

The period dealt with in this chapter—two centuries after the Deportation—was a period of unprecedented vitality in Acadian New Brunswick. It was also a period of profound social, cultural, economic, political, and literary activity. The vibrancy of the 1960s could be felt from the first year of the decade, when two simultaneous events deeply marked the years to come. In New Brunswick, 27 June 1960 saw the election of the first Acadian to lead the province, Louis J. Robichaud, who would become one of the major emblematic figures in contemporary Acadie when he introduced important progressive reforms. Five days earlier (22 June 1960) Quebec, the province next door, had elected Jean Lesage, who would later be called the father of the Quiet Revolution, a revolution that turned a traditional French Canada into a modern Quebec. As the title of a song written by Québécois Stéphane Venne summarized it, "C'est le début d'un temps nouveau." Indeed, it was the beginning of a new era for these two French-language populations, who were both undergoing a profound redefinition of their respective identities, and writers, artists, and intellectuals played active roles in the process.

Premier Robichaud himself stated that his most important legacy was the creation of the Université de Moncton in 1963, accomplished in close co-operation with Father Clément Cormier, who was the first president of the university. Establishing a French-language university in Moncton, a city where English was the dominant language, was not a short-term project, but the seeds had been planted more than half a century earlier.

During the first half of the twentieth century, several of Acadie's institutions had developed, including the clergy, colleges, financial institutions, newspapers, and radio stations. The Acadian presence in Moncton grew as urbanization took hold. As historian Patrick D. Clarke explains in "Régions et régionalismes en Acadie. Culture, espace et appartenance," Moncton's economy in the second half of the nineteenth century relied on the railway and on various textile mills in order to become, as early as 1870, a centre to which young people, including Acadians, flocked. According to Clarke, "the new Acadian bourgeoisie chose Moncton as its 'national centre,' starting at the beginning of the 20th century" (318). By 1998, the writer, artist, painter, and filmmaker Herménégilde Chiasson, born and raised in Saint-Simon on the Acadian Peninsula, was able to write that "Acadian literature was born in Moncton, a city which represents both its resting place and its driving force" ("Traversées" 79). This chapter will therefore consider Moncton's role in contemporary Acadian literary production, and will describe the literary ferments of this period and place.

SURVIVAL OF THE ACADIAN PEOPLE AND THE NATIONALIST CAUSE

In 1905, two landmark institutions set up operations in Moncton: the first was the *L'Évangéline* newspaper which had relocated from Weymouth, Nova Scotia because its owner/founder/editor Valentin Landry wanted to move closer to his readers (two-thirds of his 4,500 subscribers lived in Moncton). The second institution was the La Tour branch of the Société l'Assomption, founded in Waltham, Massachusetts. Two years later, Henri P. LeBlanc, a member of the St. Bernard Church parish, took the initial steps that would lead to the establishment of the first French-language parish in Moncton in 1914, Notre-Dame-de-l'Assomption. A church crypt on St. George Street was then officially opened on 21 March 1915. On 15 August 1915, the congregation of the new parish publicly celebrated the Acadian national holiday with other townspeople for the first time. In "Fête de l'Assomption," Father Émile Georges, who attended the festivities, recalled the occasion, which made a lasting impact on the Moncton's Acadian community:

> For the first time, the French population of Moncton, as a whole, took to the streets, you might say, and in an unprecedented demonstration took stock of its strengths, reviewed its qualities, and began to organize itself for peaceful conquests, depending on the needs which arose, for the battles it would face in the future.

A genuine transformation took place in the minds and hearts of the people as a result of this act of faith in the vitality and the energy of the population. And this transformation could be read on everyone's face; it arose unexpectedly in every conversation; it had a "je ne sais quoi" quality that showed in that calm and determined manner which is bestowed by the awareness of one's strengths and the unshakeable confidence in one's future. (63)

The first priest to serve the new parish, the visionary Henri D. Cormier, dedicated himself to building the first French-language school in Moncton. Construction began in 1919, and in 1923 the Académie du Sacré-Cœur, on the corner of Church and Victoria Streets, welcomed its first students. French-language instruction in Moncton experienced remarkable growth in the decades that followed. The school building would later be home to the offices of *L'Évangéline*, the Université Saint-Joseph (the ancestor of Université de Moncton), and a semi-professional theatre company, the Feux Chalins, founded in 1968, which produced Antonine Maillet's play *La Sagouine* at the beginning of the 1970s.

In 1922, the first library in the parish opened, making it possible to borrow French-language books. The same year, the Sœurs de la Providence religious order arrived in Moncton, and five years later opened Hôtel-Dieu Hospital, which would become the Georges L. Dumont University Hospital Centre. So rapidly was the city's Acadian population growing that less than ten years after the first French-language school opened, another one was needed for the increasing numbers of francophone children in the city: L'École Essex opened in 1932. Then in 1936, Mon. Arthur Melanson, who had founded the religious order of the Filles Marie-de-l'Assomption in Campbellton in 1922, returned to Acadie after having been appointed as bishop of Gravelbourg, Saskatchewan, in 1933. He became the first archbishop of Moncton (1937), overseeing the construction of the Notre-Dame-de-l'Assomption Cathedral on the site where the church crypt had stood. The cathedral opened its doors in 1940.

At the same time, another French church, Notre-Dame-de-Grâce, was under construction in the Georgetown section of Moncton. Clearly, the "Acadianization" of Moncton was under way, and this despite the vehement protests and formal exhortations denouncing Acadianization by Irish clergymen who were making their opinions known to church authorities, including those in Rome. However, there was no turning back: by the start of the World War Two, Moncton had become the centre of Acadie.

In August 1955, the region's Acadians marked the Bicentennial of the Deportation—and Moncton hosted the official opening ceremonies at the cathedral. The Radio-Canada reporter who was sent from Montreal to cover the event was René Lévesque, who would become a minister in the Lesage government and eventually leader of the Parti Québécois and premier of Québec. The archbishop at the time, Mon. Norbert Robichaud, asked Acadians to make themselves heard as loudly as possible, thus taking advantage of the national stage and initiating the first tintamarre. The following decades would embrace this newly found momentum with French-language company headquarters, institutions, and organizations established in Moncton. In spite of being officially unilingual until 2002, Moncton had therefore become a community that Acadians, driven by a pressing need to affirm their identity and urban presence, fully inhabited.

In her book *Histoire de la littérature acadienne*, Marguerite Maillet writes about this generation of Acadians and their writers (1929–1957). These writers, who foregrounded the themes of memory and attachment to the land, drawing their inspiration from history, religion, and the French language, were generally not well known. The exception was Napoléon Landry, a country priest who, with his second collection of poetry in 1955, put an end to the Acadian pastoral that glorified the land and history of the ancestors. Instead, he infused his poetry with Acadian place names (Caraquet, Cocagne, Memramcook), turning attention to the present and the growing urbanization of Acadie. He rejected, in other words, the trait which Clarke calls "Acadian dualism," that mix of parochialism and self-sufficiency (325) that for a long period had seemed to be enough to ensure the maintenance of community in Acadie. However, the integration of increasing numbers of Acadians into the industrial and capitalist environment of Moncton, where transcultural exchanges were much more frequent than in the country villages of Acadie, had made archaic both the rural tradition and the ideology of church authorities. Moreover, as Clarke observes, the concentration of the Acadian elite in Moncton and in the industrial economy meant that the southeastern area of the province imposed new patterns of collective organization on Acadie as a whole: "The domination of southeastern New Brunswick in the institutional development in Acadie, in the articulation of a nationalist discourse and in the entry into the political, economic and cultural realms, was by then obvious" (325). That domination may have been obvious socially and politically, but it would not become manifest in Acadian literature for several more decades.

A CRISIS OF VALUES

As was the case elsewhere in the Western world, the decade from 1960 to 1970 in Acadian New Brunswick witnessed a crisis of values that engendered such actions as the student protests in Moncton. Moncton's city government at the time was led by an anti-francophone mayor, Leonard Jones, whose confrontations with students at the newly established Université de Moncton captured national attention, especially when students tossed a pig's head onto his lawn as a symbolic gesture of defiance. The tensions of the time were deftly captured by two Quebec filmmakers, Michel Brault and Pierre Perrault, whose documentary, *L'Acadie l'Acadie* (1968/69), foregrounded those protests and the related strike at the Université de Moncton, both of which called the established order into question and demanded that Acadians be treated as full citizens. Shown for the first time in 1971, the film became a cult classic for generations of Acadian youth.

Coincident with Moncton's Acadian coming-of-age were other notable events of the decade, among them the visit of four Acadian leaders who were invited to Paris in 1968 to meet French president General de Gaulle. That visit initiated the building of much closer links between Acadie and France. The next year, in 1969, the province of New Brunswick adopted its Official Languages of New Brunswick Act, thereby becoming the first and only officially bilingual province in Canada. (The federal government followed closely behind, passing its Official Languages Act after the report of the Royal Commission on Bilingualism and Biculturalism. French and English became the official languages of Canada.)

On the eve of these large-scale administrative and judicial changes, contemporary Acadian literature reached an equally significant turning point. In an instance of literary serendipity, two young writers from southeastern New Brunswick threw themselves simultaneously into what they would later describe as the "adventure" of Acadian literature. Both were in their twenties and neither knew the other. The first was Antonine Maillet, from Bouctouche, who had studied at the Collège Notre-Dame d'Acadie in Moncton, and the second was Ronald Després, from Moncton. Maillet had just published her first novel, Després his first collection of poetry, and both writers' books were equally lauded: Maillet's *Pointe-aux-Coques* won the Prix Champlain and Després's *Silence à nourrir de sang* won the prestigious Prix David and the second prize for literature from the province of Quebec. Because of the absence of a publishing house in Acadie in 1958, both were also published in Quebec, Maillet by Fidès and Després by Éditions d'Orphée.[1] Besides this rather curious synchronicity—a synchronicity that continued for ten years—the two authors had something else in common. In their writing, both asserted the right to live in modernity. However, their very different literary aesthetics meant that the reception of Després's works, which were avant-garde for their time, would be very different from that of Maillet's books, which exemplified the transition from oral to written literature.

Although Després received more attention in 1958 than Maillet, he is still not as well known as he should be, for he is considered the first true Acadian poet. Born in 1935, he completed a classical education in 1953 after attending Collège Saint-Joseph in Memramcook, Collège l'Assomption in Moncton, and Université Sainte-Anne in Pointe-de-l'Église, Nova Scotia. He continued his studies in Paris, where he earned a graduate degree in Philosophy in 1956. He then moved to Ottawa where he began a career as a translator and interpreter, while also beginning his literary career. In 1984 the province of New Brunswick awarded him the Pascal-Poirier Prize for lifetime achievement. In critic Maurice Raymond's estimation, the Després's work represents most vividly a rupture with the past, and although that rupture is painful, it allows for two previously repressed elements to come to the surface: "First, there is the immediate repression of his situation as an Acadian. Second, there is an element that is even more silenced, and more torturous, that of a personal drama related to sexuality and the forbidden" (141). An anguished figure, Després imagines a world that is inaccessible to him, and, by symbolic extension, to Acadians.

Antonine Maillet shared a similar trajectory. Born in 1929, she had, for nearly three decades before the publication of her first novel, witnessed the growing institutionalization and urbanization of post–World War Two Acadie. More specifically, like Després, she experienced from the inside the mutations and reforms that shaped the destiny of Moncton and Acadie. Her first novel spearheaded a movement and generated a momentum that seemed impossible until it happened, namely that *Pointe-aux-Coques* entered an Acadian literary space that did not yet exist in the French-Canadian literary sphere. Her first novel therefore literally created that space, and her charismatic personality helped to give it shape. Maillet rapidly became the leading figure in Acadian literature and has, for fifty years, pursued a literary and ideological project that has spanned a lifetime.

Literary critics have been particularly interested in her work since her play *Les Crasseux* appeared. The fifth work in the influential Théâtre Vivant collection—Michel Tremblay's now-famous *Les Belles-Sœurs* was number six—Maillet's work brings an innovative vernacular to the stage, thus foregrounding cultural difference and linguistic variance at the same time as the great Quebec playwright did. Maillet, however, did not inherit her voice from a line of well-known writers; rather, she was inspired by what she experienced personally and as part of the community in Moncton when she was a professor at the Université de Moncton. While her students were taking to the streets and going to City Hall to demand their right to speak French, she was writing *Les Crasseux*, which would become the first literary text written in the Acadian language, and would be followed three years later by the monologues of the radio play *La Sagouine* (1971). Under the same title, that second play would make its mark in the 1970s in Quebec and France, as well as in Acadie, where its unprecedented success is still unrivalled.

This fomenting decade of change in Acadie was thus fuelled by a strong historical consciousness that met a status-quo anglophone politics head on. Moncton's Acadians, especially students and intellectuals, announced loudly that they had no tolerance for ambiguities around their own possibilities and utopias. Their resistance reflected a deep-rooted questioning as much as an ever-evolving present, both of which were transforming Acadie. For the first time in Acadian history, poetry, fiction, theatre, and non-fiction were daring to experiment with the allowances and consequences of modernity in order to assert a neo-nationalism and to find alternative ways to capture a very different Acadian identity. The new identity was rooted in resistance, and thus questioned conventional ideas and expressed a societal project in new language. The small but highly influential body of literature that emerged could finally be called *Acadian* literature.

"THE 1970S: A HUGE CONSPIRACY"

So said Herménégilde Chiasson when describing the years from 1970 to 1980 in New Brunswick's now-dynamic Acadie. In Chiasson's mind, the decade was a literal theatre of creations that worked to affirm a contemporary Acadian presence: "this is the point at which Acadie reached, by means of the Université de Moncton, a level of knowledge whose impact and scope it could not yet measure" ("Des années" 7). Several literary, theatrical, cultural, and artistic organizations emerged during this period and, over the years, many became leading institutions. As Chiasson indicates above, however, the Université de Moncton was at the centre of the bubbling ferment. In 1972, the university's visual arts department was launched by artist Claude Roussel, who, according to Chiasson, brought "cultural modernity ... to Acadie" ("Une Acadie triangulaire" 30). Although the

Galerie d'Art at the university had presented its first exhibition of Acadian artists in 1965, the presence of Roussel's new department led the way for a wider distribution of Acadian visual art, one manifestation of which was the opening of a new gallery in Moncton in 1975, the Galerie Sans Nom. From the time of its opening, this artist-run gallery has organized exhibitions of contemporary, multidisciplinary, and experimental art featuring the work of Yvon Gallant, Roméo Savoie, Herménégilde Chiasson, Georges Goguen, Francis Coutellier, and Nancy Morin.

Similarly, the 1971 launch of the first locally published book—an event deemed so significant that it was attended by New Brunswick premier Richard Hatfield—had a major influence on the collective imaginary. Defined by its creators as an anti-book, *L'étoile maganée* combined poems by Jacques Savoie and photos by his brother Gilles with drawings by Herménégilde Chiasson, an effort that was not only experimental but that also pushed the bounds of modernity. The founding of Éditions d'Acadie the next year was equally significant and doubly influential. Founded by a group of professors from the Université de Moncton (Melvin Gallant was the lead figure), the press fulfilled the desire for a space in which writers could take possession of a language and the expression of the Acadian consciousness. Éditions d'Acadie made an immediate impact on literary production in Acadie and gave a voice to the younger generation of Acadians who were aspiring to a new order. The press made it possible for Acadian writers to be published locally, an option that was unavailable to Maillet and Després.

The first titles from Éditions d'Acadie have become foundational works of Acadian literature: *Cri de terre*, by the young poet Raymond Guy LeBlanc; *Saisons antérieures*, by Léonard Forest; *Acadie Rock*, by Guy Arsenault; and *Mourir à Scoudouc*, by Herménégilde Chiasson. Reflecting the centrality of Moncton in the contemporary Acadian experiment, the first three writers all came from the urban Moncton area, where Chiasson had been living since starting his studies with Claude Roussel in the middle of the 1960s. With the successes of the first titles, contemporary Acadian literature took flight. To everyone watching, a Moncton of the imagination was being written that called traditional values into question.[2] Not surprisingly, Éditions d'Acadie's list of publications grew rapidly, reaching an average of ten books a year. When it closed in 2000, it had published 400 titles from a variety of genres, including non-fiction, textbooks, history, and art, as well as literature.

In the same year as Éditions d'Acadie was founded, the Parti Acadien appeared, and the year after that the Société des Acadiens du Nouveau-

Brunswick came into being. The Parti Acadien (PA) was created by a group of autonomist Acadians driven by socialist values and a nationalist sentiment—and appeared four years after the Parti Québécois (PQ) was formed in the province of Quebec. While the goal of the PQ was Quebec's political autonomy in a country separate from Canada, that of the PA, starting in 1978, was to create an Acadian province within Canada. The aim was to improve the economic conditions of francophone regions of New Brunswick that, despite the Program for Equal Opportunity put in place by the Robichaud Liberal government in 1963, continued to experience more poverty than regions where anglophones formed the majority. The PA fielded candidates in three provincial elections (1974, 1978, and 1982), but never elected an MLA. However, the party's presence was felt, for during the campaign of 1978, Premier Richard Hatfield, a noted francophile, made a commitment to increase the presence of Acadians in his government. He kept his word, and in the 1982 provincial election, his pro-francophone platform resulted in a record number of Conservative candidates winning seats in Acadian regions.

Drawing on similar energies, the Congrès des Francophones was held in Fredericton in 1972 to discuss the dangers of assimilation inherent in bilingualism. The congress led to the formation of the Société des Acadiens du Nouveau-Brunswick (SANB) in Shippagan, which was modelled on a similar Acadian organization in Nova Scotia, the Fédération des Acadiens de la Nouvelle-Écosse, founded in 1969. The SANB was an activist organization, holding press conferences, leading demonstrations, and monitoring the government's Acadian files very closely. Its effects started appearing in 1974 when the Hatfield government instituted linguistic duality in the Department of Education. However, another event that same year—the closing of the Collège Sacré-Cœur in Bathurst—would cause divisions among the province's Acadians and create feelings of hostility toward the southeast that SANB felt viscerally. The Bathurst college, which had opened in 1921, had been turned over to a civic corporation that could not make the enterprise financially sustainable. The closing of the college was not well received, particularly by Acadians in the northeast who were now deprived of an institution that had been so important to the development of their region of the province. Making matters worse was the fact that the Université de Moncton, located in the southeast, was continuing to grow and lure young people from other Acadian regions. The diversity within New Brunswick's Acadian community had asserted itself, and had done so at a time of rising Acadian fortunes.

In 1979, the SANB organized the sixteenth national Acadian convention in Edmundston to discuss these divisions and, more generally, the division of political power between anglophones and francophones. A majority of the 1,200 delegates who attended the Convention d'Orientation Nationale Acadienne (CONA) voted in favour of the creation of an Acadian province as proposed by the Parti Acadien. (This plan was dropped by the SANB, which doubted that the Acadian population, en masse, would subscribe to the idea.) Seeing an opportunity to continue to be attentive to the province's Acadians, Hatfield's government passed a law in 1981 recognizing the equality of the two official language communities of the province. A few years later, in 1986, the Parti Acadien dissolved because of internal dissent about the direction it should take.

The Acadian writing published by Éditions d'Acadie during the 1970s bore the marks of this neo-nationalism and the activist intentions of its young authors. Raymond Guy LeBlanc, the author of *Cri de Terre*, had studied in France, where young students his own age were handing out pamphlets and tracts denouncing social injustice. He returned to the Université de Moncton transformed, believing that Acadians should no longer be silent or whisper in the streets of Moncton. While Maillet's character, "La Sagouine," observes that the "censors" taking their information did not want to write "Acadjens" on their list because "*l'Acadie* ain't a country, 'n *Acadjen* ain't a nationality, cause of the fact it ain't written in Joe Graphy's books" (A. Maillet 89; Trans. de Céspedes 165), LeBlanc loudly and assuredly affirms the opposite in the epilogue of his collection: "I am Acadian." The "cry" in his collection's title is therefore meant to end the muteness of his childhood and to free his tongue to express both his identity and the Chiac language of that identity. Thus, he lets loose about the urban and linguistic realities of Acadian identity as no other poet had done before: "I curse in English every mongrel *goddam* in the book ... Before this guy here *runs me over* ... I am Acadian / Which means / stuffed dispersed bought alienated sold out rebellious / Man torn open towards the future" (R.G. LeBlanc 65; Trans. Cogswell and Elder, *Unfinished Dreams* 120).

The events in Acadie that followed the publication of his book provided ample proof that LeBlanc's hope for uncensored speech was possible. Guy Arsenault, an adolescent attending the only francophone high school in Moncton (École Vanier) when he wrote *Acadie Rock*, picked up LeBlanc's invitation to speak. His use of Chiac accommodated his sense of bitterness and revolt against feelings of being marginalized as an Acadian living in Moncton. In claiming space and physical territory for similar emancipation, Herménégilde Chiasson's *Mourir à Scoudouc* (1974) also follows LeBlanc's lead, illustrating how Acadian spaces could be revivified with new points of reference. Writers such as Claude LeBouthillier, who published *L'Acadien reprend son pays* in 1977, utilizes a utopian vision coloured with a dose of humour. And though his futuristic vision of a new country certainly breaks with literary traditions—in his novels he explores the rurality of the Acadian Peninsula—his essential energies and grievances are of a piece with the poets of the early 70s.

In 1974 three key developments further contributed to the refining of a unique Acadian voice, each leading to a proliferation of writing for the theatre and screen. In Caraquet, the Théâtre Populaire d'Acadie (TPA) was founded, and a number of plays written by authors from the Acadian Peninsula were performed: Laval Goupil's *Tête d'eau* and *Le Djibou*; Jules Boudreau and Calixte Duguay's *Louis Mailloux*; and Herménégilde Chiasson's *L'Amer à boire*. For four decades now, the TPA has toured contemporary and classic works of theatre, as well as original creations, throughout New Brunswick, Quebec, and Europe. Theatre in Acadie received another boost in 1974 when a Department of Theatre Arts was formed at the Université de Moncton. Its first graduates founded Moncton's Théâtre l'Esacouette, which has produced more than forty original plays since it was founded, including several by Herménégilde Chiasson. Film was also aligned with a maturing Acadian sensibility, and that development accelerated when the National Film Board (NFB) opened a studio in Moncton. Studio de la Francophonie Canadienne-Acadie, better known as Studio Acadie, was brought to the city with the help of Acadian filmmaker Léonard Forest, who had been working at the NFB for two decades and who had several film documentaries to his credit, including *Les Aboiteaux* (1955), *Pêcheurs de Pombcoup* (1956), *Les Acadiens de la dispersion* (1968), *La Noce est pas finie* (1969), and *Un soleil pas comme ailleurs* (1972). A prize awarded by the annual Acadian film festival (Festival International du Cinéma Francophone en Acadie [FICFA]) is now named after him: the La Vague/Léonard Forest Prize for the best Acadian medium and long film. FICFA originated in 1987 at the Francophonie Summit in Quebec City, and it has become one of the largest francophone film festivals in North America, featuring more than 100 French-language films a year from Acadie, Canada, Europe, and Africa.

In 1979 two consonant arts organizations were formed that would also add to Moncton's ever-evolving cultural ferment. The first was the province's inaugural francophone dance school and company founded in Moncton by Chantal Cadieux. Productions DansEncorps offered dance performances and productions of other forms of performing arts at a time when there was not a tradition of contemporary dance in Acadie. As well, an organization was formed for writers, the Association des Écrivains Acadiens, which quickly led to the establishment of the literary magazine *Éloizes* and the publishing house Éditions Perce-Neige in 1980. These new organizations further celebrated the specificity of Acadian culture and that culture's right to represent its difference from the majority. New Brunswick's Acadie was defining its own place, a growing territory, in highly visible public ways.

Meanwhile, three Acadian women whose careers started in Moncton were attracting unprecedented attention in Quebec. Maillet's writing project, begun on the eve of the Quiet Revolution, continued with *Don l'Orignal* in 1972 (Governor General's Literary Award), *Mariaagélas* in 1975 (Grand Prix Littéraire de la Ville de Montréal), *Les Cordes-de-bois* in 1977 (Prix des Quatre Jurys and tied for the Prix Goncourt, then rejected by the chair of the jury), and *Pélagie-la-Charrette* in 1979, which garnered the Prix Goncourt. Maillet, who had been living in Montreal since 1971, had contributed to giving new life and new diversity to Quebec literature. (She is still the only Canadian writer to have won the Prix Goncourt, and she defied the prize's two curses: that no writer gets a second chance at a Goncourt and that half of the Goncourt winners never write again.) Maillet, however, pursued her literary project with characteristic energy, publishing *Cent ans dans les bois* two years later and following that with more than thirty novels, plays, children's stories, and translations. Today, her body of work is the largest in Acadie and one of the largest in Quebec and the francophone world. She has won critical acclaim and attention from all over the world.

In ways similar to Maillet, singers Angèle Arsenault from Abram Village, Prince Edward Island, and Édith Butler from Paquetville, New Brunswick, both graduates of Collège Notre-Dame d'Acadie de Moncton and the Université de Moncton, were rising to impressive heights of popularity and record sales in French Canada. With songs she composed about Acadie and everyday life, many with touches of humour, Arsenault reached the pinnacle of her success at the end of the 1970s. In 1978 her album *Libre* was the highest-selling album in Canada, with more than 300,000 copies sold, earning her a Félix award in 1979 from Quebec's recording and performing industry association, the Association du Disque et de l'Industrie du Spectacle du Québec. During roughly the same period (1973-1985), Butler released albums of popular and traditional music, touring Canada and Europe, and performing in prestigious venues such as the Olympia in Paris. Today, after almost fifty years of performing, Butler has sold two million albums and enjoys an international reputation.

The impact of these successes in Quebec and the wider world were felt in Acadie, where countless new talents burst onto the music scene. In 1975, two popular new groups were formed. The first was Beausoleil Broussard (consisting of Isabelle Roy, Claude Fournier, Jean-Gabriel Comeau, and writer Jacques Savoie), which performed music inspired by Acadian folklore. The group met with instant success as soon as its second album, *Beausoleil Broussard*, was released in 1977. The album won a prize for new music (Prix de la Jeune Chanson Française) in Paris in 1978. The second group that met almost-instant success was 1755. Consisting of Kenneth Saulnier, Pierre Robichaud, Roland Gauvin, Donald Boudreau, and Ronald Dupuis, it sang both traditional songs and original pieces written by members of the group. Especially popular was the music it made from the lyrics of poet Gérald Leblanc. Those lyrics ("Le monde a bien changé" and "Rue Dufferin") predated much of Leblanc's poetry, which was characterized throughout his life by an urban consciousness and a questioning spirit.

In the early part of the 1970s, two books put Moncton's Acadian cultural ferment into a critical perspective and, in so doing, broke with the nationalist discourse of the times. In 1975, Jean-Paul Hautecœur's substantial volume, *L'Acadie du discours. Pour une sociologie de la culture acadienne*, was published. Hautecœur had been a professor of sociology at the Université de Moncton in the 1960s until the department was closed by the university administration, which disapproved of the influence sociology professors were exercising on rebellious students. For Hautecœur, it was imperative that Acadian society began "to understand the relationship with the past as it concerned the explicit relationship with the present [and] to articulate the type of relationship that society has with its possibilities" (*L'Acadie du discours*, 47). Not only were creative artists leading the charge, then, but influential intellectual workers were also shaping what had become a fairly cohesive activist narrative. Three years later, historian Michel Roy released *L'Acadie perdue*, a book that was extremely critical of the Church as Acadie's major cultural force—and this in face of the Church likely being the most important early institution to maintain the Acadian people's collective identity. Describing priests as "a retrograde clerical elite" (29), Roy advances the opinion that the clergy has not always played a positive role in the maintenance of Acadian identity, mostly because, for a century, they fostered an ideology and social practices that stifled Acadie's entry into the modern world. His judgment is harsh: "this progressively [more] powerful control of our nation's clergy over our minds, our collective consciousness, our mental structures, starting at the end of the last century, does it not represent a historical fact which has burdened us with consequences just as negative for the course of our history as has the justifiably famous dispersion of our people?" (33). His opinion is, of course, closely aligned with the activist discourse of the 1970s, which called into question, among other things, the place the Church held in Acadian society and its role in the transmission of values of identity based on religion and rurality.

POST-NATIONALISM AND EXISTENTIALISM

If the 1970s ended on a high note with Antonine Maillet's Goncourt award, the 1980s began equally auspiciously with the first publication from Moncton's Éditions Perce-Neige, *Graines de fées*, which was also the first collection of poetry written by a woman in Acadie, Dyane Léger. In 1981, the book was awarded the first Prix France-Acadie (literary prize), created two years earlier by the Amitiés Acadiennes and the Fondation de France. An existential exploration from a woman's perspective, Léger's collection broke away from the type of protest and advocacy written by male poets in the previous decade. Léger's work, then, ushered in a post-nationalist phase in the 1980s, exploring new possibilities and favouring a subjective, personal approach. Was she writing to compensate for what Jean-Marie Klinkenberg calls "existential insignificance"? Klinkenberg explains: "The insignificance of existence is, from the 1980s on, compensated by attention exclusively focused on the self. Personal and biographical narratives regain their place of honour. A return to the individual, then, but also to the groups that are presumed to define one's identity" (117). That Léger's second collection, *Sorcière de vent!* (1983), sustains the same themes and tones as the first would suggest that Klinkenberg's observations are correct.

Perce-Neige continued its mission of publishing new authors, including Gérald Leblanc, Rose Després, and Rémi Morin Rossignol. Starting in 1982, it also published, jointly with Éditions d'Acadie, the first dictionary of Acadian writers (*Portraits d'écrivains: Dictionnaire des écrivains acadiens*), as well as the proceedings of a conference of Acadian and Quebec writers entitled *Les Cent lignes de notre américanité*, and the first anthology to offer Acadian poetry in English translation in side-by-side format: *Poésie acadienne contemporaine / Acadian Poetry Now*.

The nationalist demands that characterized literature in the previous decade gave way in the 1980s to the emergence of a voice marked by contemporary challenges faced by both the Acadian community and its individuals. Those challenges touched on notions of space, language, the American identity, and coexistence. The poet who, above all others, would inspire Acadian writing throughout the decade was Gérald Leblanc. In 1981, Leblanc's first collection, *Comme un otage au quotidien*, was published by Éditions Perce-Neige (Leblanc was one of the founders). Three more collections followed before the end of the decade, all with titles that revealed much about Leblanc's preoccupation with naming space: *Géographie de la nuit rouge* (1984), *Lieux transitoires* (1986),[3] and *L'extrême frontière* (1988). In his writing, Leblanc, called "the cartographic writer" by Raoul Boudreau and Mylène White (40–55), maps out his psychic and mythic territory by naming the places he lives and frequents in Moncton, and in the other cities he loves: Montréal, Vancouver, and New York. These real places and "felt" spaces map out a concrete territory in place of a political territory. When he comes to write, in *Éloge du chiac* (1995), "My city is a planet," Leblanc signals a renewed emphasis on the immediacy of Moncton's urban reality. Likewise the sights, sounds, and smells of his urban life are ever-present in his work: in street names, public spaces, bars, and a nightlife with drinking and drugs. In this manner he communicates the difficulty of living in Moncton, which continues to be ambiguous and alienating for the Acadian minority, and he opts instead for linguistic touchstones in the hope of turning Moncton into a liveable space. In that desire to 'write the city,' Leblanc's work became worthy of emulation, and indeed others began to pick up the thread of examining the city's urban vitality, linguistic tensions, and North-American character.

Another young writer who made her debut on the literary scene at the time would become an important figure in Acadian literature. France Daigle began her writing career in 1983 with her first book, *Sans jamais parler du vent. Roman de crainte et d'espoir que la mort arrive à temps*, published by Éditions d'Acadie. A postmodern novel that evoked a world of emptiness, death, disorder, and contradiction, her first book was followed by *Histoire de la maison qui brûle. Vaguement suivi d'un dernier regard sur la maison qui brûle* (1985), another powerful novel in which the characters' immobility seems to abolish the notion of time.

When these novels were published, Acadie was in another state of upheaval as it was witnessing the demise, on 27 September 1982, of its only daily newspaper, *L'Évangéline*, in its ninety-fifth year. The newspaper had served as a means of communication for the Acadian population and, even more significantly, it was a strong advocate for Acadian causes. While it had a wide and lasting influence under Euclide Daigle's direction during the

1950s, promoting a more modern version of nationalism, it became even more vocal in the 1960s, joining in the chorus of Université de Moncton students who criticized the establishment and the status quo. Its positions did not sit well with those who supported traditional values, nor with the Acadian elite in the north who reproached the newspaper for favouring Moncton over other regions of Acadie. In the midst of this, *L'Évangéline* was questioning its role in bringing Acadians together, and its financial situation was growing precarious. In 1965, l'Assomption Mutuelle-Vie took charge and turned the operations over to a not-for-profit organization, where it remained until 1974. At the beginning of the 1980s, the poor state of its finances and tense labour relations led to an abrupt end to publication. In the view of France Daigle—who had been a journalist for the newspaper in the 1970s, following in the footsteps of her father, Euclide, who had written 966 editorials between 1949 and 1967—Acadie was stupefied, incredulous, and crushed. It had lost one of its vital organs.

The vacuum left by the closure of the only Acadian daily newspaper was so deeply felt that twenty-one months later, in June 1984, a group from the Acadian Peninsula started a regional daily, *L'Acadie Nouvelle*. Two years after that, in August 1986, a new provincial daily (*Le Matin*) began to serve the Francophone community with the financial support of the Hatfield government, more specifically of Minister Jean-Maurice Simard of Madawaska. Despite that support, *Le Matin* closed its doors in June 1988.

What might be called the "Saga of the Daily Newspapers" lasted a number of years and brought the tensions between the northeastern and southeastern regions of Acadie to the surface. Maillet captures these tensions in her "autofictional" novel *Le huitième jour*, published in 1986. (It was published in English as *On the Eighth Day* soon thereafter in 1989, and again in 2006 in a version translated by Wayne Grady.) Written in the carnivalesque mode, the novel tells the story of the journey made by its four protagonists, who "proudly pursue the quest and conquest of their destiny, ... stout of heart [and] firm in their resolve to let no stick be stuck into the spokes of their wheel of fortune, and no hangman come between their dreams and reality" (Grady 157). In their adventures, the four companions witness a conflict between the two regions: a fight between the North Island clan and the South Island clan. They decide to intervene, and manage to put a stop to the "Holy War that pitted the North against the South" (180). Moreover, they make the combatants acknowledge that "they must now come face to face with their new destinies" (189). A clear metaphor for the internal strife between northeastern and southeastern

Acadians, Maillet's novel challenges the political logic of such struggles, showing what they look like and what their costs are.

At the turn of the decade, two authors would take very different paths. Claude LeBouthillier, whose writings had up until then favoured narratives of a contemporary or future Acadie, opted instead for writing historical novels, aiming to fill a void in the collective memory of Acadians. *Le Feu du mauvais temps* (1989) and *Les Marées du Grand Dérangement* (1994) describe the origins of Acadian identity in testimonial fashion while pursuing narrative threads beyond the founding story of the Deportation. *Le Feu du mauvais temps*, for example, which takes place between 1740 and 1763, highlights a romantic relationship between a French settler who has just arrived in Acadie and a young Métis, born of a white father and a Mi'kmaw mother. The young settler eventually marries the Métis woman, highlighting a practice followed by many Acadians in the seventeenth and eighteenth centuries, including the author's own ancestors. The historical importance of this intercultural reality, in which settler and Indigenous mores blend, must also be carefully qualified, however, for such fictional depictions are so rare that LeBouthillier's account is a singular occurrence in the Acadian literary corpus.

Building what might be called a poetic bridge between the two decades, Gérald Leblanc continued his literary output, publishing seven collections of poetry between 1986 and 1995. Especially significant was *L'extrême frontière* (1988), which shows unequivocally that the most crucial issue for "*vivre icitte*" ("living here" [in Moncton]) is language. However, it is in *Éloge du chiac* (1995), written after the first World Acadian Congress and his stay in New York, that Leblanc exhibits the full extent of his ideas on his hybrid and ostracized language. In poem after poem, he wonders how it would be possible for him to be any prouder of his language.

THE CITY: ATTRACTION AND FEAR

The 1990s opened with the creation of the Association Acadienne des Artistes Professionnel.le.s du Nouveau-Brunswick, which absorbed the Acadian writers' association that had formed in 1986, and with the rebirth of Éditions Perce-Neige in 1991. Moncton continued, then, with its tensions between languages and cultures in contact, to be the site and the subject of the urban narrative in Acadian literature. The importance of Moncton in that literature can be explained in part by the fact that the city had been transformed over the decades into a centre of a wide and varied range of activities. It is the home of a university that has inspired literary and cultural life, and it is also the site of generative Acadian productions and exchanges. It has therefore become the intellectual and cultural driving force of Acadie, the nexus of an emerging society whose individual members have determined its parameters. The decade of the 1990s continued this evolution with Moncton emerging as an increasingly urban space in the discourse of identity. This marked a transformation for a culture that had traditionally defined itself in terms of rurality, at least in its collective discourse. In the poetry of the 1970s and 1980s, this movement toward Moncton's urbanity raised a question that preoccupied writers: how were Acadians to live in this busy hub of North American culture, which was globally anglophone, and also turn it (remake it) to their own ends? In the 1990s, Moncton appeared in Acadian prose in a more attenuated form: the question was now about how Moncton was settling into Acadian literature and how Acadian literature was settling into Moncton. The project, still in progress, involves writing Moncton in a way that provides a realistic reflection of the city, with all the paradoxes it holds for Acadians. The project itself represents a healthy passage out of a certain silence in the larger social discourse and towards the contemporary reality of Acadian collectivity—and contributes to the possibility of fulfilling the dream of reconciling the discourses of Acadie and modernity.

That Acadian literature was slow to depict urban social realities is the first observation we should make. The observation is not insignificant, as Herménégilde Chiasson points out in "Traversée." Because, as Chiasson says, "Moncton and its university would ... colour the very existence of the literature that emerged from it" (80), we should also observe that the literature that emerged from the Université de Moncton would create a literary destiny in Moncton that would likewise modify the course of the city's existence. It is this seeming paradox that preoccupied the authors who chose to write about Moncton in the 1990s, including Antonine Maillet, who published *Les Confessions de Jeanne de Valois* in 1992. Characteristically, this novel contains both Acadie's quest for urban identity, which chooses Moncton as its city, and the city that contains the literature, which chooses Moncton as the object of its imaginings. To explore this idea further, Maillet presents the Acadian experience of urbanization from the point of view of a nun, who actually lived and had an impact on her times, and whose urban quest defies the appropriation of space by laying claim, instead, to time. (That defying of space is typical in Acadie because of the long absence of a geopolitical territory.) In Maillet's text, Moncton takes its place very naturally as a space where the future of the Acadian people plays out. But the memorable episode which stands out in Moncton's imagination, and about which the protagonist explains in her confessions, is that of the presentation of the pig's head by Université de Moncton students to the anti-francophone mayor Leonard Jones in 1968. The episode revisits the site of conflict when Acadians were making the city their own, and where, for nearly a century, they had been living as second-class citizens. By foregrounding the episode, Maillet reminds her readers of how intransigent and close-minded the city and its officials were towards Moncton's francophones and towards the students of the Université de Moncton, who were simply asking for more respect from municipal officials. With this event, Maillet asserts, Moncton became a political flashpoint for Acadie. It became a dynamic city—indeed, a site of confrontation—composed of groups with competing and conflicting relations. Maillet's broader message is that the greater presence and ever-increasing confidence of Moncton's Acadian community culminated less in a utopian setting of collective and harmonious destiny and more in the reality of a disparate population living together with differences. Maillet chooses to relate this unusual episode over others because it proved to be an "exception of note" in which, to use Alain Médam's phrase, the "city [was] outside itself" (17). Thus, although it was initially difficult for Acadians to take possession of their adopted space, Moncton had already begun to grow in depth, and a new spirit would guide its social evolution. That spirit internalized the transcultural experience of the provincial city and enabled it to become, less than forty years later, a major metropolis of New Brunswick.

Shortly after Maillet's novel was published, Yves Cormier, a writer from Moncton, published the autobiographical novel *Grandir à Moncton*. With a good deal of humour, it tells the story of a young protagonist who leaves his rural community in the 1960s to go to the English city he fears, a city in which he feels alienated from the traditional Acadian space he has always known. Meeting English people for the first time presents moments of anxiety, but after a while he tames his fears and manages to adapt, honing the minority integration ethos that Acadians in Moncton, at least at that time, perfected as their way of being: "Still and all, we got used to the place. We knew where the English belonged and where the French belonged.... We knew when to speak French out loud and when to be quiet; we lived our lives in French just as long as it didn't bother anyone. And that's how I got used to living in the big city of Moncton" (34). What becomes obvious in Cormier's novel is the web of support systems that sustain the community, the paramount one being the school. The novel clearly connects

French-language schools to the maintenance of Acadian identity in the hybrid city of Moncton.

In 1994, two events occurred that would leave their mark on the Acadian population in southeastern New Brunswick: Radio Beauséjour CJSE, a community radio station located in Shediac (approximately twenty kilometres east of Moncton), went on air during the first Acadian World Congress (CMA) held in the southeast. Its success quickly surpassed all expectations, with more than 50,000 listeners tuning in. Moreover, its impact on the French-speaking community was remarkable. Acadians finally were given a voice and a public forum; until that time the local francophone population had never expressed itself on air, and therefore had never heard itself speak. From the beginning, the leaders of CJSE were visionaries. They dared to adopt, despite the protests of language purists (yes, those purists do exist in Acadie), a hiring policy that favoured radio hosts who spoke with the local accent. It was a first for a New Brunswick community that had been, for forty years, part of Radio-Canada's stronghold and had always complied with its neutral language standards. For many years, those language standards had fed a kind of linguistic insecurity in Acadie that had unconsciously driven Acadian speakers to remain silent. They often felt incompetent in their mother tongue, and as a result they suffered from a sense that they had insufficient linguistic resources from which to draw. Radio Beauséjour CJSE changed that. Being able to speak and hear their own language gradually removed the stigmas of linguistic inadequacy. Hearing the local accent and speech patterns resulted in an individual and collective liberation that made inclusivity in the public space possible, and empowered the audience to make real changes.

That this development happened when the CMA was held in southeastern New Brunswick for the first time proved to be significant. For a week and a half in 1994, 300,000 people from Acadie and the Acadian diaspora participated in a multitude of activities, including family reunions, lectures, conferences, and a variety of arts events. Themed "Retrouvailles 94" (Reunion 94), the event foregrounded Acadie's collective vitality and renewed confidence in its present and its future. The literary magazine Éloizes published a special issue on Moncton for the occasion, exploring what the city was like for writers living in its midst. Notable is an autobiographical prose piece by Léonard Forest entitled "Pour parler au monde," which recounted his childhood in Moncton. The description of the economic realities of the 1930s and the countless moves from one downtown street to another occupy most of the first half of Forest's story, setting up the focus on language in the second. After learning the languages of home and the street, Forest encounters the language of the nuns, Latin, Chiac, the beautiful French language from France, and jazz, all of which "filled our heads like a huge wave that carried us off into different countries, different worlds. To be honest, it gave us a whole lot of languages to speak to the world" (14). The multilingualism of his apprenticeship is treated positively, approached with humour, and the threats of being minoritized or assimilated are not raised. Rather, the narrator's linguistic consciousness is nurtured both by the continental reality and a sense of ancestral belonging that is invested with meaning and rootedness. Forest's experience is given critical expression in historian Patrick D. Clarke's study of regions and regionalisms in Acadie. In his work, Clarke shows that Moncton's central location at the crossroads of the Maritimes has long influenced the development of a less monolithic identity than in the northeast. In the southeast, the Acadian identity, even if founded on a community solidarity, is also the product of a dialogic process not only with the majority but also with the diaspora, in fact with the francophonie as a whole. The southeast has thus remained a space in which Acadie is turned outward and open to the rest of the world (Clarke 345), a feature that Forest corroborates in his incisive reflection.

Gérald Leblanc's novel *Moncton Mantra* (1997) would both affirm and contest that outward-reaching urbanity. Transferring the tension of his poems to the novel form, Leblanc's first novel describes the urban questioning and the slow and uncertain literary coming-of-age of his alter ego, Alain Gautreau of Bouctouche, who comes to the city to attend the Université de Moncton at the beginning of the 1970s. Seven years later, the protagonist leaves Moncton to go to the "big city," Montréal, in order to get a view from the outside of Moncton, which he calls "my town." After spending a few months in Montréal, a city he enjoys, Gautreau hears the call of Moncton getting louder and more intense: "Living in a city, having mixed feelings about the city, tinted with a sort of love-hate pull most of the time, but a city which nevertheless provided a space to explore. Moncton was all that to me. I was coming to understand that more and more ..." (Leblanc 112; Trans. Elder 97). Answering the call, he returns to Moncton, where he puts down roots in an urban reality that he can now fully inhabit. Newly returned, but altered, he becomes an advocate for the city, writing a speech about it that is authentically urban, Acadian, and North American. He references all the voices he has heard, including those of his father, mother, friends, Zachary Richard, Bob Dylan, and countless people on the streets. The voices enumerated at the end of the novel (forty-four in total) become the voices of contemporary

Moncton. As he looks at his first book, hot off the press, he realizes that he has created a space where negotiations and adjustments are possible, in effect widening the possibilities open to francophones in Moncton and thereby neutralizing some of the urban schizophrenia that is still latent.

A similarly altered Moncton is also present in several other novels published during the same decade: France Daigle's *1953. Chronique d'une naissance annoncée* (1995) and *Pas pire* (1998), and Claude LeBouthillier's *Le Borgo de l'écumeuse* (1998), to name only a few. In *Pas pire*, as in Leblanc's *Moncton Mantra*, the space to be built and to be conquered is a literary space as much as an urban one, despite the fact that the novel opens with an exhaustive description of the Dieppe of Daigle's childhood. Daigle, who is now living in the neighbouring city of Moncton, portrays her alter ego on a trip to Paris, where she appears on the popular French TV show *Bouillon de culture*. The symbolism sublimates the reality:

> [S]he takes part in the show that establishes her reputation, just as, in reality, Antonine Maillet had done twenty years earlier. The novel presents us, then, with a fictional example of a woman writer from Moncton taking it upon herself to give Acadian literature a legitimate status, and she does this by writing herself into the literary quest of Acadie. This quest, both fictional and real, had wide reverberation that resulted in international success. Though *Pas pire* was never presented on Bernard Pivot's *Bouillon de culture* show, it was awarded the France-Acadie literary prize in 1998 by a jury composed exclusively of members from France. (Lord, "Identité et urbanité" 80)

A new poet also became prominent during the 1990s: Serge Patrice Thibodeau, who published seven collections during the decade. Born and raised in Rivière-Verte, in the Madawaska region of northwest New Brunswick, Thibodeau had travelled to West Africa and communist countries such as Czechoslovakia, Poland, and Hungary, where he drew from what he had seen and experienced to develop themes that veered sharply from those that predominated in Acadian writing of the time. His first collection, *La septième chute* (1990), which was awarded the Prix France-Acadie, reflected that difference, presenting his characteristic mystical and spiritual quest that integrated Christian and Islamic elements. In 1992 he published three collections that secured his reputation: Écrits des forges brought out *Le passage des glaces suivi de Lamento,* and Éditions d'Acadie released *Le cycle de Prague,* which won the prestigious Émile-Nelligan poetry prize. The next year Hexagone published *L'appel des mots: lectures de Saint-Denys-Garneau*, a non-fiction title on the poetry of Quebec poet Saint-Denys-Garneau, for which Thibodeau received the Prix Edgar-Lespérance. Two more prize-winning collections appeared in 1995: he received the Grand Prix du Festival International de la Poésie for both *Le quatuor de l'errance suivi de La traversée du désert* and for *Nous, l'étranger*, and he received the Governor General's Literary Award for *Le quatuor de l'errance suivi de La Traversée du désert*. By the end of the decade, Thibodeau had won more literary awards than any other poet of his generation.

The year 1999 capped what had been an extraordinary decade (and century) for Acadie. A second Acadian premier, Bernard Lord, from Moncton, was elected in New Brunswick; Moncton hosted the eighth Sommet de la Francophonie; Éditions d'Acadie declared bankruptcy and closed its doors permanently; and a powerful literary work that represented the end of the decade appeared. Herménégilde Chiasson's fourth collection, *Conversations*, won the Governor General's Literary Award and seemed to sum up the turbulent times, pointing to Acadie's future. It is a book with two protagonists, She and He, who occupy a postmodern urban space that is unnamed. If the city is anonymous, implies the book, what comes next?

MAKING THE INVISIBLE VISIBLE

Literature, according to Edouard Glissant, can make the invisible visible. And so it was with Acadie. The decades of the 1960s and 1970s saw the birth of a literature that articulated, often in conditions of hardship, domination, and tension, the project of constructing a collective vision and a quest for identity. That vision and quest were anchored in modernity and urbanity. In the early 1990s, Herménégilde Chiasson would say (fittingly) that Acadian literature was born in Moncton, a city of paradox for individuals and institutions alike: "Moncton is a city, to quote Gérald Leblanc, where there are deep tensions arising from the fact that the stakes here are so great and the fact that the near-totality of Acadie's cultural infrastructures are located in this city which is two-thirds anglophone" ("Traversées" 79). It is not surprising, then, that only in the 1970s did Moncton began to write itself. And, in a broader sense, it had taken a full century for Acadians to take possession of Moncton, not just as a space of collective life, but also as a literary presence. As I explained in an earlier article, "writing Moncton, for Acadian writers at the beginning of the 1970s, meant first recognizing Moncton in its concrete forms and, second, endeavouring to give it a form on the imaginary level" (Lord, "Identité et urbanité" 69). It was when Acadian neo-nationalism gained strength that Moncton became both a problem and an unavoidable object for young writers. That it took so long for that to happen against the long history of Acadians in the region can be explained by a number of social and historical factors. In the 1950s, as Clarke has shown, two universes collided, the modern and the ancient: in such a clash, "the city predominated, but not completely" (328). The collective imaginary remained anchored in a rural Acadie that favoured belonging and rootedness; as a result, it resisted urbanization. Thus, there was an inherent contradiction in identities between the new spatial reality brought about by the "Monctonization" of Acadie and the historical matrix of Acadie, which, from the time of the return from Deportation, was agrarian and sea-based. As a city that called people to it, offering the possibility of radical change in urban modernity, Moncton was therefore slow to be accepted by a post-Deportation people.

By the 1970s that started to change, and by the 1980s that change was proceeding rapidly. By the second half of the 1980s, an entire body of literary work used the city as a construction site, a space of creation where an Acadian identity was being reimagined as urban. Reading the Acadian corpus compiled in the *Dictionnaire des œuvres littéraires de l'Acadie des Maritimes*, which lists nearly 200 Acadian works from the Maritimes in the twentieth century, it is clear that Moncton and urban spaces generally appear more often with each passing decade. And from 1970, the literary sites of urbanity double in each successive decade. In poetry, almost half of the collections published depict Moncton, while a third of the novels take place in the city. A "Moncton of the imagination" reveals, among some writers, an urban schizophrenia typified by the confrontation of Acadian cultural heritage and the immediate experience of the city. For other writers, this existential dichotomy is not a source of ambivalence. By the 1990s, this ambivalence was an accepted part of the Acadian encounter with the city. Indeed, "Moncton was being written in the multiplicity of transformations which were uprooting a city undergoing profound change; Acadian literature ... shows this creative tension, attentive to the relations not only between languages but between linguistic groups. 'Moncton of the imagination' echoes the individual and collective resilience of writers, as members of a distinct community which intends to remain that way" (Lord, "L'arrivée en ville'" 50). In the documentary *Living on the Edge, the Poetic Works of Gérald Leblanc* (*L'extrême frontière. L'œuvre poétique de Gérald Leblanc*, 2007), poet Claude Beausoleil talks about the "Moncton School," which, like a prism, projects the image of a city "where everything is possible." The city has indeed become a literary reality and has in turn acquired a literary existence. Today, the Acadian "civitas" uses Moncton as its identity centre, the point through which "Acadie" enters the continent and the world. The quest, however, is not yet over.

NOTES

This chapter was translated from French to English by Jo-Anne Elder.
1. Maillet and Després had new books published in 1962: Maillet's *On a mangé la dune* and the collection *Les Cloisons en vertige* were both published by Beauchemin, and Després's first novel, *Le Scalpel ininterrompu—Journal du docteur Jan von Fries*, was published by Éditions A. In 1968, the two authors published once again: Maillet's first play, *Les Crasseux,* was published by Holt, Rinehart and Winston, and Després published his third collection, *Le Balcon des dieux inachevés*, with Éditions Garneau.
2. Some novelists decided not to take this aesthetic route, among them prize-winning writers Louis Haché, who chose to write historical fiction, and Claude LeBouthillier, whose work includes speculative as well as historical fiction. Both came from the Acadian Peninsula.
3. This title was published by Michel Henri, who had just left Éditions d'Acadie to start his own company, which closed in 1989.

AFTERWORD

CONGRUENCE AND RECURRENCE IN THE LITERATURES OF NEW BRUNSWICK

David Creelman

One winter my eight-year-old son and I visited Ottawa. After skating on the canal in the morning, we spent an afternoon exploring the then-named Museum of Civilization. An exhibit about the nation's natural resources was designed to attract young eyes. Comprised of an enlarged map of Canada, an interactive component allowed children to press buttons along the front, an action that lit up the regions of the country that had coal or nickel, wheat or fish. Small green lights in the West and in Newfoundland appeared as we pressed "oil." Different lights appeared in British Columbia, Ontario, and Nova Scotia for "fruit." The province of New Brunswick, however, remained unlit as we pushed button after button, until finally the single light in the province brightened when we found the switch for "forestry." When we turned to the other rooms in the museum, I was unsettled that our home province, when represented in a national context, seemed quiet and dark. The image of New Brunswick as a place of little wealth and few economic opportunities is neither new nor inaccurate. But this reading of the province as an empty space, a blank signifier except for a token characteristic, is simply not true. As the essays in this collection have demonstrated, the province that has one of the lowest profiles in the nation hosts a vibrant, regenerative, and expressive cultural environment.

THE CONDITIONS OF LITERARY FERMENT
The literary culture of New Brunswick has waxed and waned over the past 240 years. This rhythm of expression and retraction is not due to any

natural cycle, but rather to shifting periods of cultural productivity that begin and end when particular social circumstances emerge, coalesce, and eventually dissipate. Moments of literary ferment have emerged in both French and English areas of the province in very similar ways. Indeed the conditions necessary to generate a period of ferment follow parallel tracks regardless of temporal, spatial, or linguistic context. Based on the evidence of the previous chapters, periods of literary productivity emerge when four socio-cultural conditions are present:

1. Compression and concentration
2. Adversarial tensions
3. Emergent aesthetic conditions
4. Individuals of daring and genius who can work together as a collective.

As the evidence of the chapters further establishes, there is no set model to determine how these four socio-cultural conditions must be established and what measure of each is required. In effect, no society can self-consciously create the web of forces necessary for ferment to begin. As Tony Tremblay has argued in his introduction, the core components of cultural production depend on a unique blend of language, history, ethnicity, economic factors, and class forces. When these elements interact with each other under particular conditions, periods of literary ferment emerge to produce rich and sustained moments of beauty and significance.

Each of the periods of literary ferment discussed in this collection emerged in historical moments characterized by a *concentration* of intellectual potential and in circumstances that forced an unusual degree of cultural *compression*. This high level of concentration was often facilitated by the urban setting within which writers studied and worked. Such a claim about New Brunswick might seem flawed. After all, the Loyalists were settler pioneers; in the decades following Confederation, the capital, Fredericton, was hardly a metropolis. Nonetheless, if we examine the particular experiences of the writers themselves, we see that their backgrounds were both varied and intensely active. Jonathan Odell was a graduate of Princeton, a doctor in the British navy, a minister of the Church of England, and a resident of Burlington and Newark, New Jersey, before the storms of revolution washed him ashore in Saint John and Fredericton. Oliver Goldsmith and Douglass Huyghue were both educated in Halifax, and Goldsmith also served in the navy before trying his hand at a number of different commercial and legal ventures. New Brunswick, following the

American Revolution, may have been a sparsely populated region of the world, but the Loyalists brought a concentrated mindset with them into the wilderness. As Malcolm Ross notes in "A Strange Aesthetic Ferment," "the influence on taste and manners of men like Odell ... made Fredericton, from the start, heir to the culture of colonial America. The well-stocked private libraries, the university itself, the urban and cultivated air of this remote frontier town, owed ... much to the American tradition" (30). Similarly, Thomas Hodd has pointed out that the capital city that nurtured Charles G.D. Roberts, Bliss Carman, Barry Straton, and Francis Sherman was small in population but richly varied in its intellectual and professional classes. Chantal Richard further notes that although Collège Saint-Joseph was not situated in an urban setting, Father Lefebvre brought together a small core of young men from a cultural context of nearly complete illiteracy and, through a focused and concise curriculum, exposed them to the sophisticated elements of French literary culture. Saint John's industrial and dock culture were likewise essential influences in the intellectual development of Ted Campbell's group, and the second Acadian Renaissance was closely tied to both Louis Robichaud's Equal Opportunity Program and Moncton's emergence as a new haven of intellectual creativity. Even when the moments of ferment were not centred in urban environments, they were always linked to institutions of intellectual production—universities, newspaper presses, publishing houses, and theatres—through which cultural and artistic literacy was supported. It was not enough, however, in any of the historical periods examined, for the key tools of the intelligentsia to be in place. Rather, there also had to be sufficient richness and variety of opinion within those concentrated and compressed settings to breed the degrees of tension and anxiety borne of this close proximity of difference.

Living within the potentiality of compression is not in itself sufficient to provoke a period of ferment. Each of the literary flowerings examined in this book emerged when *adversarial conditions* prompted members of communities to talk back, to defend themselves, or to confront a threat. As Gwendolyn Davies observes, early class and ethnic divisions soon generated among the Loyalists a sense of "discord" and "grievance" and bred a strong "subversiveness" within the common citizens, who were known for their "penchant for irony" and "kicking against the pricks." The power of the "Fifty-Five," the privileged group of Loyalists who received individual grants of 5,000 acres, was a typical provocation that generated the satire, doggerel, and invective that characterized the discourse of early New Brunswick literature. For the Confederation poets in Fredericton and the modernist voices surrounding Ted Campbell and A.G. Bailey, the local circumstances were less openly contentious, but both of those cohorts were motivated to distinguish themselves against the cultural philistinism around them. The four young men at the core of the Confederation ferment—Straton, Roberts, Carman, and Sherman—were raised within the Victorian idealism imparted by teachers George Parkin and Thomas Harrison, and then nurtured within the refined local assumptions that Bishop Medley had established. The subtext that defined the circle of their literary dreams was the demarcation line between themselves as the bearers of culture and those outside their circle, the ordinary people they sought to rise above. Fear of their provincial obscurity was the adversary that drove the Confederation poets to find a voice greater than was thought possible for men of their situation. Campbell and Bailey, in similar ways, were aware that "centralist biases" and the totalizing literary and historiographic creeds being advanced in Montreal and Toronto threatened the particularity of the local as they defined and experienced it. Whether it was Campbell's localism and the "socially conscious" work of Campbell's artists that talked back to the apolitical nationalism of the Group of Seven, or Bailey's regionalist perspective that responded to Frederick Jackson Turner's views of Manifest Destiny, the cultural producers active between 1935–1955 were motivated to create alternatives to defend their immediate circumstances.

New Brunswick's Acadians of both the first and second Renaissance were more aware than any cultural producers outside Quebec that their attempts to define themselves against hegemonies were a matter of cultural life and death. With their distinct language, historical narrative, ethnic identity, collective memory, and common folkloric heritage, the Acadians were the Maritime community most successful in achieving the cohesive homogeneity necessary to forge a national identity. Anglophone Maritimers may sometimes feel that they are part of a nation, but Acadians *are* a nation. In the later nineteenth century and in the closing decades of the twentieth, the Acadians were spurred on by clear and threatening adversaries, be they the Irish Catholic bishops who resisted the ascendency of Acadie, or the oppressive bigotry of Moncton's anglophone elites who feared the differences in their midst. If Acadians had not been motivated by the cultural tensions, not only between the French and English but also between the different regional camps within the Acadian community itself, the literary production of the two eras would have lacked an important creative spur.

Throughout the five periods of literary ferment identified in this book, New Brunswick's cultural producers have consistently opposed the inherited norms, resisted the established elites, and in most cases advanced localist and democratic principles. In this sense, provincial writers have had a long history of not being hesitant or fearful, of not being anxious about unknown exterior threats, and of not being walled within a real or metaphoric garrison. In a reversal of Northrop Frye's well-known concept of a "garrison mentality," New Brunswick writers have addressed anxieties and differences head-on and have spoken with a wider confidence that difference can be confronted, engaged, and often explored to create something new. As Christl Verduyn has noted in the Foreword to this collection, there is an inherently postcolonial dynamic at work beneath these expressions of resistance and redefinition. Indeed, from the earliest Loyalist satirists who were sued by their betters, to the sociology department that was closed in the 1960s when the Université de Moncton disapproved of the influence professors were having on rebellious students, there has been a tendency for dissenting voices to challenge established powers and recurring moments when authorities have tried to repress the upstarts. These moments when marginal voices articulate real and even threatening alternative visions of the community reflect this spirit of postcolonial resistance. Plurality even more than hybridity, then, is at work in the midst of New Brunswick's multi-voiced periods of productivity.

It is, of course, common today to speak of Canadian regional cultures as pluralist in nature. Immigration patterns in the West (the newest parts of Canada) ensured that the Prairies would emerge as one of the first thoroughly multicultural spaces, and the main urban centres of the nation—Vancouver, Toronto, and Montreal—continue to be the destination for the many diverse peoples who have transplanted (and transformed) their cultures in a new Canadian environment. Notwithstanding the rise of this new pluralism, it is important to remember that New Brunswick has had a long history of negotiating the class, ethnic, linguistic, and cultural tensions attendant in a postcolonial space. The class struggles that emerged, almost as soon as Loyalist boats grated against the rocky shores of the Fundy coast, were intensified by the waves of Irish immigration in the early and mid-nineteenth century, making Saint John not only a deeply ethnic but also a deeply divided urban landscape. Indeed, even though the education system did not formalize segregation, various religious, ethnic, and cultural differences divided the province to the point where separate religious schools were the norm in the province until late in the twentieth century. Linguistic and cultural differences are even more pronounced when considering the long divide between the Acadian community, which had settled the north and east of New Brunswick after the Great Disruption of 1755–1762, and the Loyalist-Anglo cultures that immigrated to the south and west after the American Revolution. Nowhere else in Canada have the two founding languages coexisted and struggled in such close proximity and for such a sustained period. The different and diverse communities of the province have expended enormous energy preserving, articulating, celebrating, and defending their own unique historical and cultural experiences, but the province as a whole has never knit their stories into a larger overriding narrative. As a result, there are no tourism strategies that have unified the province under a single ethnic banner or narrative, as is the case with Nova Scotia's investment in "tartanism" and Prince Edward Island's rebranding of the province around the icon of Anne of Green Gables. Rather, New Brunswick communities have fostered a host of different and sometimes conflicting forms of cultural and political expression. It is not possible for a single New Brunswick identity to materialize. Instead, as a kind a precursor to the larger nation's own experience, New Brunswick incubated a series of unique narratives that articulate the passions and concerns of single communities within a diverse society of similarly vibrant groups. And if these groups have been cohabiting rather peacefully for a generation, it does not mean that there are, even now, multiple points of connection between them. During each of the many meetings that went into the creation of this collection, the scholars noted, without fail, that it was refreshing, but unusual, for us all to be working together. Such has been the provincial legacy of interconnected isolation.

Compression/concentration and opposition/advocacy lie at the root of our pluralist province and are the anchors of ferment, but in each of the five chapters in this collection it is also evident that literary productivity did not emerge by looking only within the borders of the local experience. Writers within each of the periods of literary ferment in New Brunswick also looked outward in cosmopolitan fashion beyond their geographical and imaginative boundaries. In fact, none of the writers discussed in this volume has felt provincial. And none has hesitated to move beyond the local to seek insight from the *aesthetic codes* that were emerging in other centres. The literature from New Brunswick has always sought to capture the local context, but the forms and techniques used to articulate that context and experience were always informed by the emerging aesthetics of the larger world. Loyalist poets were deeply embedded in the aesthetics of Neoclassicism and the philosophy of the Enlightenment, for example, and they turned to these familiar philosophic assumptions and literary models to forge their own work. Goldsmith explicitly invokes his uncle as a muse when he describes the emerging settler community in *The Rising Village*. Huyghue, as Davies points out, likewise employed the established American conventions of the captivity narrative to structure his novel *Argimou: A Legend of the Micmac*. Parkin introduced the Confederation poets to Tennyson, Swinburne, and Rossetti, and thus launched Roberts and Carman into the stream of Victorian poetry that carried the Romantic overtones for which both men longed. Looking beyond their borders provided the Fredericton poets with the aesthetic models they needed to more fully explore their local circumstances. As Malcolm Ross argues in "Poets of the Confederation," if Roberts and his cohort were "thoroughgoing provincials (with a feeling for place)," they were also "thoroughgoing citizens of the world (with a feeling for time)" (89). In the first decades of the twentieth century, Ted Campbell also insisted, as Tremblay suggests in his chapter above, that "localism must be schooled in the latest European and American art theory." John Hammond turned against Post-Impressionism and employed the methods of the Boston Museum School of Art, Elizabeth Holt taught classical form to Campbell and Brittain, and Bailey admitted that, for him, Eliot's *The Waste Land* was an aesthetically transformative model. Indeed, as Tremblay notes, the circle of writers that surrounded Campbell were pouring over Ibsen, Mansfield, Woolf, Laurence, Eliot, Pound, and Yeats.

For the francophonie of the late nineteenth century, aesthetics were developed solely within a Catholicism that admitted the classical forms of tragedy and comedy into the canon, but forbade the new social realist, naturalist, and symbolist styles from taking root in local soil. Such narrow options facilitated the growth of some ideals, but also hampered other artistic possibilities. More varied were the many modernist and postmodernist aesthetics made available to the Acadian writers of the second Renaissance who employed techniques developed elsewhere to capture both the collective and subjective experiences of Acadian resistance. From Antonine Maillet's well-known use of Rabelaisian orality and the carnivalesque to Herménégilde Chiasson's visual and poetic postmodern experiments, a wider aesthetic range liberated contemporary Acadian writers. In all cases, however, New Brunswickers eagerly looked outward to learn about the currents guiding European and North American artists, and they sought aesthetic codes that allowed them to tell their own stories in fresh and original ways. Indeed, as the aesthetic code is localized, it is itself refreshed and transformed into something different. The Fredericton poets at the time of Confederation fused a Romantic interest in the natural world with a Victorian anxiety about mutability and loss, developing an aesthetic that borrowed but transformed what had been adopted. Similarly, the postmodern urban writers of the second Acadian Renaissance have taken an aesthetic that at its core problematizes questions of identity, but they use it to articulate the plural conditions that underlie the uniquely Acadian experience of the late twentieth century.

These three recurring forces that generate the conditions necessary for literary ferment still ultimately depend on imaginative women and men who are fortunate enough to optimize circumstances. A sustained and transformative period of ferment is possible only if these *imaginative individuals* join together to work, however informally, as a *collective*. Occasionally, individuals emerge and stand alone as singular and interesting figures; they prove to be innovative or even transformative, but they still may not spur a new wave of subsequent writers. James De Mille was one such figure. Born in Saint John, he was a professor at Acadia University and Dalhousie University and his more than twenty-five novels were mostly published in the 1870s. Releasing a variety of texts ranging from adventure tales for boys to historical romances and satirical novels for adults, De Mille's fiction fed a popular market but did not seem tied to (or did not influence) a New Brunswick school of writing. Indeed, his best-known novel, the posthumously published dystopian satire *A Strange Manuscript Found in a Copper Cylinder*, was without precedent, and certainly no other writer in New Brunswick has since produced its like.

Another singular voice emerged in the person of Lorne Simon, the region's first Mi'kmaq novelist. Simon was born and raised in the Elsipogtog First Nation, on the Richibucto River of New Brunswick, and his 1994 novel *Stones and Switches* chronicles the struggles of a young Mi'kmaq man, Megwadesk, as he navigates the tensions between the traditional practices and beliefs of his community and the demands and pressures of twentieth-century culture. Set in the early 1930s, at the same time as the opening of the Shubenacadie Indian Residential School in Nova Scotia was threatening the integrity of Mi'kmaw culture, Megwadesk is tempted to abandon his Indigenous heritage and seek economic security in Anglo-European practices. In the course of the novel, he discovers that he can fuse the spiritual and dream worlds of his Mi'kmaw identity with the realist conventions of his Western experience and secure his position as new father and husband: "I had this feeling, like I could make my dream real, like I could pull it into this world" (129). Lorne Simon recognized that he was a lone voice from his community and hoped to be a harbinger of a future writing community: "Currently there are hardly any Micmac writers who are vigorously taking part in this effort, yet I am sure that I will be setting an example and that others will follow. What I am doing is a ripple emanating from a pearl thrown into the pool of talent. Keep throwing pearls into the pool, for they are not wasted" (Simon, "Letter"). Simon's untimely death in a car accident, just before his novel was published, ended his promising career. Simon's voice has been heard and Mi'kmaq writers in the region continue to publish, but we still await the collective wave that Simon expected to coalesce.

Finally, David Adams Richards's situation is oddly singular. He initially followed a conventional path: he went to university, joined a circle of writers at the University of New Brunswick's Ice-House, and began to produce realist fiction about his home town. However, Richards carved a distinct path for himself, quite unlike the other writers of the Miramichi who often draw from a more pastoral, nostalgic, and even comic vein. More a maverick than a member, Richards would be hard to pin to a particular moment of literary ferment, generating as he does a singular moral vision of the world. Unique voices, then, always emerge, but the periods of literary ferment that this collection examines—the literary shifts that shape and reshape the way the people of the province have imagined themselves—are more sustainable if numerous artists align themselves with the central concerns of the period. When communities form, they do so not to speak from a single perspective, but to explore the multiple possibilities a period of ferment allows. Periods of literary ferment have short half-lives, but within the one or two decades of peak productivity, a whole cultural shift can be negotiated.

For many writers, being part of an interconnected cohort proves to be encouraging, productive, and necessary. Forming a network to encourage new talent and challenge/renovate old practices is often an essential part of the growth of a literary culture. For example, in the circle of Fredericton poets who reached their productive peak in the 1890s, Charles G.D. Roberts existed in the centre. His role as encourager, editor, promoter, anthologist, educator, and sometime-publisher lent immediate and practical support to all the poets and writers around him. But if he was the leading light, he also benefited from the interconnected group, finding in the others a critical audience, fresh ideas, and a forum to test his ever-evolving and changing artistic vision. Similarly, if Campbell and Bailey were the leading figures of their respective groups, they clearly drew strength and inspiration from the other artists around them. In his chapter above, Tremblay records Fred Ross's observation that Campbell "gave one the feeling that it was possible to be an artist, which probably wouldn't have occurred to most of us." It is that kind of mutual encouragement that allowed artistic communities to emerge and accomplish more as a collective than was possible for their members to achieve alone. Indeed, the two Acadian renaissances were inherently and deeply collectivist. Chantal Richard notes that Fred Cogswell expressed reservations about the potentially limiting power of the collective ideology of renaissance embedded in the first wave of Acadian writers; Richard counters, however, that these road maps provided direction and structure to young writers. She shows that as the collective of Acadian writers developed, it allowed a sustained narrative of resistance to emerge as the literature moved from oral to classical models. Indeed, the foundational Acadian trope of naming local places and embedding literature in locale speaks to the importance of individual writers both affirming and anchoring their work in the collective knowledge of their communities. The importance of collectivity is perhaps best captured, if unconsciously, by the subtitles that Marie-Linda Lord has used in her chapter to track the evolution of the second Acadian Renaissance. Her subtitles all hint at a tension between the individual artist and the collective experience that defines and supports each: "Crisis of Values," "Huge Conspiracy," "Post-Nationalism and Existentialism," and "The City: Attraction and Fear." At the heart of every period of literary ferment, individual talent is the driving factor, but the artistic communities are often shaping and sustaining influences that guide a single writer's effort into a larger and more compelling vision. The literary periods of ferment become part of the cultural work that has helped shape and define New Brunswick as a distinct and even pioneering social space.

NEW BRUNSWICK: A SILENT AND MULTI-VOCAL PLACE

In the records of Statistics Canada, New Brunswick is a small province. In terms of geographical size, annual income, educational achievement, health, and most other measures, New Brunswick is always in the lower ranks of comparatives. Moreover, as Tremblay notes at the beginning of this collection, the province is the least studied and least understood part of the nation, with few analyses of its culture having been produced in the previous three decades. But what exactly is the story of New Brunswick that critics and scholars should be telling?

In one way, a review of the literary history of this province would be a study of the cultures that have emerged from conditions that are sometimes isolated, occasionally claustrophobic, and always intensely localized. The size and influence of the province relative to the nation makes that inevitable. Also, the differences between the unique groups and sectors of the province have always been great. The groups and events that have shaped the anglophone community vary widely as Planter, Loyalist, Scot, Irish, Jewish, and Western and Eastern European settlers have emigrated and integrated into the social and cultural fabric. The cultural experiences of anglophone New Brunswickers are distinguished further by regional specificity, ethnicity, race, class, and gender. By contrast, Acadian cultural identity seems to be more collectively defined, though, as this study has demonstrated, clear differences emerge that define individual Acadian experience as rural/urban, working class/elite, northern/southeastern, and masculine/feminine. In truth, New Brunswick has been home to a host of different identities over the centuries and no overriding narrative or binding imagery has emerged to define this space. Powerful literary texts have emerged. Compelling poets, novelists, playwrights, and essayists have expressed their views and represented their experiences, but always there remains a large blank space ready for the next writer to fill. Nevertheless, since the first period of literary ferment emerged from within the Loyalist community, a series of productive moments have unfolded in similar ways and sometimes in parallel with each other. Those moments of cultural productivity, however, do not presage how artistic communities will evolve, and rarely have critics predicted when or how the next shifts will occur. In this sense, there has emerged, to borrow from Benedict Anderson, a number of imagined communities across the province with no single narrative accounting for those identity constructions. For example, Acadians have found in literature a number of powerful figures who are voices for their communities and coexist with each other, even as they represent very different versions of what it means to belong to Acadie. Evangeline, La Sagouine, and Pélagie-la-Charette now live in our imaginations as three unlikely sisters, and we know that in the future yet another redefining figure will likely emerge to join this complicated family. As Marie-Linda Lord has noted, the province's literary matrix has always allowed for these multiple voices.

Despite its statistically diminished standing, then, New Brunswick's cultural identity has always been expansive. Each period of literary ferment has been concentrated, cosmopolitan, and able to reach out, engage with, and contribute to national and international conversations. From the outset, writers have taken the vocabularies from local experiences and anxieties and blended those with the syntax of the aesthetics they learned from others. In taking the forms and styles from elsewhere and repurposing those forms, New Brunswick writers have created a unique creative language of their own bent to their particular local needs. In their article "Linguistic Schizophrenia: The Poetics of Acadian Identity Construction," J.P. Boudreau and Irene Gammel define a process of linguistic formation—specifically, the incubation of the distinct Acadian language Chiac—that is paradigmatic of the larger New Brunswick cultural operation. Drawing on the work of Shana Poplack, Boudreau and Gammel describe the process of code-switching, which facilitates "the juxtaposition of sentences or sentence fragments [from different languages], each of which is internally consistent with the morphological and syntactic ... rules of the language of its provenance" (53). Acadian Chiac, they suggest, emerged through a process of "borrowing," that is, "a conversational pattern of language mixing whereby lexical material is adapted and incorporated into the recipient language" (53). While some anxious linguists have read the emergence of Chiac as a sign of cultural loss and instability—"linguistically, urban language mixing can be seen as a symptom of the minority culture's alienation and colonization" (53)—Boudreau and Gammel read the emergence of a blended language as a signal of the culture's creativity: "Identity construction defies the notion of a unified front within the larger francophonie and highlights difference and fragmentation.... Acadia shares important features with Canadian identity construction. Canada is often theorized as a culture in process involving negotiating and testing, and as a result, experiencing a precarious lack of a clearly defined identity" (54).

In this sense, all literature in New Brunswick, both English and French, is and has always been written in Chiac. Our literary texts, from the outset, have been inherently pluralist and transcultural, and even if our blend of the local and cosmopolitan sounds easily on the ears of others, it is, nonetheless, a simulacrum of the bricolage that has come to define not only the province but also the nation itself.

Considered in that light, the literary culture of New Brunswick is not shadowed or silent. Our culture is not an empty signifier. To the contrary, it is a field of language in flux that has escaped the overdetermining power of neoliberal marketers and still awaits investigation by the curious. The province's literary history and its periods of ferment have been a recurring series of assertions and claims that have been unpredictable and uneven, but this instability has been and will continue to be productive. The culture at the root of these assertions is complex, multilingual, and multi-vocal, and it has anticipated the rhythms of the larger nation of which it is a part, even before the nation as a whole sensed that this is where we were going. Our past and pioneering periods of literary ferment speak the promise of equally potent moments to come.

WORKS CITED

Abell, Walter. "Jack Humphrey, Painter." *Canadian Forum* (June 1936): 16–18.

———. *Representation and Form: A Study of Aesthetic Values in Representational Art.* New York, NY: Scribner's, 1936.

"Acadians (1752 to 1784): Table of the French Acadian population from 1749 to 1771." Statistics Canada: Censuses of Canada 1665 to 1871. http://www.statcan.gc.ca/pub/98-187-x/4064810-eng.htm

Acheson, T.W. Introduction to *The Economic History of the Maritime Provinces,* by S.A. Saunders, 5–14. Fredericton, NB: Acadiensis, 1984.

Action Plan to Transform Post-Secondary Education in New Brunswick. Fredericton, NB: Province of New Brunswick, 2008.

Adams, John Coldwell. *Sir Charles God Damn: The Life of Sir Charles G.D. Roberts.* Toronto, ON: University of Toronto Press, 1986.

Album historique publié à l'occasion des fêtes du 75e anniversaire 13–14 juin 1939 / Historical Album Published on the Occasion of the 75th Anniversary June 13–14, 1939. Memramcook, NB: Université Saint-Joseph/St. Joseph's University, 1939.

L'Album souvenir des noces d'argent de la Société Saint-Jean-Baptiste du Collège Saint-Joseph. Memramcook, NB: Collège Saint-Joseph, 1893–1894.

Allain, Greg, Isabelle McKee-Allain, and Joseph Yvon Thériault. "La société acadienne: lectures et conjonctures." In *L'Acadie des Maritimes,* edited by Jean Daigle, 341–85. Moncton, NB: Institut d'études acadiennes, 1993.

Anderson, Benedict. *Imagined Communities: Reflections on the Origin and Spread of Nationalism.* 1983. London, UK: Verso, 2006.

WORKS CITED

Andrew, Sheila. "Mother's helper? Factors Affecting the Feminization of Teaching in New Brunswick Acadian Public Schools, 1861–1881." In *L'Acadie au féminin: un regard multidisciplinaire sur les Acadiennes et les Cadiennes,* edited by M. Basque, I. McKee-Allain, L. Cardinal, P.E. LeBlanc, and J.L. Pallister, 45–69. Moncton, NB: Institut d'études acadiennes, 2000.

L'Annuaire UNJ, Collège de St. Joseph. Memramcook. 1878–89, 9–16. Montréal, QC: Eusebe Sénécal, 1879.

Appadurai, Arjun. *Modernity at Large: Cultural Dimensions of Globalization.* Minneapolis, MN: University of Minnesota Press, 1996.

Armstrong, Sally. *The Nine Lives of Charlotte Taylor.* Toronto, ON: Vintage Canada, 2007.

Armstrong, Tammy. "Sherman, Francis Joseph." In *New Brunswick Literary Encyclopedia,* edited by Tony Tremblay. St. Thomas University, 2011– . http://w3.stu.ca/stu/sites/nble/s/sherman_francis_joseph.html

"The Art Exhibition." *Daily Telegraph* (Saint John, NB), March 23, 1887, 3.

Bailey, Alfred G. "Address." n.d. Alfred G. Bailey Collection. TS. UA RG80. Case 89, file 1. Archives and Special Collections, University of New Brunswick Libraries, Fredericton.

———. "The Basis and Persistence of Opposition to Confederation in New Brunswick." *Canadian Historical Review* 23, no. 4 (1942): 374–97.

———. "Creative Moments in the Culture of the Maritime Provinces." 1949. In *Culture and Nationality,* 44–57. Toronto, ON: McClelland & Stewart, 1972.

———. *Culture and Nationality.* Toronto, ON: McClelland & Stewart (Carleton Library No. 58), 1972.

———. "d'Avray, Marshall De Brett Maréchal, Joseph." In *Dictionary of Canadian Biography.* Vol. 10. University of Toronto/Université Laval, 2003–. http://www.biographi.ca/en/bio/marshall_de_brett_marechal_joseph_10E.html

———. "Early Foundations, 1783–1829." In *University of New Brunswick Memorial Volume,* edited by Alfred G. Bailey, 15–21. Fredericton, NB: University of New Brunswick, 1950.

———. "The Fiddlehead." *The Fiddlehead* 1 (February 1945): 1.

———. Foreword to *Minutes of the Bliss Carman Society of Fredericton,* n.p. Fredericton, NB: Harriet Irving Library, [1940?].

———. Introduction to *The Development of the Theory and Practice of Education in New Brunswick, 1784–1900,* by Katherine F.C. MacNaughton, 1–2. Fredericton, NB: University of New Brunswick Historical Studies, 1947.

———. "Literary Memories, Part II." 1974. Alfred G. Bailey Collection. TS UA RG80. Box 108, file 3. Archives and Special Collections, University of New Brunswick Libraries, Fredericton.

WORKS CITED

———. "Literature and Nationalism in the Aftermath of Confederation." *University of Toronto Quarterly* 25 (July 1956): 409–24.

———. "Miramichi Lightning." In *Border River*, by A.G. Bailey, 16. Toronto: McClelland & Stewart, 1952.

———. "Overture to Nationhood." In *Literary History of Canada. Vol. 1: Canadian Literature in English*, 2nd ed., edited by Carl F. Klinck, 69–81. Toronto, ON: University of Toronto Press, 1976.

Baker, Ray Palmer. *A History of English-Canadian Literature to the Confederation.* Cambridge, MA: Harvard University Press, 1920.

Bannerji, Himani. *The Dark Side of Nation: Essays on Multiculturalism, Nationalism and Gender.* Toronto, ON: Canadian Scholars' Press, 2000.

Barkley, Murray. "The Loyalist Tradition in New Brunswick: The Growth and Evolution of an Historical Myth: 1825–1914." *Acadiensis* 4, no. 2 (Spring 1975): 3–45.

Basque, Maurice, and Amélie Giroux. "Dossier 150 ans du Collège Saint-Joseph." *Bulletin* 122 (Fall 2013): 8–15.

Bates, Walter. *Henry More Smith. The Mysterious Stranger.* Fredericton, NB: Non-Entity Press, 1975.

———. *The Mysterious Stranger, or, Memoirs of Henry More Smith, alias Henry Frederick Moon, alias William Newman, who is now confined in Simsbury Mines, in Connecticut, for the crime of burglary: containing an account of his extraordinary conduct during his confinement in the goal of King's County, province of New-Brunswick, where he was under sentence of death: with a statement of his succeeding conduct, before and since his confinement in Newgate.* New Haven, CT: Maltby, Goldsmith & Co, 1817.

Beavan, Mrs. F. *Sketches and Tales Illustrative of Life in the Backwoods of New Brunswick, North America.* London, UK: George Routledge, 1845.

Belier, Patricia L. "Brunswick Press." In *New Brunswick Literary Encyclopedia*, edited by Tony Tremblay. St. Thomas University, 2011– . http://w3.stu.ca/stu/sites/nble/b/brunswisk_press.html

Bell, D.G. *Early Loyalist Saint John: The Origin of New Brunswick Politics, 1783–1786.* Fredericton, NB: New Ireland Press, 1983.

———. *Loyalist Rebellion in New Brunswick: A Defining Conflict for Canada's Political Culture.* Halifax, NS: Formac, 2013.

Bennett, Donna. "Getting Beyond Boundaries: Polybridity in Contemporary Canadian Literature." In *Moveable Margins: The Shifting Spaces of Canadian Literature*, edited by Chelva Kanaganayakam, 9–26. Toronto, ON: TSAR, 2005.

Bentley, D.M.R. "50 Years—The UNB Arts Centre." *Arts Atlantic* 41 (Fall 1991): 44–45.

———. "Charles G.D. Roberts's Use of 'Indian Legend' in Four Poems of the Eighteen Eighties and 'Nineties." *Canadian Poetry* 51 (Fall/Winter 2002): 18–38.

WORKS CITED

———. *The Confederation Group of Canadian Poets, 1880–1897*. Toronto, ON: University of Toronto Press, 2004.

———, ed. *The Essays and Reviews of Archibald Lampman*. London, ON: Canadian Poetry, 1996.

———. "Oliver Goldsmith and *The Rising Village*." *Studies in Canadian Literature/ Études en Littérature Canadienne* 15, no. 1 (1990): 21–61.

———. "Reflections on the Situation and Study of Early Canadian Literature in the Long Confederation Period." In *Home Ground and Foreign Territory: Essays on Early Canadian Literature*, edited by Janice Fiamengo, 17–43. Ottawa, ON: University of Ottawa Press, 2014.

Bersianik, Louky, Nicole Brossard, Louise Cotnoir, Louise Dupré, Gail Scott, and France Théorie. *La Théorie, un dimanche*. Montréal, QC: Les Éditions du Remue-ménage, 1988.

Birney, Earle. "As I Remember: 1926–1937." In *Spreading Time: Remarks on Canadian Writing and Writers. Book 1: 1904–1949*, by E. Birney, 24–30. Montréal, QC: Véhicule, 1980.

Blatch, George. "Mr. Blatch's Lecture on 'Common Errors.'" *Amaranth* 3 (February 1843): 48–61.

Book of Common Prayer. Toronto, ON: Anglican Book Centre, 1959.

Boone, Laurel. "Roberts, George Goodridge." In *Dictionary of Canadian Biography*. Vol. 13. University of Toronto/Université Laval, 2003– . http://www.biographi.ca/en/bio/roberts_george_goodridge_13E.html

Boudreau, J.P., and Irene Gammel. "Linguistic Schizophrenia: The Poetics of Acadian Identity Construction." *Journal of Canadian Studies* 32, no. 4 (1998): 52–68.

Boudreau, Raoul. "Poetry as Action." Introduction to *Unfinished Dreams: Contemporary Poetry of Acadie*, edited by Fred Cogswell and Jo-Anne Elder, xvii–xxvii. Fredericton, NB: Goose Lane, 1990.

Boudreau, Raoul, and Marguerite Maillet. "Acadian Literature." In *Acadia of the Maritimes*, edited by Jean Daigle, 679–719. Moncton, NB: Chaire d'études acadiennes, 1995.

Boudreau, Raoul, and Jean Morency, eds. *Le postmoderne acadien*. Special issue, *Tangence* 58 (October 1998).

Boudreau, Raoul, and Mylène White. "Gérald Leblanc: écrivain cartographe." In *Paysages imaginaires d'Acadie. Atlas littéraire*, edited by Marie-Linda Lord and Denis Bourque, 40–55. Moncton, NB: Chaire d'études acadiennes, 2009.

Bourque, André-Thadée. *Chez les Anciens Acadiens (Causeries du Grand-Père Antoine)*. Moncton, NB: Presses de L'Évangéline, 1911.

Bourque, Denis. "Le nationalisme acadien et l'émergence de la littérature acadienne (1875–1957)." *Journal of New Brunswick Studies/Revue d'études sur le Nouveau-Brunswick* 6, no. 2 (2015): 48–67.

WORKS CITED

———. "Représentations identitaires des Acadiens et des Acadiennes dans les Conventions nationales acadiennes (1881–1937)." Paper presented at the Atlantic Canada Studies Conference, St. Thomas University, Fredericton, NB, May 3, 2014.

Bourque, Denis, and Denise Merkle. "De 'Evangeline' à l'américaine à 'Évangéline' à l'acadienne: une transformation idéologique?" In *Traduire depuis les marges/Translating from the Margins,* edited by Denise Merkle, Jane Koustas, Glen Nichols, and Sherry Simon, 121–45. Montréal, QC: Éditions Nota Bene, 2008.

Bourque, Denis, and Chantal Richard. *Les conventions nationales acadiennes.* Vol. 1 (1881–1890). Moncton, NB: Institut d'études acadiennes, 2013.

Bradbury, Malcolm. *The Social Context of Modern English Literature.* New York, NY: Schocken, 1971.

Bradley, Rhonda J. "Making a Place: The Life and Work of Lucy Jarvis as Cultural Educator and Community Catalyst in Atlantic Canada." M.A. thesis, Carleton University, 1997.

Brandon, Laura. *Pegi by Herself: The Life of Pegi Nicol MacLeod.* Montreal & Kingston: McGill-Queen's University Press, 2005.

Brison, Jeffrey D. "The Kingston Conference, the Carnegie Corporation and a New Deal for the Arts in Canada." *American Review of Canadian Studies* 23, no. 4 (Winter 1993): 503–22.

———. *Rockefeller, Carnegie, and Canada: American Philanthropy and the Arts and Letters in Canada.* Montreal & Kingston: McGill-Queen's University Press, 2005.

Brückner, Martin. "Geography, Reading, and the World of Novels in the Early Republic." In *Early America Re-Explored: New Readings in Colonial, Early National, and Antebellum Culture,* edited by Klaus H. Schmidt and Fritz Fleischmann, 385–410. New York, NY: Peter Lang, 2000.

Brydon, Diana. "Metamorphoses of a Discipline: Rethinking Canadian Literature within Institutional Contexts." In *Trans.Can.Lit: Resituating the Study of Canadian Literature,* edited by Smaro Kamboureli and Roy Miki, 1–15. Waterloo, ON: Wilfrid Laurier University Press, 2007.

———. "Negotiating Belonging in Global Times: The Hérouxville Debates." In *Crosstalk: Canadian and Global Imaginaries in Dialogue,* edited by Diana Brydon and Marta Dvořák, 253–71. Waterloo, ON: Wilfrid Laurier University Press, 2007.

Brydon, Diana, and Marta Dvořák, eds. *Crosstalk: Canadian and Global Imaginaries in Dialogue.* Waterloo, ON: Wilfrid Laurier University Press, 2012.

Bumsted, J.M. "Loyalists and Nationalists: An Essay on the Problem of Definitions." *Canadian Review of Studies in Nationalism* 2 (Fall 1979): 218–32.

Butler, Marilyn. *Romantics, Rebels and Reactionaries: English Literature and Its Background 1760–1830.* Oxford, UK: Oxford University Press, 1981.

Cairncross, Frances. *The Death of Distance: How the Communications Revolution Is Changing Our Lives.* Boston, MA: Harvard Business School, 1997.

Calder, Alison. "Reassessing Prairie Realism." In *A Sense of Place: Re-Evaluating Regionalism in Canadian and American Writing*, edited by Christian Riegel and Herb Wyile, 51–60. Edmonton, AB: University of Alberta Press, 1998.

Calder, Alison, and Robert Wardhaugh, eds. *History, Literature, and the Writing of the Canadian Prairies*. Winnipeg, MB: University of Manitoba Press, 2005.

Cameron, Elspeth. *Irving Layton: A Portrait*. Toronto, ON: Stoddart, 1985.

Campbell, Charles. "Loyalist Day." *St. John (NB) Daily Sun*, May 19, 1904, 5.

Campbell, Wanda. *Hidden Rooms: Early Canadian Women Poets*. London, ON: Canadian Poetry Press, 2000.

Careless, J.M.S. "Aspects of Metropolitanism in Atlantic Canada." In *Regionalism in the Canadian Community, 1867–1967*, edited by Mason Wade, 117–29. Toronto, ON: University of Toronto Press, 1969.

———. *Frontier and Metropolis: Regions, Cities, and Identities in Canada before 1914*. Toronto, ON: University of Toronto Press, 1989.

———. "Frontierism, Metropolitanism, and Canadian History." In *Approaches to Canadian History*, edited by Ramsay Cook, Craig Brown, and Carl Berger, 63–83. Toronto, ON: University of Toronto Press, 1970.

Carman, Bliss. Review of *The Algonquin Legends of New England*, by Charles G. Leland. *University Monthly* 4, no. 2 (November 1884): 28.

———. *Letters of Bliss Carman*, edited by H. Pearson Gundy. Montreal & Kingston: McGill-Queen's University Press, 1981.

———. *Low Tide on Grand Pré: A Book of Lyrics*. New York, NY: Charles L. Webster, 1893.

———. "Sir George R. Parkin," *Daily Province*, August 31, 1922, 24.

———. Review of *Winter Sunshine*, by John Burroughs. *University Monthly* 4, no. 8 (May 1885): 123–24.

Carman, Bliss, and Richard Hovey. *Songs from Vagabondia*. Boston, MA: Copeland and Day, 1894.

Carpenter, Humphrey. *A Serious Character: The Life of Ezra Pound*. New York, NY: Delta, 1988.

Catta, Étienne. *Le Révérend Père Camille Lefebvre et la renaissance acadienne*. Vols. 1, 2, 3. Saint-Joseph, NB: Province acadienne des Pères de Sainte-Croix, 1983.

Chamard, Maurice, Anselme Chiasson, Clément Cormier, and Hector Léger. *Le Père Camille Lefebvre, C.S.C.* Montréal, QC: Fides, 1998.

Cheadle, Norman, and Lucien Pelletier, eds. *Canadian Cultural Exchange/Échanges Culturels au Canada: Translation and Transculturation/Traduction et Transculturation*. Waterloo, ON: Wilfrid Laurier University Press, 2007.

Chiasson, Herménégilde. "Des Années soixante-dix à aujourd'hui." In *Cause célèbre. 25 ans à la Galerie Sans Nom*, 7–8. Moncton, NB: Galerie Sans Nom Coop., 2003.

———. "Traversées." *Tangence* 58 (October 1998): 77–92.

———. "Une Acadie triangulaire: Essai de géo-esthétique." *Journal of New Brunswick Studies/Revue d'Études sur le Nouveau-Brunswick* 1 (2010): 29–41.

Chiasson, Zénon. "Acadian Theatre: A Cultural Institution." In *Acadia of the Maritimes*, edited by Jean Daigle, 721–56. Moncton, NB: Chaire d'études acadiennes, 1995.

Christian, William. *Parkin: Canada's Most Famous Forgotten Man*. Toronto, ON: Blue Butterfly, 2008.

Les 50 Ans du Collège Sainte-Anne. n.d. Fonds Université Sainte-Anne. MG1. Boîte 38, dossier 284. Centre acadien, Church Point.

Clarke, Patrick D. "Régions et régionalisme en Acadie. Culture, espace, appartenance." *Recherches sociographiques* 13, no. 2 (2000): 299–365.

Cody, H.A. *The King's Arrow: A Tale of the United Empire Loyalists*. Toronto, ON: McClelland & Stewart, 1922.

Cogswell, Frederick. "Bates, Walter." In *Dictionary of Canadian Biography*. Vol. 7 (1836–1850), 53–54. Toronto, ON: University of Toronto Press, 1988.

———. "English Poetry in New Brunswick Before 1880." In *A Literary and Linguistic History of New Brunswick*, edited by R. Gair et al., 107–15. Fredericton, NB: Fiddlehead & Goose Lane, 1985.

———. "Literary Traditions in New Brunswick." *Transactions of the Royal Society of Canada*. Ser. 4, vol. 15 (1977): 287–99.

———. "The Maritime Provinces (1720–1880)." In *Literary History of Canada*. Vol. 1, *Canadian Literature in English*. 2nd ed., edited by Carl F. Klinck, 85–97. Toronto, ON: University of Toronto Press, 1976.

———. "Modern Acadian Poetry." *Canadian Literature* 68–69 (Spring 1976): 62–75.

———. "New Brunswick." *A Long Apprenticeship: Collected Poems*, 12. Fredericton, NB: Fiddlehead Poetry Books, 1980.

Cohen, Daniel A. *Pillars of Salt, Monuments of Grace: New England Crime Literature and the Origins of American Popular Culture, 1674–1860*. New York, NY: Oxford University Press, 1993.

Coleman, Daniel. *White Civility: The Literary Project of English Canada*. Toronto, ON: University of Toronto Press, 2008.

Condon, Ann Gorman. *The Loyalist Dream for New Brunswick*. Fredericton, NB: New Ireland Press, 1984.

———, ed. "'Young Robin Hood Society': A Political Satire by Edward Winslow." *Acadiensis* 15, no. 2 (Spring 1986): 120–43.

Conrad, Margaret R., and James K. Hiller. *Atlantic Canada: A Region in the Making*. Don Mills, ON: Oxford University Press, 2001.

Cooney, Robert. *Autobiography of a Wesleyan Methodist Missionary*. Montreal, QC: E. Pickup, 1856.

———. *A Compendious History of the Northern Part of the Province of New Brunswick, and of the District of Gaspe, in Lower Canada*. Halifax, NS: Joseph Howe, 1832.

Cormier, Yves. *Grandir à Moncton*. Moncton, NB: Éditions d'Acadie, 1993.

Creelman, David. *Setting in the East: Maritime Realist Fiction*. Montreal & Kingston: McGill-Queen's University Press, 2003.

Currie, Margaret Catharine Gill. *Gabriel West, and Other Poems*. Fredericton, NB: H.A. Cropley, 1866.

Cuthbertson, Brian. *Stubborn Resistance: New Brunswick Maliseet and Mi'kmaq in Defence of their Lands*. Halifax, NS: Nimbus, 2015.

Daniells, Roy. "Confederation to the First World War." In *Literary History of Canada*. Vol. 1, *Canadian Literature in English*. 2nd ed., edited by Carl F. Klinck, 205–21. Toronto, ON: University of Toronto Press, 1965.

Davies, Gwendolyn. "Currie, Margaret Catharine." In *Dictionary of Canadian Biography*. Vol. 13. University of Toronto/ Université Laval, 2003– . http://www.biographi.ca/en/bio/gill_margaret_catharine_13E.html

———. "Huyghue, Samuel Douglass Smith." In *Dictionary of Canadian Biography*. Vol. 12 (1891–1900), 462–63. Toronto, ON: University of Toronto Press, 2003.

———. *Studies in Maritime Literary History*. Fredericton, NB: Acadiensis Press, 1991.

d'Avray, Marshall. "The Editor's Table." *Head Quarters*, May 10, 1854, 3.

Deichmann, Erica. "Remembrance of Things Past." Special issue, *Kay Smith. Cormorant* 9, no. 2 (1992): 55.

De Mille, James. *Fire in the Woods*. Boston: Lee and Shepard, 1872.

Djwa, Sandra. *Giving Canada a Literary History: A Memoir by Carl F. Klinck*. Montreal & Kingston: McGill-Queen's University Press, 1991.

———. *Journey with No Maps: A Life of P.K. Page*. Montreal & Kingston: McGill-Queen's University Press, 2012.

Dobson, Kit. *Transnational Canadas: Anglo-Canadian Literature and Globalization*. Waterloo, ON: Wilfrid Laurier University Press, 2009.

Donaldson, Marjory. *Art UNB: 1940–1985*. Fredericton, NB: University of New Brunswick, 1985.

Doucet, Philippe. "La politique et les Acadiens." In *Les Acadiens des Maritimes*, edited by Jean Daigle, 235–92. Moncton, NB: Centre d'études acadiennes, 1980.

Dugas, Louis J. "L'alphabétisation des acadiens, 1700–1850." M.A. thesis, University of Ottawa, 1993.

Eliot, T.S. "Tradition and the Individual Talent." In *The Sacred Wood: Essays on Poetry and Criticism*, by T.S. Eliot, 47–59. London, UK: University Paperbacks (Methuen), 1964.

"Everybody remembers ..." *Head Quarters,* October 3, 1866, 2.

"The Faith of Sam Slick." Editorial. *Busy East* 16 (October 1925): 3.

Faragher, John M. *A Great and Noble Scheme: The Tragic Story of the Expulsion of the French Acadians from Their American Homeland.* New York, NY: Norton & Company, 2005.

Findlay, Len. "The Long March to 'Recognition': Sa'ke'j Henderson, First Nations Jurisprudence, and *Sui Generis* Solidarity." In *Shifting the Ground of Canadian Literary Studies,* edited by Smaro Kamboureli and Robert Zacharias, 235–48. Waterloo, ON: Wilfrid Laurier University Press, 2012.

Fingard, Judith. "The 1820s: Peace, Privilege, and the Promise of Progress." In *The Atlantic Region to Confederation: A History,* edited by Phillip A. Buckner and John G. Reid, 263–83. Toronto, ON: University of Toronto Press, 1998.

"First of July." *Head Quarters,* July 3, 1867, 2.

Firth, Frances A. "King's College 1829–1859." In *University of New Brunswick Memorial Volume,* edited by Alfred G. Bailey, 22–32. Fredericton, NB: University of New Brunswick, 1950.

Fisher, Peter. *The Lay of the Wilderness. A Poem in Five Cantos.* By a Native of New Brunswick [pseud.]. Saint John, NB: H. Chubb, 1833.

———. *Notitia of New Brunswick, for 1836, and Extending into 1837.* Saint John, NB: H. Chubb, 1838.

———. *Sketches of New Brunswick. Containing an Account of the First Settlement of the Province. By an Inhabitant of the Province.* Saint John, NB: H. Chubb, 1825.

Fleischmann, Aloys N.M., Nancy Van Styvendale, and Cody McCarroll, eds. *Narratives of Citizenship: Indigenous and Diasporic Peoples Unsettle the Nation-State.* Edmonton, AB: University of Alberta Press, 2011.

Fleming, Patricia Lockhart. *Atlantic Canadian Imprints: A Bibliography: 1801–1820.* Toronto, ON: University of Toronto Press, 1991.

Fleming, Patricia Lockhart, Gilles Gallichan, and Yvan Lamonde, eds. *History of the Book in Canada: Beginnings to 1840.* Vol. 1. Toronto, ON: University of Toronto Press, 2004.

Florida, Richard. *The Rise of the Creative Class.* New York, NY: Basic Books, 2002.

Forbes, Ernie R. *Challenging the Regional Stereotype: Essays on the 20th Century Maritimes.* Fredericton, NB: Acadiensis Press, 1989.

———. *The Maritime Rights Movement, 1919–1927: A Study in Canadian Regionalism.* Montreal & Kingston: McGill-Queen's University Press, 1979.

Forest, Léonard. "Pour parler au monde." *Éloizes* 20/21 (1994): 11–14.

Foster, Walter E. "Justice for the Maritimes." *Busy East* 12 (August 1921): 12.

"Fourth Great Provincial Exhibition." *New Brunswick Reporter and Fredericton Advertiser,* August 19, 1870, 2.

Frost, Sarah. "Extracts from the Diary kept by Sarah Frost on the voyage from New York to St. John N.B. in one of the Loyalists Fleets of 1783." William O. Raymond Collection. Notebook 1, file 17-1. New Brunswick Museum, Saint John.

"The Frosting on the Cake." By Literary Chef [pseud.]. *Busy East* 4, no. 3 (October 1913): 42–44.

Frye, Northrop. "Conclusion to a *Literary History of Canada*." 1965. In *The Bush Garden: Essays on the Canadian Imagination*, 215–54. Concord, ON: House of Anansi, 1995.

Fuller, Danielle. *Writing the Everyday: Women's Textual Communities in Atlantic Canada*. Montreal & Kingston: McGill-Queen's University Press, 2004.

Gaeneye. "Life in Saint John. The Speculator." *Amaranth* 1 (August 1841): 223–30.

Gape, John. Letters. *New-Brunswick Courier,* January 5, 1833, 2; January 12, 1833, 2; January 19, 1833, 2; January 26, 1833, 2.

Gaudet, Placide. "Les Auteurs Paternels et Maternels de feu Monsieur Napoléon Bourassa." *La Revue acadienne* 1, no. 1 (January 1917): 12–14.

Georges, Émile. "Fête de l'Assomption. 15 août 1915." In *La Cathédrale Notre-Dame-de-l'Assomption. Monument de la Reconaissance,* by Robert Pichette, 63. Moncton, NB: Chaire d'études acadiennes, 2012.

Gérin, Pierre-M. *Le Glossaire acadien de Pascal Poirier*. Critical edition. Moncton, NB: Éditions d'Acadie/Centre d'études acadiennes, 1993.

Gerson, Carole. *A Purer Taste: The Writing and Reading of Fiction in English in Nineteenth-Century Canada*. Toronto, ON: University of Toronto Press, 1989.

Gibbs, Robert. "English Poetry in New Brunswick, 1940–1982." In *A Literary and Linguistic History of New Brunswick,* edited by R. Gair et al., 125–44. Fredericton, NB: Fiddlehead & Goose Lane, 1985.

———. Introduction to *The New Brunswick Poems of Jonathan Odell,* by Jonathan Odell, v–ix. Kingston, ON: Loyal Colonies Press, 1982.

———. "Portents and Promises." In *Fiddlehead Gold: 50 Years of* The Fiddlehead *Magazine,* edited by Sabine Campbell, Roger Ploude, and Demetres Tryphonopoulos, 11–16. Fredericton, NB: Fiddlehead & Goose Lane, 1995.

———. "Three Decades and a Bit Under the Elms." In *The Atlantic Anthology*. Vol. 3, *Critical Essays,* edited by Terry Whalen, 231–39. Charlottetown, PE: ECW/Ragweed, 1985.

Gilbert, Anne, Michel Bock, and Joseph Yvon Thériault. *Entre lieux et mémoire: l'inscription de la Francophonie canadienne dans la durée*. Ottawa, ON: University of Ottawa Press, 2009.

Godard, Barbara. "Canadian? Literary? Theory?" In *Canadian Literature at the Crossroads of Language and Culture: Selected Essays by Barbara Godard, 1987–2005,* edited by Smaro Kamboureli, 175–200. Edmonton, AB: NeWest, 2008.

Godfrey, W.G. "Glenie, James." In *Dictionary of Canadian Biography*. Vol. 5. University of Toronto/ Université Laval, 2003– . http://www.biographi.ca/en/bio/glenie_james_5E.html

———. "James Glenie and the Politics of Sunbury County." In *People and Place: Studies of Small Town Life in the Maritimes*, edited by Larry McCann, 19–29. Fredericton, NB: Acadiensis Press, 1987.

Godin, Sylvain, and Maurice Basque. *Histoire des Acadiens et des Acadiennes du Nouveau-Brunswick*. Tracadie-Sheila, NB: Éditions La Grande Marée, 2007.

Goldmann, Lucien. "The Sociology of Literature: Status and Problems of Method." *International Social Science Journal* 9, no. 4 (1967): 493–516.

Goldsmith, Oliver. *The Rising Village*. 1825. Edited by Gerald Lynch. London, ON: Canadian Poetry Press, 1989.

———. "The Rising Village." In *Canadian Poetry from the Beginnings Through the First World War*, edited by Carole Gerson and Gwendolyn Davies, 47–66. Toronto, ON: McClelland & Stewart, 2010.

———. *The Rising Village, with Other Poems. By Oliver Goldsmith, a Descendant of the Author of "The Deserted Village."* Saint John, NB: McMillan, 1834.

Grady, Wayne. *On the Eighth Day*. Translation of *Le huitième jour* by Antonine Maillet. Fredericton, NB: Goose Lane, 2006.

Gregg, Milton F. Foreword to *The Development of the Theory and Practice of Education in New Brunswick, 1784–1900*, by Katherine F.C. MacNaughton, edited by A.G. Bailey, n.p. Fredericton, NB: University of New Brunswick Historical Studies, 1947.

Gross, John. *The Rise and Fall of the Man of Letters*. Harmondsworth, UK: Pelican, 1973.

"Growing Prosperity of St. John." Editorial. *The Morning News*, April 28, 1845, 2.

Gubbins, Joseph. *New Brunswick Journals of 1811 and 1813*, edited by Howard Temperley. Fredericton, NB: New Brunswick Heritage Press, 1980.

Gunew, Sneja. *Haunted Nations: The Colonial Dimensions of Multiculturalisms*. New York, NY: Routledge, 2004.

Gwyn, Sandra. "The Newfoundland Renaissance." *Saturday Night* (April 1976): 38–45.

Haché, Bernard. "Les feuilletons littéraires dans les journaux acadiens (1867–1900)." Ph.D. diss., Université de Moncton, 2013.

Hale, Katherine. *Canadian Cities of Romance*. Toronto, ON: McClelland & Stewart, 1922.

Hall, S.K. "[Sir] Charles G[eorge] D[ouglas] Roberts 1860–1943." In *Twentieth-Century Literary Criticism*, Vol. 8, edited by S.K. Hall, 312–30. Detroit, MI: Gale, 1982.

Hamilton, W.D. "Braithwaite, Henry A." *Dictionary of Canadian Biography*. Vol. 15. University of Toronto/Université Laval, 2003– . http://www.biographi.ca/en/bio/braithwaite_henry_a_15E.html

Hare, John, and Jean-Pierre Wallot. "The Business of Printing and Publishing." In *History of the Book in Canada,* Vol. 1, edited by Patricia Lockhart Fleming et al. Toronto, ON: University of Toronto Press, 2004.

Harper, J. Russell. *Christopher Sower, 1754–1799: Notes Collected from Various Sources."* 1953. S-146-6. New Brunswick Museum, Saint John.

———. "Pegi Nicol MacLeod: A Maritime Artist." *Dalhousie Review* 43, no. 1 (Spring 1963): 40–50.

Harvey, D.C. "The Intellectual Awakening of Nova Scotia." *Dalhousie Review* 13 (April 1933): 1–21.

Hautecœur, Jean-Paul. *L'Acadie du discours.* Quebec, QC: Presses de l'Université Laval, 1975.

———. "L'Acadie: ideologies et sociétés." Ph.D. diss., Université Laval, 1972.

Hay, Denys. *The Italian Renaissance in Its Historical Background.* London, UK: Cambridge University Press, 1961.

Headon, Christopher. "The Influence of the Oxford Movement on the Church of England in Eastern and Central Canada." Ph.D. diss., McGill University, 1974.

Hegel, G.W.F. *Hegel's Aesthetics.* Translated by T.M. Knox. Oxford: Clarendon, 1975.

Henderson, James (Sákéj) Youngblood. "First Nations Legal Inheritances in Canada: The Mikmaq Model." *Manitoba Law Journal* 23, no. 1 (1995): 1–31.

———. "Postcolonial Indigenous Legal Consciousness." *Indigenous Law Journal* 1 (2002): 1–56.

Herring, Karen. "Creating a Centre/Recreating the Margin: Ted Campbell and His Studio, Saint John, New Brunswick, in the 1930s and 40s." M.A. thesis, Carleton University, 1993.

High, Steven. "The Forestry Crisis: Public Policy and Richard Florida's Clock of History." *Our Times* 28, no. 6 (March 2010): 27–33.

Hill, Charles. "Interview with Ted Campbell." 29 October 1973. *Canadian Painting in the Thirties.* National Gallery of Canada Collection, LAC. 1–51. Exhibition Records, National Gallery of Canada, Ottawa.

Hodd, Thomas. "Let's Get Creative: The Forgotten Role of Culture in New Brunswick's Quest for Self-Sufficiency." In *Exploring the Dimensions of Self-Sufficiency for New Brunswick,* edited by Michael Boudreau, Peter Toner, Tony Tremblay, 196–209. Fredericton, NB: New Brunswick and Atlantic Studies Research Centre, 2009.

Holy Bible. Authorized King James Version. Glasgow: William Collins, Sons & Co., 1946.

Huyghue, Samuel Douglas Smith. *Argimou: A Legend of the Micmac.* 1842. Sackville, NB: R.P. Bell Library/Mount Allison University, 1977/1979.

Ignatieff, Michael. *The Russian Album.* 1987. New York, NY: Picador, 2001.

Inch, Cassandra. "New Brunswick Reporter and Fredericton Advertiser." In *New Brunswick Literary Encyclopedia,* edited by Tony Tremblay. St. Thomas University, 2011– . http://w3.stu.ca/stu/sites/nble/n/new_brunswick_reporter_and_fredericton_advertiser.html

Innis, Harold Adams. *Changing Concepts of Time.* Toronto, ON: University of Toronto Press, 1952.

Jack, D.R. *Centennial Prize Essay on the History of the City and County of St. John.* Saint John, NB: McMillan, 1883.

Jasanoff, Maya. *Liberty's Exiles: American Loyalists in the Revolutionary World.* New York, NY: Knopf, 2011.

Junius. "A Journey To Fredericton." *Amaranth* 2 (October 1842): 318–20.

Kamboureli, Smaro, ed. *Canadian Literature at the Crossroads of Language and Culture: Selected Essays by Barbara Godard (1987–2005).* Edmonton, AB: NeWest Press, 2008.

Kamboureli, Smaro, and Roy Miki, eds. *Trans.Can.Lit: Resituating the Study of Canadian Literature.* Waterloo, ON: Wilfrid Laurier University Press, 2007.

Kamboureli, Smaro, and Christl Verduyn, eds. *Critical Collaborations: Indigeneity, Diaspora, and Ecology in Canadian Literary Studies.* Waterloo, ON: Wilfrid Laurier University Press, 2014.

Kamboureli, Smaro, and Robert Zacharias, eds. *Shifting the Ground of Canadian Literary Studies.* Waterloo, ON: Wilfrid Laurier University Press, 2012.

Kanaganayakam, Chelva, ed. *Moveable Margins: The Shifting Spaces of Canadian Literature.* Toronto, ON: TSAR, 2005.

———. "Pedagogy and Postcolonial Literature; or, Do We Need a Centre for Postcolonial Studies?" *University of Toronto Quarterly* 73, no. 2 (Spring 2004): 725–38.

The Kino-nda-niimi Collective. *The Winter We Danced: Voices from the Past, the Future, and the Idle No More Movement.* Winnipeg, MB: ARP Books, 2014.

Klinkenberg, Jean-Marie. "Langue et deficit identitaire." In *Les langues du roman. Du plurilinguisme comme stratégie textuelle,* edited by Lise Gauvin, 109–27. Montreal, QC: Presses de l'Université de Montréal, 1999.

Labelle, Ronald. "Tintamarre: a New Acadian 'Tradition.'" *Encyclopedia of French Cultural Heritage in North America.* http://www.ameriquefrancaise.org/en/article-319/Tintamarre:__a_New_Acadian_"Tradition"__.html

Landry, Charles. *The Creative City: A Toolkit for Urban Innovators.* London, UK: Earthscan, 2000.

Landry, Nicolas, and Nicole Lang. *Histoire de l'Acadie.* Québec, QC: Septentrion, 2001.

[Fonds] Landry, Pierre A. Fonds 5.1, dossiers 1–10. Centre d'études acadiennes Anselme-Chiasson, Université de Moncton, Moncton.

WORKS CITED

Lane, M. Travis. "Bailey, Alfred Goldsworthy." In *New Brunswick Literary Encyclopedia*, edited by Tony Tremblay. St. Thomas University, 2011–. http://w3.stu.ca/stu/sites/nble/b/bailey_alfred_goldsworth.html

———. "Interview with Alfred Goldsworthy Bailey, September 1985." September 1985. Alfred G. Bailey Collection. TS. MS4. 4.7.3. Archives and Special Collections, University of New Brunswick Libraries, Fredericton. Reprinted, "An Interview with Alfred Goldsworthy Bailey." *Studies in Canadian Literature/Études en Littérature Canadienne* 11, no. 2 (Fall 1986): 226–45.

Larocque, Peter J. "Fine Intentions: An Account of the Owens Art Institution in Saint John, New Brunswick, 1884–1893." M.A. thesis, University of New Brunswick, 1996.

Leavis, Q.D. *Fiction and the Reading Public*. London, UK: Chatto & Windus, 1965.

Leblanc, Gérald. *Moncton Mantra*. Moncton, NB: Perce-Neige, 1997. Translated by Jo-Anne Elder. Fredericton, NB: Goose Lane, 2001.

LeBlanc, Raymond Guy. *Cri de terre*. Moncton, NB: Éditions d'Acadie, 1972.

———. "Cri de terre [Land Cry]." Translated by Frederick Cogswell and Jo-Anne Elder. *Unfinished Dreams: Contemporary Poetry of Acadie*, edited by Frederick Cogswell and Jo-Anne Elder, 120. Fredericton, NB: Goose Lane, 1990.

Lee, SKY. *Disappearing Moon Café*. Vancouver: Douglas & McIntyre, 1990.

Léger, Antoine. *Une Fleur d'Acadie: un épisode du grand dérangement*. Moncton, NB: Imprimerie acadienne, 1946.

Lighthall, William D., ed. *Songs of the Great Dominion: Voices from the Forests and Waters, the Settlements and Cities of Canada*. London, UK: Walter Scott, 1889.

List of Books Imported by the Society in 1816. Ward Chipman Papers. MG23/D1. Ser. 1, vol. 2. Library and Archives Canada, Ottawa.

A Literary and Linguistic History of New Brunswick, edited by Reavley Gair, with Richard Guerin, Robert Whalen, and Henri-Dominique Paratte. Fredericton, NB: Fiddlehead & Goose Lane, 1985.

Lockwood, Anthony, Jr. "A Map of New Brunswick: Compiled from Actual Surveys and from Documents in the Surveyor General's Office." 1826. Archives, M203-1826q. New Brunswick Museum, Saint John.

Logan, H.J. "Some of the Maritime Problems." *Busy East* 14 (April 1924): 23.

Lord, Marie-Linda. "Identité et urbanité dans la littérature acadienne." In *Regards croisés sur l'histoire et la littérature acadiennes*, edited by Madeleine Frédérick and Serge Jaumain, 67–85. Brussels: Peter Lang, 2006.

———. "L'arrivée en ville' de l'avenir féminin de l'Acadie dans *Les confessions de Jeanne de Valois* d'Antonine Maillet." In *Écrire au féminin au Canada français*, edited by Johanne Melançon, 49–63. Sudbury, ON: Prise de Parole, 2013.

Loriggio, Francesco. "The Question of the Corpus: Ethnicity and Canadian Literature." In *Future Indicative: Literary Theory and Canadian Literature*, edited by John Moss, 53–70. Ottawa, ON: University of Ottawa Press, 1987.

Lukàcs, Georg. *History and Class Consciousness*. 1923. Translated by Rodney Livingstone. Cambridge, MA: MIT Press, 1971.

———. *The Historical Novel*. 1937. Translated by Hannah and Stanley Mitchell. London: Merlin, 1962.

———. *Studies in European Realism*. 1950. London: Merlin, 1962.

MacCallum, Lindsey. "Foster, Annie Harvie (Ross)." In *New Brunswick Literary Encyclopedia*, edited by Tony Tremblay. St. Thomas University, 2011– . http://w3.stu.ca/stu/sites/nble/f/FosterAnnieHarvieRoss.html

McCann, Larry. "'Living a Double Life': Town and Country in the Industrialization of the Maritimes." In *Geographical Perspectives on the Maritime Provinces*, edited by Douglas Day, 93–113. Halifax, NS: St. Mary's University, 1988.

MacDonald, Elizabeth Roberts. *Dream Verses and Others*. Toronto, ON: Copp, Clark, 1906.

———. *Our Little Canadian Cousin*. Boston, MA: L.C. Page, 1904.

Macfarlane, Heather, and Armand Garnet Ruffo, eds. *Introduction to Indigenous Literary Criticism in Canada*. Peterborough, ON: Broadview Press, 2016.

MacFarlane, W.G. *New Brunswick Bibliography: The Books and Writers of the Province*. Saint John, NB: Sun Printing, 1895.

McKay, Ian. *Rebels, Reds, Radicals: Rethinking Canada's Left History*. Toronto, ON: Between the Lines, 2005.

MacLeod, Alistair. *No Great Mischief*. Toronto, ON: McClelland & Stewart, 1999.

McLeod, Neal, ed. *Indigenous Poetics in Canada*. Waterloo, ON: Wilfrid Laurier University Press, 2014.

[MacLeod], Pegi Nicol. "Miller Brittain." *Maritime Art* 1, no. 4 (April 1941): 14–18.

McLuhan, Marshall. *The Gutenberg Galaxy: The Making of Typographic Man*. Toronto, ON: University of Toronto Press, 1962.

MacNaughton, Katherine. *The Development of the Theory and Practice of Education in New Brunswick, 1784–1900*, edited by Alfred G. Bailey. Fredericton, NB: University of New Brunswick Historical Studies, 1947.

MacNutt, W.S. *The Atlantic Provinces: The Emergence of Colonial Society 1712–1857*. 1965. Toronto, ON: McClelland & Stewart, 1972.

———. "Gowan, Robert." In *Dictionary of Canadian Biography*. Vol. 10. University of Toronto/Université Laval, 2003–. http://www.biographi.ca/en/bio/gowan_robert_10E.html

———. *New Brunswick: A History, 1784–1867*. 1963. Toronto, ON: Macmillan, 1984.

Mailhot, Raymond. "La 'Renaissance acadienne' (1864–1888), l'interprétation traditionnelle et *Le Moniteur Acadien*." M.A. thesis, Université de Montréal, 1969.
Maillet, Antonine. *La Sagouine*. Montreal, QC: Leméac, 1971. Translated by Luis de Céspedes. Toronto, ON: Simon & Pierre, 1985.
———. *Le huitième jour*. Montreal, QC: Leméac, 1986.
———. "Rabelais et les traditions populaires en Acadie." Ph.D. diss., Université Laval, 1971.
Maillet, Marguerite. *Histoire de la littérature acadienne: De rêve en rêve*. Moncton, NB: Éditions d'Acadie, 1983.
Maillet, Marguerite, Gérard LeBlanc, and Bernard Émont. *Anthologie de textes littéraires acadiens 1606–1975*. Moncton, NB: Éditions d'Acadie, 1979.
Maxwell, Lilian. *The River St. John and Its Poets*. Sackville, NB: Tribune, 1947.
Médam, Alain. *Montréal interdite*. Montreal, QC: Liber, 2004.
Meyrowitz, Joshua. *No Sense of Place: The Impact of Electronic Media on Social Behavior*. New York, NY: Oxford University Press, 1985.
"Mille vies" (Thèmes). Bibliothèques publiques de Montréal. http://bibliomontreal.com/1000-vies/?p=2829&pageint=theme
Miller, Muriel. *Bliss Carman: Quest and Revolt*. St. John's, NL: Jesperson, 1985.
Monro, Alexander. *History, Geography, and Statistics of British North America*. Montreal, QC: John Lovell, 1864.
Moss, Laura, ed. *Is Canada Postcolonial? Unsettling Canadian Literature*. Waterloo, ON: Wilfrid Laurier University Press, 2003.
"The Mother of the Roberts." *Canadian Magazine* (August 1918): 342–43.
Mowat, Helen F. "The Fredericton School of Poets." *St. John (NB) Daily Sun*, Feb. 5, 1904, 7.
Mukherjee, Arun. *Oppositional Aesthetics: Readings from a Hyphenated Space*. Toronto, ON: TSAR, 1994.
Mullaly, Edward. "Thomas Hill: The Fredericton Years." *Studies in Canadian Literature* 11, no. 2 (Fall 1986): 190–205.
Murray, David R., and Robert A. Murray. *The Prairie Builder: Walter Murray of Saskatchewan*. Edmonton, AB: NeWest, 1984.
Murray, Joan, ed. *Daffodils in Winter: The Life and Letters of Pegi Nicol MacLeod, 1904–1949*. Moonbeam, ON: Penumbra, 1984.
Myatt, Rev. Wilfrid E, ed. *Autobiography of Oliver Goldsmith. A Chapter in Canada's Literary History*. Hantsport, NS: Lancelot Press, 1985.
Nealis, Jean E.U. *Drift*. Saint John, NB: T. O'Brien, 1884.
Nicholas, Andrea Bear. "Acquin, Gabriel." *Dictionary of Canadian Biography*. Vol. 13. University of Toronto/Université Laval, 2003– . http://www.biographi.ca/en/bio/acquin_gabriel_13E.html

———. "Settler Imperialism and the Dispossession of the Maliseet, 1758-1765." In *Shaping an Agenda for Atlantic Canada*, edited by John G. Reid and Donald J. Savoie, 21–57. Halifax & Winnipeg: Fernwood Publishing, 2011.

———. "The Role of Colonial Artists in the Dispossession and Displacement of the Maliseet, 1790s–1850s." In *Meeting Places/Lieux de Rencontre*, edited by Renée Hulan and Christl Verduyn. Special issue, *Journal of Canadian Studies* 49, no. 2 (Spring 2015): 25–86.

Niergarth, Kirk. "'Missionary for Culture': Walter Abell, *Maritime Art* and Cultural Democracy, 1928–1944." *Acadiensis* 36, no. 1 (Autumn 2006): 3–28.

Obituaries. "Ira Ingraham." *Gleaner* (Fredericton, NB), September 14, 1894; "Mrs Susan Pearson." *Daily Telegraph* (Saint John, NB), January 26, 1892; "Eleanor Parker." *Daily Telegraph* (Saint John, NB), February 25, 1884.

O'Flaherty, Patrick. *The Rock Observed: Studies in the Literature of Newfoundland*. Toronto, ON: University of Toronto Press, 1979.

"The Old Boys' Society." *Capital* (Fredericton, NB), October 15, 1881, 4.

Ong, Walter. *Interfaces of the Word: Studies in the Evolution of Consciousness and Culture*. Ithaca, NY: Cornell University Press, 1977.

O.P. [pseud.]. "The Triumph of Intrigue." *New-Brunswick Courier*, February 23, 1833, 2–3.

Ortiz, Fernando. *Contrapunteo cubano del tabaco y el azúcar: Advertencia de sus contrastes agrarios, económicos, históricos y sociales, su etnografía y su transculturación*. Madrid: Cuba España, 1999.

Ouellet, Fernand. "Démographie, développement économique, fréquentation scolaire et alphabétisation dans les populations acadiennes des Maritimes avant 1911: une perspective régionale et comparative." *Acadiensis* 26, no. 1 (Autumn 1996): 3–31.

P., F., prêtre de Sainte-Croix. *Notions élémentaires de littérature et de style épistolaire mises sous forme de cathéchistique à l'usage des élèves du cours commercial du Collège Saint-Joseph de Memramcook*. Shédiac, NB: Typographie du Moniteur Acadien, 1889.

Pacey, Desmond. "A.G. Bailey." *Canadian Literature* 68–69 (1976): 49–60.

———. "Archibald Lampman." In *Ten Canadian Poets*, 114–40. Toronto: Ryerson, 1958.

———. "Sir Charles G.D. Roberts." In *Essays in Canadian Criticism, 1938–1968*, 172–98. Toronto, ON: Ryerson, 1969.

———. "The Humanist Tradition." In *University of New Brunswick Memorial Volume*, edited by Alfred G. Bailey, 64–65. Fredericton, NB: University of New Brunswick, 1950.

Padolsky, Enoch. "Canadian Ethnic Minority Literature in English." In *Ethnicity and Culture in Canada: The Research Landscape*, edited by J.W. Berry and J.A. Laponce, 361–86. Toronto, ON: University of Toronto Press, 1994.

———. "Cultural Diversity and Canadian Literature: A Pluralistic Approach to Majority and Minority Writing in Canada." *International Journal of Canadian Studies* 3 (1991): 111–26.

Page, P.K. "Poetry and Mars Bars." *Kay Smith*. Special issue, *Cormorant* 9, no. 2 (1992): 64–65.

Perley, Moses. *Camp of the Owls: Sporting Sketches and Tales of Indians*, edited by Peter Mitcham. Hantsport, NS: Lancelot, 1990.

Philip, Marlene Nourbese. *Frontiers: Essays and Writings on Racism and Culture, 1984–1992*. Stratford, ON: Mercury Press, 1992.

Pichette, Robert. *La Cathédrale Notre-Dame-de-l'Assomption. Monument de la Reconaissance*. Moncton, NB: Chaire d'études acadiennes, 2012.

Pierce, Lorne. "Francis Sherman: A Memoir." In *The Complete Poems of Francis Sherman*, edited by L. Pierce, 1–18. Toronto, ON: Ryerson, 1935.

Pinsky, Alfred. "Painting in New Brunswick, 1880–1946." In *Arts in New Brunswick*, edited by R.A. Tweedie, Fred Cogswell, and W. Stewart MacNutt, 149–61. Fredericton, NB: Brunswick Press, 1967.

[Fonds] Poirier, Pascal. Fonds 6.1, dossiers 1–12. Centre d'études acadiennes Anselme-Chiasson, Université de Moncton, Moncton.

Poirier, Pascal. "Collèges et Couvents en Acadie." *La Patrie*, January 3, 1903, 9.

———. *L'Impartial*. Tignish, PE. January 15, 1903, 4.

———. *Le Père Lefebvre et l'Acadie*. Montréal, QC: C.O. Beauchemin et fils, 1898.

———. *Le Parler franco-acadien et ses origines*. Québec, QC: Imprimerie Franciscaine Missionaire, 1928.

———. *Les Acadiens à Philadelphie; suivi de Accordailles de Gabriel et d'Évangéline*, edited by Judith Perron. Moncton, NB: Éditions d'Acadie, 1998.

——— and L. J. Belliveau. *L'Évangéline*. Weymouth, NS. January 30, 1902, 2.

Pomeroy, E.M. *Sir Charles G.D. Roberts: A Biography*. Toronto, ON: Ryerson, 1943.

Porter, Roy. *English Society in the 18th Century*. London, UK: Penguin, 1991.

Postman, Neil. *Technopoly: The Surrender of Culture to Technology*. New York, NY: Vintage, 1993.

Postman, Neil, and Charles Weingartner. *The Soft Revolution: A Student Handbook for Turning Schools Around*. New York, NY: Delacorte, 1971.

"Prologue on Opening a Little Theatre in This City, on Monday the 5th January Inst." *Royal Gazette and the New Brunswick Advertiser*, January 20, 1795, 4.

Raddall, Thomas H. *In My Time: A Memoir*. Toronto, ON: McClelland & Stewart, 1976.

[Fonds] Rameau de Saint-Père, Fraçois-Edme. Fonds 2.1, dossiers 1–36. Centre d'études acadiennes Anselme-Chiasson, Université de Moncton, Moncton.

Rameau de Saint-Père, François-Edme. *La France aux colonies. Études sur le développement de la race française hors de l'Europe. Les Français en Amérique, Acadiens et Canadiens.* Paris: A. Jouby libraire-éditeur, 1859.

Rawlyk, George. "The Atlantic Provinces: History and Politics." In *Read Canadian: A Book about Canadian Books,* edited by Robert Fulford, Abraham Rotstein, and David Godfrey, 30–36. Toronto, ON: James, Lewis & Samuel, 1972.

Raymond, Maurice. "Abréaction et littérature: le 'cas' Ronald Després." *Port Acadie: revue interdisciplinaire en études acadiennes / Port Acadie: An Interdisciplinary Review in Acadian Studies* 20–21 (2011–12): 141–48.

Record of Alfred Goldsworthy Bailey. n.d. Alfred G. Bailey Collection. TS UA RG80. Box 32, file 4. Archives and Special Collections, University of New Brunswick Libraries, Fredericton.

Rees, Ronald. *Land of the Loyalists: Their Struggle to Shape the Maritimes.* Halifax, NS: Nimbus, 2000.

Reid, Dennis. *A Concise History of Canadian Painting.* Toronto, ON: Oxford University Press, 1973.

Reid, John. "Health, Education, Economy: Philanthropic Foundations in the Atlantic Region in the 1920s and 1930s." *Acadiensis* 14, no. 1 (Autumn 1984): 64–83.

———. *Six Crucial Decades: Times of Change in the History of the Maritimes.* Halifax, NS: Nimbus, 1987.

Richard, Camille. "L'idéologie de la première Convention nationale acadienne." M.A. thesis, Université Laval, 1960.

Richard, Chantal. "La Déportation comme mythe de création dans l'idéologie des Conventions nationales acadiennes (1881–1937)." *Acadiensis* 36, no. 1 (Fall 2006): 69–81.

———. "Poèmes acadiens de Napoléon-P. Landry." M.A. thesis, Université de Moncton, 1998.

Richard, Chantal, Anne Brown, Margaret Conrad, Gwendolyn Davies, Bonnie Huskins, and Sylvia Kasparian. "Markers of Collective Identity in Loyalist and Acadian Speeches of the 1880s: A Comparative Analysis." *Journal of New Brunswick Studies/Revue d'Études sur le Nouveau-Brunswick* 4 (2013): 13–30.

Riordan, Liam. *Many Identities, One Nation: The Revolution and Its Legacy in the Mid-Atlantic.* Philadelphia, PA: University of Pennsylvania Press, 2007.

Risteen, Frank. *Fredericton, the Celestial City and the River St. John, for the Tourist and Sportsman.* Fredericton, NB: Fredericton Tourist Committee, 1897.

Roberts, Charles G.D. "The Beginnings of Canadian Literature." *University Monthly* 2, no. 4 (June 1883): 59–64.

———. "Bliss Carman." *Dalhousie Review* 9, no. 4 (October 1939): 409–17.

———. *The Canadian Guide-Book: The Tourist's and Sportsman's Guide to Eastern Canada and Newfoundland.* New York, NY: D. Appleton, 1891.
———. *The Collected Letters of Sir Charles G.D. Roberts,* edited by Laurel Boone. Fredericton, NB: Goose Lane, 1989.
———. "Francis Sherman." *Dalhousie Review* 14, no. 4 (January 1935): 419–27.
———. *In Divers Tones.* Boston, MA: D. Lothrop, 1886.
———. "New Brunswick." In *Picturesque Canada; the Country as It Was and Is.* 2 vols. Edited by George Monro Grant, 741–88. Toronto, ON: Belden Bros., 1882.
———. "On Reading the Poems of Sidney Lanier." *University Monthly* 4, no. 7 (April 1885): 109.
———. *Orion, and Other Poems.* Philadelphia, PA: J.B. Lippincott, 1880.
———. "The Outlook for Literature: Acadia's Field for Poetry, History and Romance." *Halifax Morning Herald,* New Year's Supplement, January 1, 1886, 7. http://www.uwo.ca/english/canadianpoetry/confederation/roberts/non-fictional_prose/outlook.htm#cite
———. Prefatory Note to *The Watchers of the Trails: A Book of Animal Life,* by Charles G.D. Roberts, vii–ix. 1904. Boston, MA: L.C. Page, 1907.
———. "To Bliss Carman, with a Copy of Lang's 'Helen of Troy.'" *University Monthly* 4, no. 7 (April 1885): 109.
Roberts, J. Elizabeth Gostwycke. *Poems.* Fredericton, NB: E.R. MacDonald, 1885.
Roberts, Lloyd. *The Book of Roberts.* Toronto, ON: Ryerson, 1923.
Roberts, William Carman, Theodore Roberts, and Elizabeth Roberts MacDonald. *Northland Lyrics,* selected and arranged with a prologue by Charles G.D. Roberts and an epilogue by Bliss Carman. Boston, MA: Small Maynard, 1899.
Robertson, Ian Ross. "The 1850s: Maturity and Reform." In *The Atlantic Region to Confederation: A History,* edited by Phillip A. Buckner and John G. Reid, 333–59. Toronto, ON: University of Toronto Press, 1998.
Robichaud, Domitien. "Travaux sur l'Acadie publiés depuis 1921." *L'Évangéline,* October 6, 1927, 11.
Robidoux, Ferdinand-J. *Memramcook, Miscouche, Pointe de l'Église, 1881, 1884, 1890. Vol. 1* of *Conventions nationales des Acadiens. Receuil des travaux et délibérations des six premières conventions.* Shédiac, NB: Imprimerie du Moniteur Acadien, 1907.
Ross, Malcolm. "Medley, John." In *Dictionary of Canadian Biography.* Vol. 12. University of Toronto/ Université Laval, 2003– . http://www.biographi.ca/en/bio/medley_john_12E.html
———. "Poets of the Confederation." In *The Impossible Sum of Our Traditions,* 87–92. Toronto, ON: McClelland & Stewart, 1986.

———. "A Strange Aesthetic Ferment." In *The Impossible Sum of Our Traditions*, 27–42. Toronto, ON: McClelland & Stewart, 1986.
Roy, Michel. *L'Acadie perdue*. Montreal, QC: Éditions Québec/Amérique, 1978.
Roy, Muriel K. "Démographie et démolinguistique en Acadie, 1871–1991." In *L'Acadie des Maritimes,* edited by Jean Daigle, 141–206. Moncton, NB: Institut d'études acadiennes, 1993.
Roy, Thérèse B. "L'évolution de l'enseignement chez les Acadiens du Nouveau-Brunswick, 1755–1855." M.A. thesis, Université de Moncton, 1972.
Rudin, Ronald. *Remembering and Forgetting in Acadie: A Historian's Journey through Public Memory*. Toronto, ON: University of Toronto Press, 2009.
Runte, Hans R. *Writing Acadia: The Emergence of Acadian Literature, 1970–1990*. Amsterdam: Rodopi, 1997.
Savoie, Donald J. "Reviewing Canada's Regional Development Efforts." *Royal Commission on Renewing and Strengthening Our Place in Canada*, 147–84. Ottawa, ON: Government of Canada, 2003.
———. *Visiting Grandchildren: Economic Development in the Maritimes*. Toronto, ON: University of Toronto Press, 2006.
Scott, Allen J. "The Cultural Economy: Geography and the Creative Field." *Media, Culture and Society* 21 (1999): 807–17.
Scott. F.R. "The Canadian Authors Meet." In *Selected Poems*, 70. Toronto, ON: Oxford University Press, 1966.
Shaw, Avery. "The Art of Miller Brittain." *New Brunswick Museum Educational Review*. n.d., n.p.
Sheier, Libby, Sarah Sheard, and Eleanor Wachtel, eds. *Language in Her Eye: Views on Writing and Gender by Canadian Women Writing in English*. Toronto, ON: Coach House, 1990.
Sherman, Francis. *Matins*. Boston, MA: Copeland and Day, 1896.
Shives, Robert. "An English Spelling Book." *The Amaranth* 1, no. 3 (March 1841): 96.
Siemerling, Winfried, and Sarah Phillips Casteel, eds. *Canada and Its Americas: Transnational Navigations*. Montreal & Kingston: McGill-Queen's University Press, 2010.
Simon, Lorne Joseph. Letter to Jeanette Armstrong. In *Stones and Switches*, n.p. Penticton, BC: Theytus Books, 1994.
———. *Stones and Switches*. Penticton, BC: Theytus Books, 1994.
Slemon, Stephen. "Climbing Mount Everest: Postcolonialism in the Culture of Ascent." In *Postcolonizing the Commonwealth: Studies in Literature and Culture*, edited by Rowland Smith, 51–74. Waterloo, ON: Wilfrid Laurier University Press, 2000.

Smart, Patricia. "The 'Pure Laine' Debate." *Canadian Forum* 76, no. 864 (November 1997): 15–19.

Smith, A.J.M. "The Fredericton Poets." In *Towards a View of Canadian Letters: Selected Critical Essays, 1928–71*, 65–76. Vancouver, BC: University of British Columbia Press, 1973.

Smith, Goldwin. *Canada and the Canadian Question*. Toronto, ON: Hunter Rose, 1891.

Smith, Mary Elizabeth. "English Drama in New Brunswick." In *A Literary and Linguistic History of New Brunswick*, edited by R. Gair et al., 167–91. Fredericton, NB: Fiddlehead & Goose Lane, 1985.

———. *Too Soon the Curtain Fell: A History of Theatre in Saint John: 1789–1900*. Fredericton, NB: Brunswick Press, 1981.

Southgate, Rev. Horatio, D.D. *A Sermon Preached at the Consecration of Christ Church Cathedral, Fredericton, N.B. 31 August 1853*. Boston: Ticknor, Reed, and Fields, 1853.

"Special Agreement bet. William Durant & Walter Bates Esq. Saint John." January 17, 1826. Durant Family Papers. Microform. MS23. Microfilm F9083. Provincial Archives of New Brunswick, Fredericton.

"A Spectator." *Royal St. John's Gazette and Nova-Scotia Intelligencer*, January 29, 1784, 2.

Spray, W.A. "Perley, Moses Henry." In *Dictionary of Canadian Biography*. Vol. 9. University of Toronto/ Université Laval, 2003– . http://www.biographi.ca/en/bio/perley_moses_henry_9E.html

Stanley, George F.G. "John Clarence Webster, The Laird of Shediac." *Acadiensis* 3, no. 1 (Autumn 1973): 51–71.

Statistics Canada. Censuses of Canada 1665 to 1871. http://www.statcan.gc.ca/pub/98-187-x/4064810-eng.htm

———. "Economic Importance of Culture and Sport across Canada, 2010." http://www.statcan.gc.ca/pub/13-604-m/2015079/eco-eng.htm1

Straton, Barry. *The Building of the Bridge, an Idyll of the River Saint John*. Saint John, NB: J. & A. McMillan, 1887.

———. *The Hunter's Handbook*. Boston, MA: Lee & Shepard, 1885.

———. *Lays of Love, and Miscellaneous Poems*. Saint John, NB: J. & A. McMillan, 1884.

Sugars, Cynthia, ed. *Home-Work: Postcolonialism, Pedagogy and Canadian Literature*. Ottawa, ON: University of Ottawa Press, 2004.

———, ed. *Unhomely States: Theorizing English-Canadian Postcolonialism*. Peterborough, ON: Broadview, 2004.

Sugars, Cynthia, and Gerry Turcotte, eds. *Unsettled Remains: Canadian Literature and the Postcolonial Gothic*. Waterloo, ON: Wilfrid Laurier University Press, 2009.

Surette, Leon. *The Birth of Modernism: Ezra Pound, T.S. Eliot, W.B. Yeats, and the Occult*. Montreal & Kingston: McGill-Queen's University Press, 1993.

———. "Ezra Pound, Bliss Carman, and Richard Hovey." *Canadian Poetry* 43 (Fall/Winter 1998): 44–69.

Swanick, Eric. "Hill, Thomas." In *Dictionary of Canadian Biography*. Vol. 8. University of Toronto/ Université Laval, 2003–. http://www.biographi.ca/en/bio/hill_thomas_8E.html

Swanick, Lynne Struthers. "Madge Smith." *Canadian Women's Studies* 2, no. 3 (Summer 1980): 34–37.

Sweet, Jean M. "Ted Campbell's Studio." *Atlantic Advocate* 59, no. 7 (March 1969): 30–35.

Tator, Carol, F. Henry, and W. Mathis. *Challenging Racism in the Arts*. Toronto, ON: University of Toronto Press, 1998.

The Telling It Book Collective [SKY Lee, Lee Maracle, Daphne Marlatt and Betsy Warland]. *Telling It: Women and Language across Cultures*. Vancouver, BC: Press Gang, 1990.

Thacker, Robert. *The Great Prairie Fact and Literary Imagination*. Albuquerque, NM: University of New Mexico Press, 1989.

Thiesse, Anne-Marie. "Des fictions créatrices: les identités nationales." *Romantisme* 110, no. 4 (2000): 51–62.

Thomas, Peter, and Nicholas Tracy. *Master and Madman: The Surprising Rise and Disastrous Fall of the Hon. Anthony Lockwood RN*. Fredericton, NB: Goose Lane, 2012.

Thorburn, Hugh G. *Politics in New Brunswick*. Toronto, ON: University of Toronto Press, 1961.

Toole, Janet. "[Interview with] Dr. A.G. Bailey—The Literary Tradition—Part II." April 3, 1974. TS MS4 7.4.1. Archives and Special Collections, University of New Brunswick Libraries, Fredericton.

Tremaine, Marie. *A Bibliography of Canadian Imprints, 1751–1800*. 1952. Toronto, ON: University of Toronto Press, 1999.

Tremblay, Tony. "Harnessing Cultural and Human Capital for Economic Sustainability: A New Brunswick Model." *Journal of Enterprising Communities: People and Places in the Global Economy* 3, no. 4 (2009): 369–77.

———. "'People Are Made of Places': Perspectives on Region in Atlantic-Canadian Literature." In *The Oxford Handbook of Canadian Literature,* edited by Cynthia Sugars, 657–75. New York, NY: Oxford University Press, 2016.

Tremblay, Tony, and Ellen Rose. "The Canadian Little Magazine Past and Present: Can Digitizing a Literary Subculture Make a Movement?" *Canadian Literature* 200 (Spring 2009): 16–35.

Turner, Frederick Jackson. "The Significance of the Frontier in American History." In *The Frontier Thesis and the Canadas: The Debate on the Impact of the Canadian Environment,* edited by Michael S. Cross, 12–22. Toronto, ON: Copp Clark, 1970.

Tyler, Moses Coit. *The Literary History of the American Revolution 1763–1783.* Vol. 2. New York, NY: Putnam's Sons, 1897.

"An Unlikely Time, An Unlikely Place." *Kay Smith.* Special issue, *Cormorant* 9, no. 2 (1992): 39–54. Originally aired on *Maritime Magazine.* Narr. Jackie Good et al. Prod. Costas Halavrezos. CBC Radio, Saint John. August 17, 1980.

Van Buskirk, Judith L. *Generous Enemies: Patriots and Loyalists in Revolutionary New York.* Philadelphia, PA: University of Pennsylvania Press, 2002.

Verthuy, Maïr. "Pan Bouyoucas: le principe des vases communicants ou de la nécessité de 'sortir de l'ethnicité.'" In *Literary Pluralities,* edited by Christl Verduyn, 172–83. Peterborough, ON: Broadview Press, 1998.

Verduyn, Christl. "Critical Allegiances." In *Critical Collaborations: Indigeneity, Diaspora, and Ecology in Canadian Literary Studies,* edited by Smaro Kamboureli and Christl Verduyn, 227–39. Waterloo, ON: Wilfrid Laurier University Press, 2014.

Viau, Robert. "L'Épée et la plume: La persistance du thème de la Déportation acadienne en littérature." *Acadiensis* 36, no. 1 (Autumn 2006): 51–68.

———. *Les Grands Dérangements: La déportation des Acadiens en littératures acadienne, québécoise et française.* Beauport, QC: Publications MNH, 1997.

Vincent, Thomas B., ed. *Narrative Verse Satire in Maritime Canada 1779–1814.* Ottawa, ON: Tecumseh P, 1978.

———. *Jonathan Odell. An Annotated Chronology of the Poems 1759–1818.* Kingston, ON: Loyal Colonies Press, 1980.

Wallace, C.M. "Hogg, James." In *Dictionary of Canadian Biography.* Vol. 9. University of Toronto/ Université Laval, 2003–. http://www.biographi.ca/en/bio/hogg_james_9E.html

Wallace-Casey, Cynthia. "Environment Canada, Parks Canada, Christ Church Cathedral, National Historic Site: 1983." *Material Culture Review* 26 (Fall 1987): 46–52.

Ware, Martin. Introduction to *That Far River: Selected Poems of Theodore Goodridge Roberts,* edited by Martin Ware, xv–xxiv. London, ON: Canadian Poetry Press, 1998.

Ware, Tracy. "Arthur Symons' Reviews of Bliss Carman." *Canadian Poetry* 37 (Fall/Winter 1995): 100–13.

Webster, J.C. Letter to C.C. Jones. 14 June 1937. Presidents' Papers, 1909–1945, UA RG 136. Box 14, file 3 (1937, U–Z). Archives and Special Collections, University of New Brunswick Libraries, Fredericton.

Whalen, Terry, ed. and intro. "Lorne Pierce's 1927 Interview with Charles G.D. Roberts (As Reported by Margaret Lawrence)." *Canadian Poetry: Studies, Documents, Reviews* 21 (Fall/Winter 1987). http://www.uwo.ca/english/canadian poetry/cpjrn/cpjrn/vol21/whalen.htm

White, Hayden. "The Problem of Change in Literary History." *New Literary History* 7, no. 1 (1975): 97–111.

White, Stephen A. "The True Number of Acadians." *Du Grand Dérangement à la Déportation: Nouvelles perspectives historiques*. edited by Ronnie-Gilles LeBlanc. Moncton, NB: Chaire d'études acadiennes, 2005.

Whiteman, Bruce. Introduction to *The Letters of John Sutherland, 1942–1956*, edited by Bruce Whiteman, ix–xxxv. Toronto, ON: ECW Press, 1992.

William Reynolds, Bookseller and Stationer. [Advertisement.] *St. John (NB) City Gazette,* July 10, 1816, 1.

Williams, Lorna. "From Agricultural Improvement to Industrial Affirmation: The Evolution of the New Brunswick Provincial Exhibitions, 1852–1883." M.A. thesis, University of New Brunswick, 2003.

Williams, Raymond. "Culture." In *Keywords. A Vocabulary of Culture and Society*, 87–93. 1976. Hammersmith, London, UK: Fontana, 1988.

Wright, Esther Clark. *The Loyalists of New Brunswick*. Fredericton, NB: Esther Clark Wright, 1955.

———. *The Saint John River*. Toronto, ON: McClelland & Stewart, 1949.

———. *Saint John Ships and Their Builders*. Wolfville, NS: The Author, 1976.

Wright, Robert. *Virtual Sovereignty: Nationalism, Culture, and the Canadian Question*. Toronto, ON: Canadian Scholars' Press, 2004.

Wyile, Herb. *Anne of Tim Hortons: Globalization and the Reshaping of Atlantic-Canadian Literature*. Waterloo, ON: Wilfrid Laurier University Press, 2011.

Wynn, Graeme. "'Deplorably Dark and Demoralized Lumberers'? Rhetoric and Reality in Early Nineteenth-Century New Brunswick." *Journal of Forest History* 24, no. 4 (October 1980): 168–87.

———. *Timber Colony: A Historical Geography of Early Nineteenth Century New Brunswick*. Toronto, ON: University of Toronto Press, 1981.

CONTRIBUTORS

DAVID CREELMAN is Professor of Literature and has taught at the University of New Brunswick (Saint John) for more than twenty-five years. He has published articles on a variety of Canadian and Maritime writers, and in 2003 he published a study of Maritime fiction entitled *Setting in the East: Maritime Realist Fiction*. In 2015 he was named as a 3M Teaching Fellow.

GWENDOLYN DAVIES, FRSC, is Emerita Professor and Dean at the University of New Brunswick. Author of sixty articles and book chapters on pre-1950 Canadian literature, she has written or edited six books, including a scholarly edition of *The Mephibosheth Stepsure Letters*; *Studies in Maritime Literary History, 1760–1930*; and *Fiction Treasures by Maritime Writers: Best-Selling Novelists from Canada's Maritime Provinces 1860–1950*.

THOMAS HODD is Associate Professor of English at Université de Moncton. His essays on Confederation-era writers have appeared in *Canadian Poetry*, the University of Ottawa Can Lit Symposium series, and most recently *The Great War: From Memory to History* (2015). He is co-editor of a special issue on early Canadian literature for *Canadian Literature* (2012). His guest-edited issue on Atlantic-Canadian poetry is forthcoming in *Canadian Poetry*.

MARIE-LINDA LORD is Professor of Communication at Université de Moncton. With funding from the Social Sciences and Humanities Research

193

CONTRIBUTORS

Council of Canada, she conducts research on representation and discourse in the literature and media of Acadie and New Brunswick. She has written more than thirty chapters and scholarly papers and edited four books. She is currently working on Moncton and its literature.

CHANTAL RICHARD is Associate Professor at the University of New Brunswick. A specialist in Acadian Studies, she is the principal investigator of Vocabularies of Identity/Vocabulaires identitaires, co-author of the three-volume *Conventions nationales acadiennes (1881–1937)*, and author of *Poèmes acadiens de Napoléon-P. Landry*. She is also co-editor of the *Journal of New Brunswick Studies/Revue d'études sur le Nouveau-Brunswick*.

TONY TREMBLAY is Canada Research Chair in New Brunswick Studies at St. Thomas University. He is founding editor of the *Journal of New Brunswick Studies/Revue d'études sur le Nouveau-Brunswick* and general editor of the *New Brunswick Literary Encyclopedia*. His recent work includes *Fred Cogswell: The Many-Dimensioned Self* (2012), *Last Shift: The Story of a Mill Town* (2011), and *David Adams Richards of the Miramichi* (2010).

CHRISTL VERDUYN is Professor of English and Canadian Studies at Mount Allison University, where she holds the Davidson Chair in Canadian Studies and is Director of the Centre for Canadian Studies. She is the author, editor, and co-editor of over a dozen volumes, most recently *Critical Collaborations: Indigeneity, Diaspora, and Ecology in Canadian Literary Studies* (2014).

INDEX

Abell, Walter, 118; on democratic use of art, 113
Abrams, M.H., 10; *The Mirror and the Lamp*, 8
Académica (journal), 59
Acadian literature: and Acadian dualism, 132; and collective memory, 46, 145; French-language publishers, 133–34, 136, 140, 142, 150–51; golden-age myth, 47; Moncton of the imagination, 136, 153n3; for theatre and screen, 139–40
Acadian national holiday, 55, 56–57; Fête de l'Assomption, 130–31
Acadian Nationalism period, 11, 12
Acadian Renaissance, 70–71n1, 157, 164; bicentennial celebrations, 65, 67–68, 72n13, 132; and Collège Saint-Joseph, 53, 71n2; creation of national identity, 63, 158; French-language newspapers, impact of, 61–62; golden-age myth of pre-Renaissance work, 47; local and historical literary consciousness, 61; narratives of resistance, 65–67; nationalism, and collective identity, 12, 45–47, 50, 65–67, 68–69, 72n13; Rameau's program for Acadian rebirth, 55–57; youth literature, 66–67
Acadians: Acadianization of Moncton, 130–32; Chiac, and Acadian identity, 138–39, 166; collective memory, and cultural identity, 12, 45–47, 50, 65–67, 68–69, 72n13; demographic changes pre- and post-Expulsion, 47–50; *Evangeline*, as founding myth, 56; French/English divisions post-Expulsion, 2, 47–50; French-language school system, 50–55; identity, consciousness of, 13–14, 133–35; intercultural relationships, 145; isolation of by Colonial governments, 47–48, 49; literacy, and access to education, 46, 47–50; negative stereotypes of, 49, 50; oral tradition of, 57–59, 61, 65, 69; outmigration of, 65; Rameau's program for Acadian rebirth, 55–57; as vanquished people, 3
Acadian World Congress (CMA), 148

195

INDEX

Acadie: as colony of France, 57; concept of, 45–47; *Evangeline*, as mythology of resistance, 62–63; isolation of under English, 47–48, 49; links to France, 133; as model of pluralism, 14; Monctonization of, 152; national hymn, 57; national symbol of, 55, 57; rebirth of, 55–57; regions and regionalisms of, 149
L'Acadie l'Acadie (film), 133
Acadie Rock (Arsenault), 136, 138
Achard, Eugène, 66
Acheson, T.W., 106
Acquin, Gabriel, 92
Adams, John Coldwell, 74, 94
Adney, Tappan, 91
adversarial tensions, 15, 156–58
aesthetic conditions, 15, 160–62
Agricultural and Emigrant Society, 29
Albert, Laurent: *Les Splendides Têtus*, 66
Albion (New York), 37
Algonquin group (later Group of Seven), 109
Allan, Peter John, 79, 123
Allen, George W., 89
The Amaranth (journal), 12, 37–38, 43n5; engagement with landscape, and identity-formation, 41; historical fiction, 38, 43n6; local heritage material, 38; sporting sketches, 40
Amitiés Acadiennes, 142
Anderson, Patrick: *Preview*, 122
Anglican Creed, 42n1
Anthologie de textes littéraires acadiens (M. Maillet, Leblanc, Émont), 46–47
Appadurai, Arjun, 17
Argimou (Huyghue), 38, 41, 43n6, 161
Armstrong, Sally, 2
Armstrong, Tammy, 94
Arnold, Matthew, 7
Around the Campfire (Roberts), 90

Arsenault, Angèle: *Libre* (album), 140
Arsenault, Guy, 14, 70–71n1; *Acadie Rock*, 136, 138
Association Acadienne des Artistes Professionnel.le.s du Nouveau-Brunswick, 145
Association des Écrivains Acadiens, 140
Association du Disque et de l'Industrie du Spectacle du Québec, 140
The Atlantic Provinces (MacNutt), 35
"Attic Portfolio" magazine, 86, 89
Austen, Jane, 30
Ave Maris Stella, as national hymn, 57

Bailey, Alfred G., 16, 36, 83, 93, 158; activist research agenda, 120–21; and Bliss Carman Society, 121; and Campbell's studio, 13, 103, 110, 114; change through institutional means, 126–27; as custodian of heritage, 123; Fiddlehead School, 116–27; innovation, and socio-cultural environment, 6, 10, 74; landscapes as source of spiritual renewal, 91; move to Fredericton, 115–16, 119; and New Brunswick modernism, 119–21; Parkin as mentor, 87; as social historian, 127; and the "Tea Pot School," 118; at UNB, 119–22, 125
Bailey, Alfred G. – works: *The Conflict of European and Eastern Algonkian Cultures*, 122; "Creative Moments," 15; *Culture and Nationality*, 6; "Northwest Passage," 122; *Tâo*, 115; "The Unreturning," 122
Bailey, Jacob, 20, 28
Bailey, Loring Woart, 119
Baillie, Thomas, 35
Baker, Ray Palmer, 20–21
balkanization, and insularity of settlement, 3
Barkley, Murray, 34

INDEX

Bates, Walter: Loyalism of, 31; *The Mysterious Stranger*, 12, 30–31, 32, 42–43n3
Bayley, Robin, 121
Beausoleil, Claude: "Moncton School," 152–53
Beausoleil Broussard, 141
de Beauvoir, Simone, 60
Beavan, Emily, 38
Beaverbrook, Lord, 125, 127
Behind the Arras (Carman), 101
Bell, David, 21–22
Bellivau, Philippe-Louis, 71n2
Belliveau, Fidèle, 71n2
Belliveau, Philéas, 58
Belyea, Eleanor, 122
Bentley, D.M.R., 36, 74, 99n1; on Mi'kmaq-inspired work of Roberts, 93; settler community evolution, 33
Birney, Earle, 119, 121, 126
The Birth of Modernism (Surette), 101–2
Blatch, George, 37–38
Bliss, Emma Wetmore, 82, 85–86
Bliss, Sarah, 85–86
Bliss, Sophia, 85–86
Bliss Carman Society, 115, 118; founding and growth of, 121–22
Bock, Michel, 69, 70
The Book of Roberts (L. Roberts), 85, 97
de Bossuet, Jacques-Bénigne, 60
Boston Museum School of Art, 109, 161
Boston Painters Workshop, 111
Boudreau, Donald, 141
Boudreau, J.P., 166
Boudreau, Jules: *Louis Mailloux*, 139
Boudreau, Raoul, 10, 15, 143
Bourassa, Napoléon: *Jacques et Marie*, 63
Bourgeois, Philéas-Frédéric, 71n2
Bradbury, Malcolm, 8–9
Braithwaithe, Henry, 92
Branch, James, 12, 69; *Jusqu'à la mort! Pour nos écoles*, 65; *L'Émigrant acadien*, 65; *Vivent nos écoles catholiques! Ou la résistance de Caraquet*, 65
Brandon, Laura, 117
Brault, Michel, *L'Acadie l'Acadie* (film), 133
Brewster, Elizabeth, 13, 16, 103, 122, 123
Brison, Jeffrey, 113
Britain: book exports from, 30; "Free Port Act," 29; Robin Hood Club (London), 27; War of 1812, 29
Brittain, Miller, 109, 112, 118, 161
Brooker, Bertram, 111–12
Brückner, Martin, 41
Brunswick Press, 13, 103, 127
The Building of the Bridge (Straton), 96
Bumsted, J.M., 19, 20
Burroughs, John: *Winter Sunshine*, 95
The Busy East magazine, 108, 114; response to Maritime malaise, 106–7
Butler, Édith, 140–41
Butler, Marilyn, 41

Cadieux, Chantal: Productions Dans-Encorps, 139–40
Cairncross, Frances, 17
Calder, Alison, 16, 17
Campbell, Ted (Daniel Edwin), 13, 158, 161; cross-fertilization of ideas, 115; mural work, 112; post-Confederation critique, 110–11; at Provincial Normal School, 116; socially conscious art of, 112; studio group, 103, 108–16, 157; visual art activism, 114
Campbell, William Wilfred, 73
Canada and the Canadian Question (Smith), 104
Canadian Authors Association, 102, 115
Canadian Group of Painters, 111–12
Canadian Magazine, 86
Canadian Monthly and National Review, 96

INDEX

Cape Cod School, 111
The Capital (newspaper): coverage of "Old Boys Society of the Collegiate School," 88–89
Careless, J.M.S., 105, 125
Carleton, Sir Guy, 21
Carleton, Thomas: College of New Brunswick, 76; resistance to as Governor, 25, 42n1
Carlyle, Thomas, 7
Carman, Bliss, 3, 13, 98, 123, 127; avant-garde aesthetic of, 101–2; on Cody, 103; experience of Confederation, 83–84; family linkages, 84–86; on Parkin as mentor, 81, 82, 87; publishing collaborations, 89; relationship to Charles Roberts, 73–74, 99n1; *The University Monthly* (newspaper), 92, 95
Carman, Bliss – works: *Behind the Arras*, 101; *Low Tide on Grand Pré*, 96; *Songs from Vagabondia* (Carman, Hovey), 89, 101
Carman, Elizabeth: *Dream Verses*, 97; *Our Canadian Cousin*, 97
Carman, Jean Murray, 86
Carman, William, 97
Carnegie Corporation, 111, 119
Casgrain, Henri-Raymond, 60
Catholic Church: Acadians within, 54; aesthetics within, 161; criticism of, 141–42; and French-language school system, 49, 50–55; *Index Librorium Prohibitorum*, 59–61; influence of, 48, 49–50; Irish clergy, dominance of, 49–50
CCF, 126; Regina Manifesto, 108
censorship: *Index Librorium Prohibitorum*, 59–61
Cent ans dans les bois (A. Maillet), 140
Chateaubriand, François-Rene de, 60
Chiasson, Herménégilde, 14, 16, 70–71n1, 135, 136, 161; Acadian literature in Moncton, 130, 146, 151
Chiasson, Herménégilde – works: *Conversations*, 151; *L'Amer à boire*, 139; *L'étoile maganée* (Savoie, Chiasson), 136; *Mourir à Scoudouc*, 136, 139
Chiasson, Zénon, 10
Christian, William, 77
Chronique d'une naissance annoncée (Daigle), 150
Chubb, Henry, 35
Clarke, George Frederick, 123
Clarke, Patrick D., 130, 132, 152; regions and regionalisms of Acadie, 149
class issues: and literary production, 37–38
Cody, H.A., 103
Cody, Norman, 109
Coffin, John, 27
Cogswell, Frederick, 10, 13, 16, 103, 112, 123, 126, 164; and Fiddlehead Poetry Books, 127; on *The Mysterious Stranger*, 32; *The Stunted Strong*, 111
collective creativity, 15
collective memory, 69; and cultural identity, 12, 45–47, 50, 65–67, 68–70, 72n13, 158; role of in historical tropes, 46
collective production of imaginative individuals, 162
Collège l'Assomption, 134
Collège Notre-Dame d'Acadie, 133
Collège Sacré Cœur, 137
Collège Saint-Anne (Nova Scotia), 58, 59
Collège Saint-Joseph, 12, 70–71n1, 134, 157; and Acadian Renaissance, 53, 71n2; approved reading list, 60–61; bilingual approach of, 52; Expulsion as inspiration for student's writing, 63–64; and Rameau de Saint-Père, 56; religious censorship,

59–61; Saint-Patrick's Academy, 59; "séances publiques," 58; Société Littéraire Saint-Jean-Baptiste, 58–59; as Université de Moncton, 52–53
Collège Saint-Louis, 53–54
Collegiate School: and Confederation poets, 86–90; "Old Boys Society of the Collegiate School," 88–89; *Progress* (journal), 89; tradition of educational leadership, 88
Comeau, Jean-Gabriel, 141
commercial enterprises: and north-south division of labour and settlement, 2
Comme un otage au quotidien (Leblanc), 143
A Compendious History of the Northern Part of the Province of New Brunswick (Cooney), 34
Compton, Anne, 16
Condon, Ann, 24
Confederation: experiences of, 83–84; imperialism, and national autonomy, 13; provincial divisions over, 83–84
Confederation Awakening period, 11, 13
Confederation poets, 68; camping expeditions, 90–92; factors influencing, 74, 157–58; family linkages, 84–86; fear of provincial obscurity, 158; and First Nations peoples, 92–93; influence of UNB on, 93–95; leisure as virtue of literary success, 98–99; mentors, 13, 74; nature writing, 90–92; Ottawa School, 16; publishing collaborations, 89–90; publishing successes, 96–97; Sherman's Wharf, 90–91; sites of influence, 13, 73–74, 85–90
confessional crime literature: popularity of, 31–32
Congrès des Francophones (1972), 137

Contemporary Verse magazine, 122
Conventions Nationales Acadiennes (CNA), 12, 68; and Acadian identity, 53, 56–57
Conversations (Chiasson), 151
Cooney, Robert: *A Compendious History of the Northern Part of the Province of New Brunswick*, 34
Cormier, André D., 71n2
Cormier, Father Clément, 68, 129
Cormier, François-Xavier, 71n2
Cormier, Henri D., 131
Cormier, Yves: *Grandir à Moncton*, 147–48
Coutellier, Francis, 136
Crawford, Julia, 109
Crawley, Alan, 115; *Contemporary Verse* magazine, 122
Creelman, David, 14–15, 16
Creighton, Donald, 125
Cri de terre (LeBlanc), 136, 138, 139
Cropley, Henry, 81
Crosskill, John H., 43n5
cultural compression, 156, 157
cultural economies, and creative communities, 16–17, 18
cultural geography: diversity of microcultures, 4; of New Brunswick, 1–4
cultural sociology: in analysis of New Brunswick literature, 9–11; and literary ferment, 6–10, 155–56; and Lukàcsian Marxism, 6–7
culture: cultural custodianship as business of universities, 124–25; as interaction between individuals and environment, 1; as regional, 120–21; scholarly explorations of NB culture, 3–4, 10–15
Culture and Nationality (Bailey), 6
Cunningham, Margaret, 122
Currie, Margaret Catharine Gill, 80–81; *Gabriel West, and Other Poems*, 31

Daigle, Euclide, 143, 144
Daigle, France, 144; *Chronique d'une naissance annoncée*, 150; *Histoire de la maison qui brûle*, 143; *Pas pire*, 150; *Sans jamais parler du vent*, 143
Dalhousie Review, 123
Dames de la Congrégation de Montréal, 54
Daniells, Roy, 114, 116–17, 119, 121, 126
David, Robert, 88
Davies, Gwendolyn, 12, 157, 161
d'Avray, Marshall, 80, 90, 94
Deichmann, Kjeld and Erica, 110, 115, 117
Delille, Jacques, 60
De Mille, James, 15; *Fire in the Woods*, 41; *A Strange Manuscript Found in a Copper Cylinder*, 162
Denys, Nicolas, 47
Descartes, René, 60
The Deserted City (Sherman), 95
Després, Ronald, 67, 133–34, 153n2; Pascal-Poirier Prize, 134; *Silence à nourrir de sang*, 133
Després, Rose, 3, 70–71n1, 142
dialogues, as expression of resistance, 20–21, 22, 23
Dictionnaire des œuvres littéraires de l'Acadie des Maritimes, 152
Diderot, Denis, 60
Djwa, Sandra, 115
Doak, James, 78, 99n4
doggerel, as expression of resistance, 20–21, 22, 24
Don l'Orignal (A. Maillet), 140
Douglas, Sir Howard: King's College, 76
Duchamp, Marcel, 111
Dudek, Louis, 126
Duguay, Calixte: *Louis Mailloux*, 139
Dumas, Alexandre, 60
Duncan Commission (1926), 106, 107

Dupuis, Ronald, 141
Durant, William, 30–31
Durkheim, Émile, 8

Écrits des forges, 150
Éditions d'Acadie, 136, 138, 142, 143, 150, 151
Éditions d'Orphée, 133–34
Éditions Perce-Neige, 140, 142, 143, 145
education: access to, impact on literacy, 46, 47–50; advances in, 50–55; Collège Saint-Joseph, 12; roaming teachers (maîtres ambulants), 49; for seasonal workers, 106. *See also* French-language education
Eliot, T.S., 111, 121, 161
Elle et Lui (Léger), 66
Éloge du chiac (Leblanc), 143, 145
Éloizes (magazine), 140, 148
Émile-Nelligan prize: *Le cycle de Prague* (Thibodeau), 150
Émont, Bernard: *Anthologie de textes littéraires acadiens*, 46–47
English New Brunswick: access to education, 49; and Confederation, 13; public expectations/response to literary expression, 14–15. *See also* French New Brunswick; New Brunswick
epochal transformation: criteria for, 10–11; and matrix events, 8–9; sociocultural conditions for, 15
ethnicity: and cultural geography, 2–3
Evangeline (Longfellow), 65; as founding Acadian myth, 56; LeMay translation, 62–63; mythology of resistance, 62–63, 66–67
existentialism, and post-nationalism, 142–45
the Expulsion: bicentennial celebrations, 65, 67–68, 72n13, 132; demographic changes pre- and

post-Expulsion, 47–50; *Evangeline*, as founding Acadian myth, 57; *Evangeline*, as mythology of resistance, 62–63, 66–67; French/English divisions, 2, 47–50; *Jacques et Marie* (Bourassa), 63; and narratives of loss and displacement, 63–64; Tintamarre, 68, 72n13, 132

federalism, as elitism, 113
Fédération des Acadiens de la Nouvelle-Écosse (Nova Scotia), 137
Fénélon, François, 60
Fenety, George, 96
Festival International du Cinéma Francophone en Acadie (FICFA): La Vague/Léonard Forest Prize, 139
Feux Chalins, 131
The Fiddlehead, 13, 103, 115, 118, 122–23, 126, 127
Fiddlehead School, 116–27
Fidès, 133
Filles Marie-de-L'Assomption, 131
Finch, Robert, 119, 121
Fingard, Judith, 75
Fire in the Woods (DeMille), 41
First Nations peoples, 1; disenfranchisement of, 41, 43n6; literary treatments of, 12; living conditions, 39; north–south division of, 2; population at 1842 census, 39; social proximity to settler populations, 92–93; St. Mary's First Nation, 92; systemic erasure of, 3; violations of Aboriginal land titles, 38–40
First Statement magazine, 114, 122
Firth, Frances, 122, 124
Fisher, Peter: *The Lay of the Wilderness*, 31; *Notitia of New Brunswick*, 31; *Sketches of New Brunswick*, 31, 34
Flaubert, Gustave, 60
Florida, Richard: urban centrism, 16–17

Fondation de France, 142
Footnote to the Lord's Prayer (Smith), 111
Forbes, E.R., 105, 106
Forest, Léonard: documentaries, 139; "Pour parler au monde," 148–49; *Saisons antérieures*, 136
forest industry: as economic driver, 33, 36–37; trading vs. timber economy, 24–25
Foster, Annie Harvie (Ross), 95
Foster, George E., 94
Foster, Walter, 107
Foucault, Michel, 7
Fournier, Claude, 141
Fraser, C.F., 85
Fraser, Raymond, 3
Fredericton: Anglican Diocese of, 77; architectural achievements, 77–78; and Bailey's influence, 103; as "Celestial City," 75, 99n3; Christ Church Cathedral, 77; Confederation poets, 13, 73–75; as destination for local talent, 80–82; early development of, 29–30; factors in development of literary community, 75–80; newspapers role in promotion of cultural literacy, 78–80; Observatory Art Centre (formerly Observatory Summer School for the Arts), 117, 118–19; political confrontations with Saint John, 24–25; population, 75, 99n2, 116; as site of influence, 13, 73–75, 156–57; social makeup, 116–17; university's influence on community culture, 117–19
Fredericton Art Club, 116
Fredericton Branch Railway, 78
Fredericton Collegiate School, 81
French-language education: Académie du Sacré-Cœur, 131; accessibility of, 55; Collège l'Assomption, 134;

Collège Notre-Dame d'Acadie, 133; Collège Saint-Joseph, 12, 51–53, 71n2, 134; Collège Saint-Louis, 53–54; education of girls, 54, 55; establishment of, 49; L'École Essex, 131; as responsibility of clergy, 51; roaming teachers (maîtres ambulants), 49; Université de Moncton, 14, 52–53, 129, 133, 139; Université Sainte-Anne (Nova Scotia), 134; Université Saint-Joseph, 131

French-language press: creation of, 61; publishers, 133–34, 136, 140, 142, 150–51

French New Brunswick: Acadian Renaissance, and collective identity, 12; demographic changes pre- and post-Expulsion, 47–50; education, advances in, 50–55; influence of Roman Catholic Church, 48, 49–50; literacy, and access to education, 46, 47–50; public expectations/response to literary expression, 14–15. *See also* English New Brunswick; New Brunswick

Frye, Northrop, 126; "garrison mentality" and, 91, 159

Fuller, Danielle, 16

Gabriel West, and Other Poems (Currie), 81
Gaeneye: "Life in Saint John," 37
Gallant, Melvin, 136
Gallant, Yvon, 136
Galloway, David, 126
Gammel, Irene, 166
Gammon, Donald, 118, 122
Ganong, William F., 86, 123
Gaudet, Placide, 15, 56, 63, 71n2
de Gaulle, General, 133
Gauvin, Roland, 141
genetic structuralism theory, 7–8

Géographie de la nuit rouge (Leblanc), 143
Georges, Father Émile, 130–31
Georges L. Dumont University Hospital Centre, 131
Gibbs, Robert, 15, 123; on Odell, 28
Gide, André, 60
Gilbert, Anne, 69, 70
Gillett, Violet, 109
Girouard, Gilbert-Anselme, 71n2
Glenie, James: "creed" of, 28, 42n1; *Substance of MR. GLENIE's Address*, 25–26; Winslow's parody of, 26–27
Glissant, Edouard, 151
globalization, vs. place and referentiality, 16–17
Le Glossaire Acadien (Poirier), 53
Godard, Barbara, 16
Godfrey, W.G., 42n1
Goguen, Georges, 136
Golding, Phil, 110, 114
Goldmann, Lucien: genetic structuralism theory, 7–8
Goldsmith, Oliver, Jr., 156; *The Rising Village*, 12, 31, 32–33, 98, 161; transfer to China, 33–34
Goldsmith, Oliver, Sr.: *The Deserted Village*, 32
Good, Jackie, 116
Goupil, Laval: *Le Djibou*, 139; *Tête d'eau*, 139
Governor General's Literary Award: *Conversations* (Chiasson), 151; *Don l'Orignal* (A. Maillet), 140; *Le quatuor de l'errance suivi de La traversée du désert* (Thibodeau), 151
Gowan, Robert: "The Triumph of Intrigue," 35
Grady, Wayne, 144
Graines de fées (Léger), 142
Grand Prix du Festival International de la Poésie: *Le quatuor de l'errance*

suivi de La traversée du désert
   (Thibodeau), 151; *Nous, l'étranger*
   (Thibodeau), 151
Grand Prix Littéraire de la Ville de Montréal: *Mariaagélas* (A. Maillet), 140
Gray, John Hamilton, 76
Gregg, Milton F., 120
Grigor, William, 80
Gross, John: *Rise and Fall of the Man of Letters*, 37
Group of Seven, 109, 111, 112, 158
Gubbins, Joseph, 39
Gwyn, Sandra, 15

Haché, Juste, 51
Haggard, Rider, 95
Haliburton, Thomas Chandler, 26
Hall, Margaret, 127
Hammond, John, 110, 111, 161; and Owens Art School, 109
Harper, J. Russell, 118
Harrison, Thomas, 13, 94, 158
Hart, Julia Catherine (Beckwith), 15, 79
Harvey, D.C., 15
Hatfield, Richard: as premier, 136; pro-Francophone platform, 137, 138, 144
Hathaway, Rufus, 103
Hautecœur, Jean-Paul: *L'Acadie du discours*, 141
have-less provinces: cultural economy of, 15–18
Hawthorne, Charles Webster, 111
Hazen, Douglas, 89
The Head Quarters (newspaper), 79–80, 83, 84, 100n5
Hexagone, 151
High, Steven, 17
Hill, Thomas, 34, 78–79, 90, 99n4, 100n5; *The Constitutional Lyrist*, 78; *Provincial Association*, 78
Histoire de la littérature acadienne (M. Maillet), 46, 132

Histoire de la maison qui brûle (Daigle), 143
historical fiction, 12, 38
Hodd, Thomas, 13
Hogg, James, 79, 123
Holt, Elizabeth Russell, 109, 111, 161
Hopkins, Gerard Manley, 126
Hovey, Richard, 89, 97
Howe, Dorothy, 121
Howe, Joseph, 26
Hugo, Victor, 60
human-centric modernism, 111–13
Humphrey, Jack, 109, 112, 118
Hunter, Lady Sir Martin, 29
Hunter's Handbook (Straton), 91, 96
Huyghue, Douglas, 12, 37, 156; *Argimou*, 38, 41, 43n6, 161

ideological interests, compression and concentration of, 15
Ignatieff, Michael, 121
immigration: Irish immigration, 3, 33, 34; and Loyalist fear of displacement, 34; plurality, and multiculturalism, 159–60
Inch, Cassandra, 79
In Divers Tones (Roberts), 4, 96
In Memorabilia Mortis (Sherman), 96
Innis, Harold, 6; staples theory, 125
innovation: epochal change, and matrix events, 8–9; and socio-cultural environment, 6–10
intellectual history, and cultural economy of have-less provinces, 15–18
Intercolonial Railway, 84, 106–7; impact on New Brunswick, 36; interprovincial trade, costs of, 104–5
Irish immigration, 33, 74; dominance of Irish clergy, 49–50; as result of famine, 3
irony, as literary trope, 41

INDEX

Jack, Bessie, 86
Jacob, Dr. Edwin, 76
Jacques et Marie (Bourassa), 63
Jarvis, Lucy, 117, 118
Jasanoff, Maya, 21, 22
"John Gape Letters," 35–36
Jones, C.C., 119, 121
Jones, Kelsey, 110
Jones, Leonard, 133, 147
Jones Commission, 107
Journal of the New Brunswick Society for the Encouragement of Agriculture, Home Manufactures, and Commerce, 79
Junius: "A Journey to Fredericton," 37
Jusqu'à la mort! Pour nos écoles (Branch), 65

Kandinsky, Wassily, 111
Kierkegaard, Søren, 115
King's College, 76, 80
Klinck, Carl, 126
Klinkenberg, Jean-Marie, 142

L'Acadie du discours (Hautecœur), 141
L'Acadie Nouvelle (newspaper), 144
L'Acadien reprend son pays (LeBouthillier), 139
L'Acadie perdue (Roy), 141–42
La douloureuse aventure d'Évangeline (Achard), 66
La Fontaine, Jean de, 60
LaFrance, Charles-Édouard, 51
LaFrance, Father François-Xavier, 52; education of girls, 54; Séminaire Saint-Thomas, 51
Lamartine, Alphonse de, 60
Lamennais, Félicité de, 60
Lampman, Archibald, 16, 73, 96
land distribution issues, 3; crown lands, 35, 36; and the "Fifty Five," 21–23; of returning Acadians, 48; violations of Aboriginal land titles, 38–40

Landry, Charles, 17
Landry, Israël, 55
Landry, Napoléon, 15, 132; *Poèmes Acadians*, 67, 69; *Poèmes de mon pays*, 69
Landry, Pierre-Amand, 56, 71n2
Landry, Valentin Augustin, 71n2, 130
language: Acadian French, as historically accurate language, 53, 54; bilingual approach of Collège Saint-Joseph, 52; bilingualism, and assimilation, 137, 159–60; Chiac, and Acadian identity, 138–39, 166; French/English differences, and cultural geography, 2–3, 148–49, 159–60; as inherited tradition, 14; linguistic inadequacy, stigma of, 148; Official Languages of New Brunswick Act, 133
La Noce est pas finie (film, Forest), 139
L'appel des mots (Thibodeau), 151
Larousse, Pierre, 60
La Sagouine (A. Maillet), 4, 131, 135
La septième chute (Thibodeau), 150
La Société Mutuelle l'Assomption, 66, 72n12
l'Assomption Mutuelle-Vie, 144
Later Poems (Roberts), 96
La touchante Odyssée d'Évangeline (Achard), 66
Lauvrière, Émile: *La Tragédie d'un peuple*, 62
Lays of Love (Straton), 96
The Lay of the Wilderness (Fisher), 31
Layton, Irving, 114
League for Social Reconstruction, 126
Leavis, Queenie: "Victorian uplift," dynamics of, 38
LeBlanc, Gérald, 16, 70–71n1, 141, 142; as cartographic writer, 143; on Moncton, 151
LeBlanc, Gérald – works: *Anthologie de textes littéraires acadiens*, 46–47; *Comme un otage au quotidien*, 143;

Éloge du chiac, 143, 145; *Géographie de la nuit rouge*, 143; *L'extrême frontière*, 143, 145; *Lieux transitoires*, 143, 153n4; *Moncton Mantra*, 149–50
LeBlanc, Henri P., 130
LeBlanc, Raymond Guy, 14, 70–71n1; *Cri de terre*, 136, 138, 139
Le Borgo de l'écumeuse (LeBouthillier), 150
LeBouthillier, Claude: *L'Acadien reprend son pays*, 139; *Le Borgo de l'écumeuse*, 150; *Le Feu du mauvais temps*, 145; *Les Marées du Grand Dérangement*, 145
Le Courrier des Provinces Maritimes (newspaper), 61, 71n2
Le cycle de Prague (Thibodeau), 150
Le Djibou (Goupil), 139
Lefebvre, Father: and Collège Saint-Joseph, 51–52
Lefebvre, Father Camille, 55, 157
Le Feu du mauvais temps (LeBouthillier), 145
Léger, Antoine, 12, 69; *Elle et Lui*, 66; *Une fleur d'Acadie*, 66, 67
Léger, Dyane, 70–71n1; *Graines de fées*, 142; *Sorcière de vent!*, 142
Leggatt, William: "Song of Thousands," 35–36
Le huitième jour (On the Eighth Day) (A. Maillet), 144–45
Leland, Charles G.: *The Algonquin Legends of New England*, 92, 95
Le Matin (newspaper), 144
LeMay, Pamphile, 60; translation of *Evangeline*, 62–63
L'Émigrant acadien (Branch), 65
Le Moniteur Acadien (newspaper), 55, 57, 61, 62, 70–71n1
Le Parler franco-acadien et ses origines (Poirier), 53
Le passage des glaces suivi de Lamento (Thibodeau), 150
Le quatuor de l'errance suivi de La traversée du désert (Thibodeau), 151
Les Aboiteaux (film, Forest), 139
Les Acadiens à Philadelphie (Poirier), 53, 64–65
Les Acadiens de la dispersion (film, Forest), 139
Lesage, Jean, 129
Lescarbot, Marc: *Histoire de la Nouvelle France*, 47; *Les Muses de la Nouvelle France*, 47; *Le Théâtre de Neptune*, 47
Les Cent lignes de notre américanité, 142
Les Confessions de Jeanne de Valois (A. Maillet), 146–47
Les Cordes-de-bois (A. Maillet), 140
Les Crasseux (A. Maillet), 134–35
Les exilés acadiens (Achard), 66
Les Intrigues de Sabine, and religious censorship, 60
Les Marées du Grand Dérangement (LeBouthillier), 145
Les Splendides Têtus (Albert), 66
L'étoile maganée (Savoie, Chiasson), 136
letters: as expression of resistance, 20–21
L'Évangéline (newspaper), 61, 71n2, 130; end of publication, 143–44; *Les Intrigues de Sabine*, 60
Lévesque, René, 132
Lewis, William, 22; libel suit against, 23
L'extrême frontière (Leblanc), 143, 145
libraries: Mechanics' Institute, 37; Saint John's Society "Library," 30; St. Andrews, 42n2
Lieux transitoires (Leblanc), 143, 153n4
Lighthall, William D.: *Songs of the Great Dominion*, 96, 97
L'Impartial (newspaper), 54, 61
Lippincott, J.B. (publisher), 96
Lismer, Arthur, 109
literary expression, public expectations/response to, 14, 15

INDEX

literary ferment: and cultural sociology, 6–10; innovation, and socio-cultural environment, 10; periods of in New Brunswick, 10–11; as result of political ferment, 35; socio-cultural conditions for, 14, 155–56; and transformational change, 4–5; and urbanization, 130
The Literary History of Canada, 126
literary modernism, 111
literary primitivism, 41
literary production, as reflection of class issues, 37–38
literary societies: Saint-Patrick's Academy, 59; Société Littéraire Saint-Jean-Baptiste, 58–59; Société Littéraire Saint-Joseph, 59; St. Patrick Literary and Dramatic Society, 59
literary sociology, 4–5
literature, and literary creation: Bradbury's definition of, 8; as collective activity, 41; epochal change as matrix events, 8–9; "great man" theories, 7; influence of visual art activism on, 114; of post–World War Two New Brunswick, 103–27; and relational totality, 8–9; relocation as dislocation, 102–3; as social reaction, 7–8; and Ted Campbell's studio group, 108–16
Livesay, Dorothy, 115, 119, 126
Living on the Edge, the Poetic Works of Gérald Leblanc (film), 152–53
localism, 13; as act of political resistance, 69–70; growth of, 30–31; humanist expression of Campbell, 110–11; identity, and cultural expressions, 125; and regional culture, 31, 161; of theme and place, 69–70; in work of Currie, 81
Lockwood, Anthony: *Map of New Brunswick*, 31

Logan, H.J., 106
Longfellow, Henry Wadsworth, 12; *Evangeline*, as founding Acadian myth, 56
Lord, Bernard, 151
Lord, Marie-Linda, 13–14, 15
Louis Mailloux (Boudreau, Duguay), 139
Lowenthal, Leo: *Literature and the Image of Man*, 8
Low Tide on Grand Pré (Carman), 96
Loyalist and Conservative Advocate (newspaper), 34, 99n4; literary content, 78–79
Loyalist Awakening period, 11, 12
Loyalist narrative experience, and settler community evolution, 33
Loyalists, 2, 3, 156; analogy to "children of Israel," 34, 43n4; commitment to British law, 31–32; the "Fifty Five," 21–23; identity, and nationhood of, 19–20; literary writing as expression of resistance, 20–21; mythologization of, 12, 34, 41, 43n4; satire as literary convention, 27–28, 35
Lukàcs, Georg, 6–7; *The Historical Novel*, 6; *History and Class Consciousness*, 7; *Studies in European Realism*, 6
Lukàcsian Marxism, 6–7
Lyman, John, 111

MacDonald, Angus L., 107
Macdonald, John A., 104
MacKenzie, Margaret, 117
MacKenzie, Norman, 117, 120
Mackenzie King, William Lyon, 107
MacLeod, Alistair, 3
MacLeod, Pegi Nicol, 111; cultural democracy of "Four Freedoms," 118; localism of, 118; and Madge Smith's studio, 117–19; on Miller Brittain,

112; "The Fishermen of New Brunswick" rug commission, 118
MacNutt, W.S., 23, 74; *The Atlantic Provinces*, 35; on Glenie, 27; insularity of settlement, 3; *New Brunswick, A History*, 123
Mailhot, Raymond, 15
Maillet, Antonine, 10, 14, 16, 67, 134–35, 153n2, 161; Governor General's Literary Award, 140; Prix Champlain, 133
Maillet, Antonine – works: *Cent ans dans les bois*, 140; *Don l'Orignal*, 140; *La Sagouine*, 4, 131, 135; *Le huitième jour (On the Eighth Day)*, 144–45; *Les Confessions de Jeanne de Valois*, 146–47; *Les Cordes-de-bois*, 140; *Les Crasseux*, 134–35; *Mariaagélas*, 140; *Pélagie-la-Charrette*, 140; *Pointe-aux-Coques*, 133, 134; *Rabelais et les traditions populaires en Acadie*, 57–58
Maillet, Marguerite, 15; *Anthologie de textes littéraires acadiens*, 46–47; *Histoire de la littérature acadienne*, 46, 132
Maliseet (Wolastoqiyik) people, 1, 2; and Confederation poets, 92–93; violations of Aboriginal land titles, 38–40
Map of New Brunswick (Lockwood), 31
Mariaagélas (A. Maillet), 140
Maritime Art Association, 114, 119
Maritime Art magazine, 114
Maritime Confederation League, 107
Maritime economy: alteration in trade patterns, 103–5; Atlantic region as anachronistic backwater, 106–7; and economic protectionism, 104
Maritime malaise: as construct of economic inequity, 104–8; response to, 106–7
Maritime Provinces Trade Commission, 107
Maritime Rights Movement, 106
Marriott, Anne, 115
Marshall, Joseph, Baron d'Avray, 119
Massey-Lévesque Commission, 127
Matins (Sherman), 96
Maxwell, Lilian, 85, 86
McCurry, H.O., 110–11, 118
McGuinty, Dalton, 16
McInnes, Graham, 112
McKay, Ian: matrix events, and epochal change, 9
McNair, John B., 123
Mechanics' Institute, 37
Médam, Alain, 147
Medley, Bishop John, 74, 158; and Christ Church Cathedral, 77; as mentor to Parkin, 81, 100n6; *New Brunswick Churchman*, 79
Melanson, Arthur, 131
Melville, David, 23
Meyrowitz, Joshua, 17
Mi'kmaq people, 1, 2, 162–63; and Confederation poets, 92–93; violations of Aboriginal land titles, 38–40
Miller, Muriel, 74, 84
Millet, Jean-François, 110
modernism, 101–2; Bailey, and New Brunswick modernism, 119–21; Bliss Carman Society, 115; *Contemporary Verse* magazine, 115; federalism, as elitism, 113; *The Fiddlehead*, 103, 115; *First Statement* magazine, 114; and French Symbolists, 101; human-centric modernism, 111–13; literary modernism, 111–13; and Maritime economy, 103–8; place-based modernism, 116; and second-generation modernism, 16; social landscape of postwar New Brunswick, 13; Ted Campbell's studio, 103, 108–16; and wilderness nationalism of Hammond, 109

INDEX

Modernism, Mid-Century Emergent period, 11, 13
Modernity and Urbanity period, 11, 13–14
Moncton: Acadianization of, 130–32; as cultural incubator, 13–14; Expulsion bicentennial celebrations, 72n13, 132; French-language instruction, 131; Galeria Sans Nom, 136; Hôtel-Dieu Hospital, 131; of the imagination, 152–53; Leonard Jones as mayor, 133, 147; as literary presence, 151–53; Notre-Dame-de-Grâce, 131; Notre-Dame-de-l'Assomption Cathedral, 131; Notre-Dame-de-l'Assomption parish, 130–31; Sœurs de la Providence, 131; student protests, 133, 147; transcultural exchanges in, 132; Université de Moncton, 14, 52–53, 129; urbanity of, 145–47; urbanization, and Acadian presence, 130
Moncton Mantra (Leblanc), 149–50
Monro, Harold, *Twentieth Century Poetry*, 115
Montreal: relocation of literary creation, 102–3; and second-generation modernism, 16
More Smith, Henry, 32
Morin, Nancy, 136
The Morning Freeman, 53
Morning News (Saint John), 33–34
Morton, W.L.: *Manitoba, A History*, 125; *The Progressive Party in Canada*, 125
Mount Allison Ladies College, 114
Mount Allison University, Bachelor of Fine Arts degree, 114
Mourir à Scoudouc (Chiasson), 136, 139
Mowat, Helen, 86
Mullaly, Edward, 78–79
multiculturalism: contemporary Acadie as model of pluralism, 14; and diversity of cultural geography, 2–3

Murray, David, 88
music, 140–41; Angèle Arsenault, 140; Beausoleil Broussard, 141; Édith Butler, 140–41; 1755, 141
The Mysterious Stranger (Bates), 12, 32, 42–43n3; printing and distribution, 30–31

Napoleonic Wars: and British protection of shipping commerce, 29
National Film Board (NFB): Studio Acadie, 139
national identity: conditions for, 45–46
National Intelligencer (New York), 28
nationalism: Acadian nationalism, and collective identity, 12, 45–47, 50, 63, 65–67; of Loyalist refugees, 19–20; of Parti Acadien, 136–37
national literature: conditions for, 45–46
nature writing: engagement with landscape, and identity-formation, 41; landscapes as source of spiritual renewal, 90–91
Nealis, Jean: *Drift*, 96
neo-liberalism: vs. place, and referentiality, 17
New Brunswick: balkanization, and insularity of settlement, 3; community social cohesion, 32–33; crown lands, 35, 36; cultural GDP of, 18; cultural geography, 1–4; demographic changes pre- and post-Expulsion, 47–50; and diversity of microcultures, 4; Equal Opportunity program, 2, 14, 137, 157; French/English divisions post-Expulsion, 47–50; Indian Act (1844), 40; inland vs. coastal interests, 24–25; Irish immigration, 3, 33, 74; land distribution issues, 21–23, 35, 36; literacy, and access to education,

46, 47–50; Loyalist population, 21; Maritime malaise, as construct of economic inequity, 104–8; multivocal cultural identity of, 164–66; north–south division of labour and settlement, 2; Official Languages of New Brunswick Act, 133, 138; Parti Acadien, 136–37, 138; periods of literary ferment, 10–11; population at first census, 29; Schools Act (1871), 64; settlement of, 1–2; Société des Acadiens du Nouveau-Brunswick (SANB), 136, 137, 138; tourism strategies, 160; trading vs. timber economy, 24–25; War of 1812, 29. *See also* English New Brunswick; French New Brunswick

New Brunswick Museum, 112, 117, 127; Dr. and Mrs. Clarence Webster Collections, 119

New Brunswick Reporter and Fredericton Advertiser, 49, 78, 79

New Critics, 111; and modernism, 102; and structural coherence, 8

newspapers: *Acadian Recorder*, 43n3; *Albion* (NY), 37; French-language papers, 61–62; *Halifax Morning Post*, 43n5; *The Head Quarters*, 79–80, 83, 84, 100n5; *L'Acadie Nouvelle*, 144; *Le Courrier des Provinces Maritimes*, 61, 71n2; *Le Matin*, 144; *Le Moniteur Acadien*, 61, 62, 70–71n1; *L'Évangéline*, 60, 61, 71n2, 130, 143–44; *Loyalist and Conservative Advocate*, 34, 78–79, 99n4; *The Morning Freeman*, 53; *Morning News*, 33–34; *National Intelligencer* (New York), 28; *The New-Brunswick Courier*, 35; *New Brunswick Reporter and Fredericton Advertiser*, 49, 78, 79; as populist literary vehicles, 12, 20–21; promotion of cultural literacy in Fredericton, 78–80; *Royal Gazette*, 24, 27, 28; *Royal St. John's Gazette*, 22–23; *Saint John City Gazette*, 30; *Saint John Freeman*, 49; *The Saint John Gazette*, 23, 27; satire as literary convention, 27–28, 35, 36; *The St. John Gazette & Daily Advertiser*, 23; *The University Monthly*, 92–93, 95; use of satire, 12

The New-Brunswick Courier: "John Gape Letters," 35

Northland Lyrics (Roberts siblings), 89, 97

Notitia of New Brunswick (Fisher), 31

Notre-Dame-de-l'Assomption parish, 130–31

Nous, l'étranger (Thibodeau), 151

Nova Scotia: Jones Commission, 107

Nowlan, Alden, 16, 111

Observatory Art Centre (formerly Observatory Summer School for the Arts), 117, 118–19; as the "Tea Pot School," 118

occupational pluralism, 2; in diversification of NB economy, 29

Odell, Jonathan, 15, 20, 123, 156; Glenie's satirization of, 28, 42n1; patriotic poems by, 28; as Provincial Secretary, 22; use of satire, 28

Odell, William Franklin, 35

O'Flaherty, Patrick, 15

Ong, Walter, 1; on creative achievement, 7–8

oral tradition: of Acadians, 57–59, 61, 65, 69; transition to written literature, 134, 164

Orion, and Other Poems (Roberts), 95

Ottawa School of Confederation poetry, 16

Owens Art School, 109

INDEX

Pacey, Desmond, 13, 103, 122, 123, 126; *Hippity Hop*, 118; Parkin as mentor, 87; *University of New Brunswick Memorial Volume*, 93–94

Page, P.K., 13, 115, 116; and Campbell's studio, 103, 110, 114; "Ecce Homo," 115

pamphlets, as expression of resistance, 20–21, 27–28

Parkin, Sir George R., 13, 74, 80, 102; Medley as mentor, 81–82, 100n6; as mentor to Confederation poets, 87, 93–94, 158, 161

parody, as expression of resistance, 20–21

Parti Acadien, 136–37

Parti Québécois, 137

Pascal, Blaise, 60

Pascal-Poirier Prize, 134

Pas pire (Daigle), 150

Passamaquoddy people, 1, 2; violations of Aboriginal land titles, 38–40

Pater, Walter, 102

Pêcheurs de Pombcoup (film, Forest), 139

Peebles, Linden, 121

Pélagie-la-Charrette (A. Maillet), 140

Perley, Moses, 12, 37; as commisioner of Indian Affairs, 39–40; recognition of Indigenous cultures, 38; sporting sketches, 40; as "Wunjeet Sagamore," 39

Perrault, Pierre, *L'Acadie l'Acadie* (film), 133

Phillips, James, 80

Picturesque Canada (Roberts), 92

Pierce, Lorne, 84, 94

Pitts, Herman H., 49

place, and referentiality of have-less provinces, 17

place names: in Acadian literature, 67, 132, 164; and localism, 69

plays: *Jusqu'à la mort! Pour nos écoles*, 65; *L'Amer à boire* (Chiasson), 139; *La Sagouine* (A. Maillet), 4, 131, 135; *Le Djibou* (Goupil), 139; *L'Émigrant acadien*, 65; *Les Acadiens à Philadelphie* (Poirier), 53, 64–65; *Les Crasseux* (A. Maillet), 134–35; *Le Théâtre de Neptune* (Lescarbot), 47; *Louis Mailloux* (Boudreau, Duguay), 139; *Provincial Association* (Hill), 78; *Tête d'eau* (Goupil), 139; *Vivent nos écoles catholiques! Ou la résistance de Caraquet*, 65

Poèmes Acadians (N. Landry), 67, 69

Poèmes de mon pays (N. Landry), 69

Poésie acadienne contemporaine/Acadian Poetry Now, 142

poetry: as expression of resistance, 20–21

Pointe-aux-Coques (A. Maillet), 133, 134

Poirier, Pascal, 12, 15, 54, 56, 58, 69, 71n2; *Le Glossaire Acadien*, 53; *Le Parler franco-acadien et ses origines*, 53; *Les Acadiens à Philadelphie*, 53, 64–65; on writings of Collège Saint-Joseph students, 63–64

political dissent, influence on literary production, 23–28

political satire, 26; as Loyalist literary convention, 27–28

Pomeroy, Elsie, 74, 84, 89, 90, 95

Porter, Roy: *English Society in the 18th Century*, 27

Portraits d'écrivains, 142

Postman, Neil, 5

Pound, Ezra, 101, 102

Preview magazine, 122

Prix Champlain: *Pointe-aux-Coques* (A. Maillet), 133

Prix David: *Silence à nourrir de sang* (Després), 133

Prix de la Jeune Chanson Française: Beausoleil Broussard, 141

Prix des Quatre Jurys: *Les Cordes-de-bois* (A. Maillet), 140
Prix Edgar-Lespérance: *L'appel des mots* (Thibodeau), 151
Prix France-Acadie: *Graines de fées* (Léger), 142; *La septième chute* (Thibodeau), 150
Prix Goncourt: *Pélagie-la-Charrette* (A. Maillet), 140
Productions DansEncorps, 139–40
Public Works of Art Project (US), 113

Quebec: pan-French nationalism, 68; Quiet Revolution, 14, 129; recognition of Acadian writers, 140–41
Queen's Quarterly, 123

Racine, Jean, 7
Raddall, Thomas H.: *In My Time*, 19, 42
Radio Beauséjour CJSE, 148
Rameau de Saint-Père, François-Edmé, 12; program for rebirth of Acadie, 55–57, 61
Rawlyk, George, 106
Raymond, Maurice, 134
Raymond, William O., 123
the Rectory, 13
Rees, Ronald, 30
regional literatures: appropriation and realignment of, 16; growth of, 30–31
Reid, John, 38, 104
religion: and cultural geography, 2–3; influence of Catholic Church, 48, 49–50; and religious censorship, 59–61; social gospel activism, 106
resource economies, and north–south division of labour and settlement, 2
responsible government, demands for, 35–36, 99n4
Reynolds, William, 30

Richard, Chantal, 12, 164
Richard, Father Marcel-François, 55–57; Collège Saint-Louis, 53–54
Richards, David Adams, 16, 163
Riordan, Liam, 19
Rise and Fall of the Man of Letters (Gross), 37
The Rising Village (Goldsmith Jr.), 12, 31, 32–33, 98, 161
Roberts, Charles G.D., 13, 16, 81, 82, 98, 123, 158; "Attic Portfolio" magazine, 86; Classics Medal, 93; experience of Confederation, 83–84; family linkages, 84–86; final tour, 102; Mi'kmaq-inspired work of, 92–93; on Parkin as mentor, 87; publishing collaborations, 89; and the Rectory, 85–86; relationship to Bliss Carman, 73–74, 99n1; travel guides, 91; *The University Monthly* (newspaper), 93, 95; as unofficial leader of writing community, 97, 163–64; wilderness writing, 41, 90–93
Roberts, Charles G.D. – works: *Around the Campfire*, 90; *In Divers Tones*, 4, 96; *Later Poems*, 96; *Northland Lyrics* (Roberts siblings), 89, 97; "On Reading the Poems of Sidney Lanier," 95; *Orion, and Other Poems*, 95, 96; *Picturesque Canada*, 92; *Red Fox*, 92; "The Departing of Gluskap," 93; "The Outlook for Literature," 93; "The Quelling of the Moose," 93; "To Bliss Carman, with a Copy of Lang's 'Helen of Troy,'" 95
Roberts, Dr. W.F., 108
Roberts, Elizabeth, 82, 86, 98; experience of Confederation, 83–84; family linkages, 84–86; *Poems*, 96
Roberts, George Goodridge, 80, 81; as pastor of Christ Church Parish Church, 82

INDEX

Roberts, Lloyd: *The Book of Roberts*, 85, 97
Roberts, "Thede," 110
Roberts, Theodore Goodridge, 84, 95, 97
Roberts, William Carman, 84
Robichaud, Louis J.: election of, 129; Equal Opportunity program, 2, 14, 137, 157; Université de Moncton, 52–53, 129
Robichaud, Norbert, 132
Robichaud, Pierre, 141
Rogers, Robert, 122
roman-feuilleton: *Les Intrigues de Sabine*, and religious censorship, 60
Roosevelt, Franklin D.: "Four Freedoms" of, 118; reconstruction ethic of, 113
Ross, Fred, 109, 110
Ross, Malcolm, 15, 74, 157, 161; Parkin as mentor, 87
Rossignol, Rémi Morin, 142
Rousseau, Jean-Jacques, 60
Roussel, Claude: visual arts, Université de Moncton, 135–36
Routhier, Adolphe-Basile, 60
Roy, Isabelle, 141
Roy, Michel: *L'Acadie perdue*, 141–42
Royal Commission on Bilingualism and Biculturalism: Official Languages Act (federal), 133
Royal Commission on Maritime Claims (Duncan Commission), 106
Royal Commission on National Development in the Arts, Sciences and Letters (1949), 125–26
Royal Gazette, 24, 27, 28
Royal St. John's Gazette: "A Plain Dealer" (dialogue), 23; "A Spectator" (poem), 22–23
Runte, Hans R., 15
Ruskin, John, 81
Ryan, John, 22; libel suit against, 23

Saint-Jean-Baptiste Day, 56
Saint John: as destination point for immigration, 75; diversity and difference within, 23–24; growth of as mercantile centre, 28, 36–37, 75; incorporation of as city, 21; literary production and distribution, 12, 30–31; Lower Cove, 21, 23–24; as Loyalist city, 20, 21; modernism in, 13; Owens Art School, 109; political confrontations with Fredericton, 24–25; role in Atlantic communications system, 36; ship building, 36, 75; Ted Campbell's studio, 13, 103, 108–16, 157; trade unionism, 108; Upper Cove, 21, 23–24
Saint John Art Club, 109, 119
Saint John City Gazette, 30
Saint John Freeman, 49
Saint John's Society "Library," 30
Saint John Vocational School, 109
Saint John Gazette, 23, 27
St. John Gazette & Daily Advertiser, 23
Saisons antérieures (Forest), 136
Sans jamais parler du vent (Daigle), 143
Sartre, Jean-Paul, 60
satire, as literary convention, 27–28, 35, 36
Saulnier, Kenneth, 141
Savoie, Donald, 104
Savoie, Gilles, 136
Savoie, Jacques, 136, 141
Savoie, Roméo, 136
Sayre, Rev. John, 22–23
scholarly explorations of culture, 15–18
Scott, Allen, 9
Scott, Duncan Campbell, 73
Scott, F.R.: "The Canadian Authors Meet," 102
Scott, Sir Walter: popularity of, 30, 38
Séminaire Saint-Thomas, 51. *See also* Collège Saint-Joseph

serialized novels, 62
sermons, as expression of resistance, 20
settler community evolution: "four stages theory," 33
1755 (musical group), 141
Shackleton, Kathleen, 110
Shaw, Avery, 110, 112
Sherman, Francis, 13, 16, 81, 84, 85, 97, 98, 102, 158; at Collegiate School, 87, 88; *The University Monthly* (newspaper), 95
Sherman, Francis: *The Deserted City*, 95; *Matins*, 96; *In Memorabilia Mortis*, 96
Shives, Robert: *The Amaranth* and, 37, 38, 43n5
Silence à nourrir de sang (Després), 133
Simard, Jean-Maurice, 144
Simon, Lorne: *Stones and Switches*, 162
Sisters of Charity, 54
sites of influence: the Collegiate School, 86–90; the Rectory, 85–86; role of environment, 73–74; Sherman's Wharf, 90–91
sites of innovation, 126
Sketches of New Brunswick (Fisher), 31, 34
Smith, A.J.M., 98, 111, 126
Smith, Edith Marjorie (Madge): influence on art culture in Fredericton, 117–19
Smith, Goldwin: *Canada and the Canadian Question*, 104
Smith, Kay, 13, 109, 116; and Campbell's studio, 103, 110, 114; *Footnote to the Lord's Prayer*, 111
social systems, and agents of changes, 4–5
Société des Acadiens du Nouveau-Brunswick (SANB), 137, 138
Société L'Assomption, La Tour branch, 130

Société Littéraire Saint-Jean-Baptiste: *Académica*, 59; objectives, 58; practice of oratory skills, 58–59
Société Littéraire Saint-Joseph, 59
Société Mutuelle L'Assomption, 72n12
Société Nationale des Acadiens, 68
Société Nationale L'Assomption, 55, 68, 72n12
sociology: of rural vs. urban communities, 2–3
Sœurs de la Providence: Hôtel-Dieu Hospital, 131
Sommet de la Francophonie, 151
Songs from Vagabondia (Carman, Hovey), 89, 101
Songs of the Great Dominion (Lighthall), 96, 97
Sorcière de vent! (Léger), 142
Southgate, Horatio, 77
Spigelman, Martin S., 49
sporting sketches, 12; of Perley, 40
St. Andrews: Subscription Library, 42n2
Stansbury, Joseph, 20, 28
Stendhal (Henri Beyle), 60
St. Francis Xavier University, 106
St. Mary's First Nation, 92
Stockley, William F.S., 94–95
Stones and Switches (Simon), 162–63
St. Patrick Literary and Dramatic Society, 59
A Strange Manuscript Found in a Copper Cylinder (DeMille), 162
Straton, Barry, 13, 84, 98, 158; at Collegiate School, 87; experience of Confederation, 83–84; family linkages, 84–86; publishing collaborations, 89; *University Monthly* (newspaper), 95; University of New Brunswick (UNB), 100n7
Straton, Barry – works: *The Building of the Bridge*, 96; *Hunter's Handbook*, 91, 96; *Lays of Love*, 96

Street, Samuel Denny: *Creon*, 27–28
Studio Acadie (NFB), 139
Surette, Leon: *The Birth of Modernism*, 101–2
Sutherland, Betty, 109
Sutherland, John, 13, 110, 116; and Campbell's studio, 103, 114–15; *First Statement* magazine, 114, 122
Swanick, Eric, 99n4
Sweet, Jean M., 114
Symons, Arthur: on Carman, 101
Synge, J.M.: *The Shadow of the Glen*, 114

Tâo (Bailey), 115
Tête d'eau (Goupil), 139
Thacker, Robert, 16
Theatre Guild of Saint John, 114
Théâtre l'Esacouette, 139
Théâtre Populaire d'Acadie (TPA), 139
Théâtre Vivant, 134–35
theatrical prologues: *All The World's A Stage*, 24; as expression of resistance, 20–21; as populist literary vehicles, 12, 24–25; *Speed the Plough*, 25
Thériault, Joseph Yvon, 69, 70
Thibodeau, Serge Patrice, 16; *L'appel des mots*, 151; *La septième chute*, 150; *Le cycle de Prague*, 150; *Le passage des glaces suivi de Lamento*, 150; *Le quatuor de l'errance suivi de La traversée du désert*, 151; *Nous, l'étranger*, 151
Thiesse, Anne-Marie, 45
Thomas, Dylan, 121
Thomson, Tom, 109
Thorburn, Hugh, 103
Tilley, Sir Leonard, 84
timber industry. *See* forest industry
Tompkins, James, 106
Toronto: and Maritime tourism, 107; relocation of literary creation, 102–3; and second-generation modernism, 16
tourism, 160
tradition, and contemporaneity, 121
transformational change, and literary ferment, 4–5
Tremblay, Michel: *Les Belles-Sœurs*, 134
Tremblay, Tony, 13
Trois villes martyres (Achard), 66
Tupper, Sir Charles, 84
Turner, Frederick Jackson, 124, 158

Underhill, Frank, 119
Une fleur d'Acadie (Léger), 66, 67
Université de Moncton, 14, 52–53, 129; Department of Theatre Arts, 139; Galeria d'Art, 136; growth of, 137; sociology department, 141, 159; strike, 133; visual arts department, 135–36
Université Sainte-Anne (Nova Scotia), 134
Université Saint-Joseph, 131
University of New Brunswick (UNB): Anglican administration of, 76; Bailey's involvement with, 119–22, 127; and Confederation poets, 13, 74; creative environment of, 95; expansion of, 13; founding and development of, 75–77; influence over community culture, 117–19; Roberts at, 93, 100n7; *University Monthly* (newspaper), 92–93, 95
University of New Brunswick Memorial Volume, 93–94
Un soleil pas comme ailleurs (film, Forest), 139
urban centrism: "3T's," 16–17; and "renaissance cities," 17

Van Rensselaer, Stephan, 28
Venne, Stéphane, 129

Verduyn, Christl, 11–12, 159
Vincent, Thomas, 27–28
Vivent nos écoles catholiques! Ou la résistance de Caraquet (Branch), 65
Voltaire (François-Marie Arouet), 60

Wallace, C.M., 79
Wardhaugh, Robert, 16
Ware, Martin, 95
War of 1812, 28
wealth distribution, and cultural geography, 2–3
Webster, J.C., 121, 123; endorsement of Bailey as curator, 120
Weingartner, Charles, 5
Western Canada: frontier mythology of, 105
Whistler, James, 110, 111
White, Hayden, 10, 11
White, Mylène, 143
"wilderness nationalism," 109
wilderness writing: of Confederation poets, 90–93; engagement with landscape, and identity-formation, 41

Williams, Raymond, 1; *Culture and Society*, 8
Wilmot, Lemuel Allan, 99n4
Wilson, Lorna, 78
Winslow, Edward: parody of Glenie, 26–27; *Young Robin Hood Society*, 26–27
Wolastoqiyik (Maliseet) people, 1, 2; violations of Aboriginal land titles, 38–40
Woodcock, George, 126
Wright, Esther Clark, 33
Wyile, Herb, 16
Wynn, Graeme, 24; occupational pluralism, 29

Yeats, W.B., 101
Young Aspirant (journal), 79
youth literature: Acadian national ideology, 66–67

Zola, Émile, 60

www.ingramcontent.com/pod-product-compliance
Lightning Source LLC
Chambersburg PA
CBHW072152100526
44589CB00015B/2192